Research About Leisure:
Past, Present, and Future

Second Edition

Lynn A. Barnett, Ed.
University of Illinois

Sagamore Publishing
Champaign, Illinois

Production supervision: Brian J. Moore
Cover design: Amy L. Todd and Michelle R. Dressen
Proofreader: Phyllis L. Bannon

Library of Congress Catalog Card Number: 94-67271
ISBN: 0-915611-96-1

For our mentors, colleagues, and students . . .
Thank you.

Contents

Acknowledgments

The principal acknowledgment in a collective work of original chapters is to the authors themselves and to their various sources of support and assistance. These are indicated, wherever appropriate, as acknowledgments in the individual chapters. Thank you.

The whole of the book is different from the sum of its parts, and its existence as an entity should be appropriately acknowledged as well. It is an ill-kept secret that many more people than the authors participate in the creation of any book. A debt of gratitude is extended to Sagamore Publishing. The final shepherding of the book into print was overseen by Brian Moore, Production Supervisor for the project, and Amy Todd, Design Assistant, who designed the cover. Thanks to both of you.

And finally, to Steven and Courtney, Jordan, and Emily who offer the insight and thirst for play and leisure.

Preface

All purely material research conducted by a human scientist is purely inquisitive behavior—appetitive behavior in free operation. In this sense, it is play behavior. All scientific knowledge . . . arose from playful activities conducted in a free field entirely for their own sake . . . Anybody who has seen in his own activities the smooth transition from inquisitive childhood play to the life-work of a scientist could never doubt the fundamental identity of play and research.

—Konrad Lorenz
Psychology and Phylogeny
1976

Within the past 25 years we have witnessed a dramatic increase in empirical research on leisure, both in terms of research articles published in professional journals, and in research-based books on leisure such as the present volume. A major thrust of this research has focused on the role of leisure in the person's life—in what ways does leisure influence development, or consolidate or reinforce it, or simply reflect the individual's developmental history? In a complementary vein, there has been interest in another important way of examining leisure. That is, how do leisure behaviors themselves develop? What are the antecedent conditions and behavioral correlates of various forms of leisure at different developmental levels and for different populations? What is the conceptual relationship between leisure and other epistemic-ludic behaviors, such as reality testing, exploration, insightful problem-solving, learning, humor, metaphor comprehension, ritualistic behavior, or language itself?

This surge of research productivity has certainly hammered the last nails into the coffin of the condemnation of the study of leisure on the grounds that the construct is vague, superfluous, and scientifically useless. As we have seen, conceptual and methodological advancements over the years (and a fair amount of true grit) has rendered leisure more and more empirically manageable. As a consequence, it has become more scientifically respectable to conduct research on leisure and recreation. This second edition of the book strongly attests to the thirst for scholarly information about our discipline.

A major purpose of the present book is to bring together in a single volume work that reflects the wide range of interests that social and behavioral scientists have in leisure, recreation, and the environment. The book had its beginnings in 1987 when we began to make plans for a special commemorative celebration of the ten-year anniversary of the Leisure Research Symposium. We wanted a volume presenting a comprehensive and provocative view of the extant scientific research to articulate the leisure research movement through the reflection, insight, and vision of its major contributors. Moreover, the intent of the book would be to refine and extend concepts and methodologies within and beyond one's usual area of study. Our thinking was that this formula and direction would yield novel information and fresh insights. After diligent organizational and editorial work, not to mention the excellent contributions of the authors and co-authors of the chapters in the present volume, we have an excellent product that encompasses a wealth of topics concerning structural, functional, and pragmatic aspects of leisure, and a product that includes strong emphasis on methodological as well as substantive content concerns.

The empirical and theoretical research and scholarship compiled in this volume reflect a common theme. The works may be said to have evolved within a common framework that the study of leisure is relevant and indeed necessary for fully comprehending human development. Some of the researchers represented may be primarily interested in leisure as expressive behavior and others in leisure for its constitutive role in society. In both cases, leisure is held to provide a foundation for interpersonal and intrapersonal qualities and characteristics, and the significance of the study of leisure is regarded as extending over the life course. The chapters of this text suggest Lorenz's notion of continuity across the life stages, and are a testimonial to Researcher the Player.

It is hoped that the chapters of this book will inspire a new generation of research extending knowledge both in theoretical and applied areas. As this book suggests, a critical mass in the area of research is being reached, thus validating and legitimatizing leisure as an important area of empirical study. On the other hand, to be sure, there are yet many within our ranks still swayed by early prejudices about the futility of empirically studying leisure. For these less informed or hard-nosed among us who still condemn leisure research as frivolous, let us keep up the momentum displayed in these pages and accept the challenge to obtain even higher levels of excellence and methodological rigor in the years ahead.

—Lynn A. Barnett

— Prologue —
In Celebration of Leisure Research:
A Reflective Look Back

Lynn A. Barnett
Department of Leisure Studies
——————— **University of Illinois** ———————

Michael G. Wade
School of Physical Education, Recreation,
and School Health Education
——————— **University of Minnesota** ———————

Not to know what has been transacted in former times is to be always a child. If no use is made of the labors of past ages, the world must remain always in the infancy of knowledge.

Cicero, 100 BC

Our earliest research writing focused on the recreation patterns of the affluent, as observed and described with great verve by Riis in How the Other Half Lives (1890) and by Thorstein Weblen in The Theory of the Leisure Class (1899). Stemming from the pervasive Protestant Ethic at the time, and the corollary that leisure was the domain of the upper class, detailed reports of recreational activities and the use and abundance of free time for leisure were published. While these "scientific" observations were for the most part unstructured, and even though there was usually no reliability or validity issues addressed, we nevertheless can tentatively identify these writings as the earliest examples of recreation and leisure research.

The birth of the Recreation Movement in the United States served as a catalyst for many of our earliest recreation studies. Three major developments were associated with the Recreation Movement (Kraus, 1984):

(a) the development of a network of national, state, and municipal parks (e.g., Central Park, Boston Sand Gardens, Yellowstone National Park);

(b) the development of national voluntary organizations and settlement houses (e.g., YMCA, Girl Scouts, Boys Club, Camp Fire Girls); and,

(c) the development of playground movements in many cities and towns.

The Play Movement quickly evolved at the turn of the century from the Recreation Movement, and was primarily attributed to Joseph Lee, Jane Addams, and Luther Gulick. These landmark beginnings served as the impetus for most of our early research in recreation, specifically studies in the areas of recreational activity needs and interests of the community and park planning, development, and design. The majority of these early research efforts were undertaken by civic-minded lay people, governmental agencies, young organizations in physical education and recreation, and a few professionals in the field.

THE TURN OF THE CENTURY:
EARLY RESEARCH EFFORTS

The first published experimental study explored play and playground use in the 1890s and was conducted by Joseph Lee, the first President of the Playground Association of America. Lee was very active in the playground movement in Boston, and, by the end of the decade, he had set up his own experimental playground to determine the best type of administration, leadership, design, and programs for play areas (Knapp & Hartsoe, 1979). His field experiments on playground design and play activities for children made a significant contribution to the Playground Movement in the United States, as well as to developing standards for the operation of playgrounds nationwide. These studies were published by Lee in two books, dated 1905 and 1907. Lee's early experiments motivated others to investigate these issues which continued into the 1920s and later, as the Play Movement became much more clearly defined (cf., Appleton, 1905; Curtis, 1914; Cutten, 1926; Lehman & Witty, 1927; May & Petgen, 1928; Nash, 1927; National Recreation Association, 1925, 1934; Rainwater, 1922; Steiner, 1933).

The growth of recreation and leisure research was given a significant boost by the formation of the National Recreation Association (formerly the Playground and Recreation Association of America), created in 1906. The purpose of the Association was to help communities establish playgrounds and create public support for the local movement. One of the major efforts undertaken by the Playground and Recreation Association was numerous nationwide surveys conducted by field secretaries in order to learn what people needed for recreation and to discover the available public, private, and commercial facilities. These field secretaries traveled extensively across the nation, collecting data for descriptive and comparative purposes.

One of the first of these recreation surveys was administered for the city of Detroit in 1913 by Rowland Haynes. The Detroit Recreation Survey explored four major questions: (a) part one treats the need for recreation in Detroit: what, how much, and where; (b) part two treats the facilities and supervision of recreation, both at present and what is needed; (c) part three treats administration of public recreation at present and the needed form of administration for an adequate system in Detroit; (d) part four outlines a program for securing the needed elements of a system, covering supervision, facilities, and administration (Haynes, 1913; p. 7). Due to the success of the survey technique and findings, Weir (who was the first field secretary of the Association) published a lengthy book entitled *A Manual of Municipal and County Parks*. The book was the product of field research in public recreation and a comprehensive survey of municipal and county parks. Weir's detailed study became a springboard for NRA activity in research and publication. The comprehensive park study was reported in 1925 and 1926, and thereafter the Association issued the Park Manual and County Parks (Recreation and Park Yearbook, 1950). Three nationwide surveys were again conducted in 1930, 1935, and 1940 in cooperation with several agencies (Recreation and Park Yearbook, 1950).

And, in 1950, the Association presented the Recreation and Park Yearbook as a review of the local and county recreation and park development from 1900 to 1950.

The first recreation research study published in a journal delineated the play interests of young children. The study was conducted by W.S. Monroe of State Normal School in Westfield, MA, and was published in the December 1899 issue of the American Physical Education Review. The method and findings of this research were also presented in the Physical Education session at the National Education Association held in Los Angeles, CA on July 14, 1899; this may well be the earliest presentation of recreation or leisure research. It is interesting that it took us only 77 short years hence to convene our own conference for the presentation of leisure and recreation research.

MOVING INTO THE 1900S: EARLY RESEARCH PUBLICATIONS

There were, in fact, few early journals which were available sources for the publication of recreation research. The Research Quarterly, first published in 1930 by the American Association for Health, Physical Education, and Recreation (AAHPER; formerly known as the American Physical Education Association), provided an outlet for the dissemination of recreation, leisure, and play research. It was natural that recreation research be published in a physical education journal, since the majority of the authors of recreation research studies were physical education professionals; indeed, the majority of our research in the early and mid-1900s focused on recreational needs and interests of school-aged children, particularly in physical activities, and many times in school settings. For example, a study of physical recreational activities of St. Stephens College graduates conducted by W. Haynes was published in the March 1931 issue of the Quarterly. Thirty-seven years later, the Journal of Leisure Research came into being, followed by Recreation Research Review in 1973, Leisurability in 1974, Leisure Sciences in 1977, and Leisure Studies in 1982.

While the majority of early research had been conducted by organizations and related disciplines, recreation professionals and scholars also made their contributions. AAHPER takes credit for publishing most of this research in its Journal of Health, Physical Education, and Recreation and in The Research Quarterly. In 1940, the Quarterly presented for the first time a bibliography of master's theses and doctoral dissertations documenting research in recreation from 1917 to 1939, compiled and published by G.M. Gloss of Louisiana State University in 1940. This bibliography was the first compilation of recreation research conducted in various education institutions across the country. The first recorded master's thesis was completed in 1917 and was titled, "Recreation For All In High School Through Better Organization and Supervision" by I.O. Ash at the University of Nebraska. The first recorded recreation-related dissertation was completed in 1926 by Ethel J. Saxman of Teacher's College, Columbia University, and was titled, "Student's Use In Leisure Time of Activities Learned in Physical Education in State Teacher's College".

Thomas K. Cureton, one of the pioneering spirits in research in physical education, recreation, and health, compiled two sets of recreation research bibliographies - one for master's theses (Cureton, 1952), and one for doctoral dissertations (Cureton, 1949). The American Association of School Administrators under the Department of the National Education Association of the United States produced a pamphlet titled, "Reference On Leisure Education" in 1937 that chronicled research work done by professionals in the physical education, parks and recreation fields.

There have been several attempts made to keep abreast of current recreation research and to chart its course by publishing research bibliographies. Butler (1958) published a bibliographic index of recreation research studies for the National Recreation Association and Anderson (1951) earlier prepared such an index for research related specifically to industrial recreation. Cureton (1954, 1961) covered the range of years from 1924-1960, as did Hubbard and Weiss (1959, 1960) starting from a later date. This trend continues through the present (cf., Crandall et al, 1977; Van Doren, 1972; Van Doren & Solan, 1979) even though the use of microfilm techniques and abstracting publications, as well as the increase in cross-indexing and the number of published journals, has diminished its frequency.

RECREATION RESEARCH AND THE GOVERNMENT:
FEDERAL AND LOCAL INTEREST

Outdoor recreation research was early promoted by federal and state governments with the establishment of the National Park Service in 1916. Upon the approval of Congress, President Roosevelt transferred jurisdiction of all parks and monuments previously administered by other departments to the National Park Service. In 1936, the Park, Parkway, and Recreation Area Study Act was passed by Congress and signed by the President. The study was national in scope and addressed four major objectives: (a) to obtain all available information concerning existing recreational facilities, areas, and systems: (b) to analyze legislation, existing plans, populations, and other factors affecting recreational problems; (c) to determine requirements for recreation over a period of years on a nationwide scale; and, (d) to formulate definite plans and recommendations for adequately meeting the present and future recreational requirements of the country. The comprehensive result of the study became the 1937 Yearbook: Park and Recreation Progress. By 1938, another Yearbook was published. However, the content of this book differed, and contained articles by authorities in the field of parks and recreation outside of the federal government, supplemented by reports and discussion by National Park Service personnel. Some of the articles in the Yearbook are in-depth evaluations and analyses of existing public recreational facilities and sites, with accompanying proposals and recommendations to further improve recreation services. The extensive study by the National Park Service became a stepping stone for some practitioners in public park and recreation agencies to become involved in research. Moreover, the 1938 study resulted in publication of a pamphlet titled, "Park Use Studies and Demonstrations." The pamphlet is divided into two parts: part 1A is a report documenting attendance, activity participation, and preference studies conducted in cooperation with 248 state parks and related recreational areas in 1938; part 2A covers the organization, conduct, and results of park use program demonstrations in 1939 (Park Use Studies and Demonstrations, 1941).

In 1941, the National Park Service prepared a report: A Study of National Recreation Problems. This report reflected, to some degree, the preliminary findings of various states cooperating in the study and embodied the recommendation of the National Park Service for coordinated nationwide planning. Further, it also provided a useful guide to correlate planning by agencies on all levels of government cooperating in the nationwide program. The early field studies and surveys conducted by the National Park Service reflected a national consciousness and interest in the preservation and care of our national parks, forests, historic sites, monuments, and wildlife. In addition, it extensively contributed to the development and expansion of research specifically in recreation planning, site development, and parks and recreation regulations and standards between 1930 and 1950. This mission was carried on after the 1950 assessment in several ways and by several different agencies. Significant research, for example, was contributed by the National Advisory Council on Regional Recreation Planning, presenting intensive analyses of land needs and land saturation (Anderson, 1959).

Interest in research in recreation areas, facilities, and resources continued in the 1950s, and 1960s (c.f., AAHPER, 1965; Butler, 1962; California Committee on Planning for Recreation, Park Areas, and Facilities, 1956; Community Service Council of Metropolitan Indianapolis, 1966; Denver Area Welfare Council, 1956; National Recreation and Park Association, 1965; National Regional Council on Regional Planning, 1959). The descriptive community recreation survey grew out of the need of individual community recreation districts to provide programs and facilities for their constituents (cf., Bachelor, 1952; Bradburn, 1963; Brightbill, et al, 1965; Boston Committee of Citizens, 1949; Council of Social Agencies, 1952; Detroit Metropolitan Regional Planning Commission, 1960; National Recreation and Park Association, 1964; Norman, 1966; Recreation and Youth Services Planning Council, 1957, 1958, 1960; Sapora, 1954; Sapora & Kenney, 1960; UNESCO, 1962; United Community Service, 1963; Washington State Recreation and Cultural Resources, 1946; Westchester County of New York Recreation Commission, 1961). The American Recreation Society Committee on Research and the National Advisory Committee on Recreation Research developed a comprehensive list of research completed and research in progress in the broader recreation field. They also identified a list of topics for recreation research, and, based upon a national inquiry, identified very specific research questions in need of empirical study (Brightbill 1950; Butler & National Advisory Committee on Recreation Research, 1950; Staley, 1950).

THE POST-WAR YEARS: LEISURE RESEARCH APPEARS

The 1950s also witnessed a surge of interest in leisure beyond its previously narrowly defined scope relating to parks, recreation and physical activity. The publications and inquiry carried on at the Center for the Study of Leisure at the University of Chicago from 1955 to 1959 resulted in research about leisure and its relationship to broader societal issues; for example, suburbia, industrial settings, and mass media (cf., Larabee & Meyersohn, 1958). These studies have been published and disseminated in over 40 books and articles, and, in addition, several research journals published issues devoted exclusively to the subject of recreation in modern society (cf., American Journal of Sociology - May 1957 issue; Annals of the American Academy of Political and Social Sciences - September 1957 issue). The Center was operated from funds obtained through a temporary foundation grant, and was regretfully discontinued when the funding source expired.

In 1953, the National Council on Recreation Research was formed. The formation of the Council was a product of the previous works and interests of dedicated leaders and members of the National Recreation Association. The formation of the Council was preceded by many early research panels and discussions held at National Recreation Association congresses. George Butler was one of the key figures who initiated the need to upgrade research standards in the field and he spoke to the need to establish a central "clearinghouse for recreation research" (Proceedings of the 31st National Recreation Congress, 1949). In 1954, Recreation magazine of the National Recreation Association first included a research section in the index; and for the first time the magazine contained a permanent section entitled "Research Review and Abstracts." Some of the early research reviews published in the November 1954 issue of the magazine were: "Study of Group Work and Recreation for United Community Service of Metropolitan Detroit" by L.R. Barrett; "Public Recreation as a Municipal Service in Alabama" by R. Daland;

"Cooperative Use and Maintenance of Recreation Areas in New Jersey Communities" by R. Sisco; and "Pattern of Recreation Administration in Wisconsin" by Dr. H.C. Hutchins (Butler, 1954).

The late 1950s and early 60s saw increased specialization of recreation and leisure research. As new and different needs arose, as a knowledge base was becoming established, and as education and academic curricula became more widely established and specialized, existing research directions similarly responded and new ones appeared. While content became more specific and more conceptual, methodological issues also emerged as part of the quest for empirical techniques which could address some of the specific leisure research issues. Since the first health, physical education, and recreation research methods book appeared in 1949 (commissioned and published by the Board of Directors of AAHPER), very little discussion about research design or quantitative methods had been conducted. The new 60s also witnessed an interest in method, as well as in substance.

These new directions for research carry on into the present day, and can be summarized as primarily representing three new areas:

(a) attempts at precisely and more specifically defining leisure both conceptually and operationally (cf., Barnett, 1978; Bergier, 1981; Burdge, 1985; Cesario, 1978; Crawford et al, 1986; Crompton, 1977; Dunn, 1980; Graefe et al, 1981; Gunter, 1987; Hammitt, 1980; Harper, 1981, 1986; Hawes, 1978; Iso-Ahola, 1979a, b, 1986; Kelly, 1978, 1980; Mills, 1985; Roadburg, 1983; Shaw, 1985; Smith, 1985; Snepenger & Crompton, 1984, 1985; Stover & Garbin, 1982; Tinsley & Kass, 1978, 1979; Tinsley & Tinsley, 1986; Wade, 1985; Young & Kent, 1985);

(b) the effects of recreation activities and programs on people (cf., Chenery, 1981; Goodale, 1965; Henkel, 1967; Heywood, 1978; Kelly et al, 1987; Miller et al, 1966; Parker, 1967; Sessoms, 1965; Stevens, 1966; Tinsley et al, 1987; Ulrich & Addoms, 1981; van der Smissen, 1965; Wingo, 1964); and,

(c) efforts toward developing more sophisticated and sensitive measurement and analytical techniques (cf., Baxter & Ewing, 1986; Beaman, 1974; Beard & Ragheb, 1980; Becker & Iliff, 1983; Becker et al, 1980, 1987; Biskin, 1983; Brown, 1984; Brown & Tinsley, 1983; Buhyoff, 1979; Buhyoff et al, 1985; Christensen,

1979, 1980, 1982, 1983, 1985; Cosper & Shaw, 1985; Ellis & Witt, 1984; Hammitt & McDonald, 1982; Holbrook, 1980; Holland et al, 1986; Johnson & Field, 1981; Kreimer, 1977; Levine & Hunter, 1983; Mills et al, 1981; Moeller et al, 1980; Noe, 1987; Oderwald, 1980; Olivera et al, 1983; Perdue & Ditton, 1983; Peterson & Stynes, 1986; Ragheb & Beard, 1982; Rosenthal et al, 1983; Shaw, 1986; Shelby & Harris, 1985; Stynes, 1980; Tate, 1984; Tinsley, 1983; Trafton & Tinsley, 1980; Tyre & Siderelis, 1979; Um & Crompton, 1986; Wellman et al, 1980; Yu, 1980, 1981).

The proliferation of research and the development of subdisciplinary research into recreation and leisure issues that grew rapidly from the 60s to the present. This is expertly reviewed in the following chapters by subdisciplinary content areas.

SUMMARY

The evolutionary development of research in recreation and leisure was reflective of the societal needs within that period of time. The Recreation Movement during the early 1900s stimulated an investigation of recreation needs, habits, and interests of the community residents, particularly the school children. Physical education professionals were the first to conduct systematic studies on the physical activity participation and preferences of the children. Soon after, early recreation leaders began to investigate community public recreation, which often included assessments of recreational facilities and sites.

The development of recreation and leisure research can also be attributed to the growth of municipal parks. For example, when the federal and state governments stepped forward to conduct a nation-wide study of parks and monuments, other areas were examined: analyses of sites, evaluations of organizations, management, personnel, and administration. The results of these comprehensive surveys produced standards and guidelines for parks and recreation service operations.

There were several other factors that promoted research in recreation and leisure. More recreation studies were conducted when colleges and universities instituted recreation curricula into organized and formally established programs and departments. When graduate programs in recreation were expanded, research topics began to diversify. Moreover, the publication of research articles in professional journals and magazines, and the establishment of research sections and a research council in The National Recreation Association and the American Association for Health, Physical Education, and Recreation encouraged professionals to conduct research studies with applied significance.

As recreation research began to gain momentum, research questions began to change in focus to more basic issues. Questions such as, "What is recreation?" "Why do people recreate?" "What benefits does recreational participation offer the individual, group, community, society?" were posed and treated with serious discussion and scientific inquiry. "Leisure" research emerged as the fundamental and encompassing study of recreation and a new and broad-based disciplinary approach to research in our field was born. The blossoming of leisure research continues.

Grateful appreciation is extended to Benita M. Barros and Karen Fox for their assistance with the preparation of this chapter.

BIBLIOGRAPHY

American Association for Health, Physical Education, and Recreation (1949). *Recreation and Park Yearbook: A Review of Local and County Recreation and Park Developments 1900-1950.* Washington, D.C.: American Association for Health, Physical Education, and Recreation.

American Association for Health, Physical Education and Recreation (1965). *Planning Areas and Facilities for Health, Physical Education, and Recreation.* Washington, D.C.: American Association for Health, Physical Education, and Recreation.

American Association for Health, Physical Education, and Recreation, & National Recreation and Park Association (1965). *Recreation Research: A Collection of Papers from the National Conference on Recreation Research, November 1965.* Washington, D.C.: American Association for Health, Physical Education, and Recreation.

Anderson, J.M. (1951). A Survey of Recent Research Findings in Industrial Recreation. *Research Quarterly,* (3), 273-285.

Anderson, K.R. (1959). *A User Resource Recreation Planning Method.* Loomis, CA: National Advisory Council on Regional Recreation Planning.

Appleton, L.E. (1905). *Comparative Study of the Play Activities of Adult Savages and Civilized Children.* Chicago, IL: University of Chicago Press.

Bachelor, W. (1952). *Public Recreation Survey of Columbus, Ohio.* Columbus, OH: City of Columbus.

Barnett, L.A. (1978). Theorizing about Play: Critique and Direction. *Leisure Sciences, 1* (2), 113-130.

Baxter, M.J., and G. O. Ewing (1986). A Framework for the Exploratory Development of Spatial Interaction Models: A Recreation Travel Example. *Journal of Leisure Research, 18* (4), 320-336.

Beaman, J. (1974). Distance and the 'Reaction' to Distance as a Function of Distance. *Journal of Leisure Research, 6* (3), 220-231.

Beard, J.G., and M. G. Ragheb (1980). Measuring Leisure Satisfaction. *Journal of Leisure Research, 12* (1), 20-33.

Becker, R.H., and T. J. Iliff (1983). Non-respondents in Homogeneous Groups: Implications for Mailed Surveys. *Leisure Sciences, 5* (3), 257-268.

Becker, R.H., G. D. Dottavio, and K. K. Mengak (1987). Engagement as a Criterion for Defining Homogeneous Groups: Implications for Mailed Surveys. *Leisure Sciences, 9* (2), 135-140.

Becker, R.H., W. A. Gates, and B. J. Niemann (1980). Establishing Representative Sample Designs with Aerial Photographic Observations. *Leisure Sciences, 3* (3), 277-300.

Bergier, M.J. (1981). A Conceptual Model of Leisure-Time Choice Behavior. *Journal of Leisure Research, 13* (2), 139-148.

Biskin, B.H. (1983). Multivariate Analysis in Experimental Leisure Research. *Journal of Leisure Research, 15* (4), 344-358.

Boston Committee of Citizens (1949). *Greater Boston Community Survey.* Boston, MA: Boston Committee of Citizens.

Bradburn, N.M. (1963). *In Pursuit of Happiness.* Chicago, IL: University of Chicago National Opinion Research Center (Report No. 92).

Brightbill, C.K.B. (1950). Research in Recreation—A Growing Need. (mimeographed copy.)

Brightbill, C.K., A. V. Sapora, E. H.Storey, J. Ver Lee, L. B. Huston, J. G. Coke, and P. H. Lewis (1965). *Parks and Recreation in Minneapolis, Vol. I, II, III.* Urbana, IL: University of Illinois, Department of Recreation and Municipal Park Administration.

Brown, M.T., and H. E. A. Tinsley (1983). Discriminant Analysis. *Journal of Leisure Research, 15* (4), 290-310.

Brown, T.L. (1984). Non-Respondents in Homogeneous Groups: Implications for Mailed Surveys—A Comment. *Leisure Sciences, 6* (4), 509-512.

Buhyoff, G.J. (1979). A Methodological Note on the Reliability of Observationally Gathered Time-Spent Data. *Journal of Leisure Research, 11* (4), 334-342.

Buyhoff, G.J., R. B. Hull IV, H. M. Rauscher, and R. C. Kirk (1985). Statistical Microcomputing: A Critical Look. *Leisure Sciences, 7*(1), 101-114.

Burdge, R.J. (1985). The Coming Separation of Leisure Studies from Parks and Recreation Education. *Journal of Leisure Research, 17* (2), 133-141.

Butler, G.D. (1958). *Research in Recreation Completed in 1957.* New York: National Recreation Association.

Butler, G.D. (1962). *Standards for Municipal Recreation Areas.* New York: National Recreation and Park Association.

Butler, G.D., and the National Advisory Committee on Recreation Research (1957). *Meriting Study on Research.* Washington, D.C.: National Advisory Committee on Recreation Research.

California Committee on Planning for Recreation, Park Areas, and Facilities (1956). *Guide for Planning Recreation Parks in California.* Sacramento, CA: State Documents Section.

Cesario, F.J. (1978). A New Method for Analyzing Outdoor Recreation Trip Data: A reply. *Journal of Leisure Research, 10* (2), 153-155.

Chenery, M.F. (1981). Effects of Summer Camp on Child Development and Contributions of Counselors on Those Effects. *Journal of Leisure Research, 13* (3), 195-207.

Christensen, J.C. (1979). The Correlation Coefficient and Problems of Inference in Recreation Research. *Leisure Sciences, 2* (3&4), 291-304.

Christensen, J.C. (1980). A Second Look at the Informal Interview as a Technique for Recreation Research. *Journal of Leisure Research, 12* (3), 183-186.

Christensen, J.C. (1982). On Generalizing About the Need for Follow-Up Efforts in Mail Recreation Surveys. *Journal of Leisure Research, 14* (3), 263-265.

Christensen, J.C. (1983). An Explosion of Canonical Correlation in Leisure Research. *Journal of Leisure Research, 15* (4), 311-322.

Christensen, J.C. (1985). Multiple Comparison Tests for Cross Classified Recreation Data. *Journal of Leisure Research, 17* (4), 296-304.

Community Service Council of Metropolitan Indianapolis (1966). *An Approach to Analyzing Leisure Time Services.* Indianapolis, IN: Community Service Council of Metropolitan Indianapolis, Inc.

Cosper, R.L., and S. M. Shaw. The Validity of Time-Budget Studies: A Comparison of Frequency and Diary Data in Halifax, Canada. *Leisure Sciences, 7* (2), 205-226.

Council of Social Agencies (1952). *The Cincinnati Report.* Cincinnati, OH: Council of Social Agencies.

Crandall, R.C., S. M. Altengarten, S. M. Carson, M. M. Nolan, and J. T. Dixon (1977). A General Bibliography of Leisure Publications. *Journal of Leisure Research, 9* (1), 15-54.

Crawford, D.W., G. Godby, and A. C. Crouter (1986). The Stability of Leisure Preferences. *Journal of Leisure Research, 18* (2), 96-115.

Crompton, J.L. A Recreation System Model. *Leisure Sciences, 1* (1), 53-66.

Cureton, T.K. (1949). Doctorate Theses Reported by Graduate Departments of Health, Physical Education, and Recreation 1930-1946 Inclusively. *Research Quarterly, 20,* 21-59.

Cureton, T.K. (1952). *Masters Theses in Health, Physical Education, and Recreation.* Washington, D.C.: American Association of Health, Physical Education and Recreation.

Cureton, T.K. (1954). *Thesis Abstracts in Physical Education 1924-1953.* Champaign-Urbana, IL: University of Illinois.

Cureton, T.K. (1961). *Thesis Abstracts in Health, Physical Education, and Recreation, 1953-1960.* Champaign-Urbana, IL: University of Illinois.

Curtis, H.S. (1914). *Play and Recreation.* New York: Ginn and Company.

Curtis, H.S. (1917). *The Play Movement and Its Significance.* New York: McMillan Company.

Cutten, G.B. (1926). *The Threat of Leisure.* New Haven: Yale University Press.

Denver Area Welfare Council (1956). *Criteria for Recreation and Leisure Time Agencies.* Denver, CO: Denver Area Welfare Council, Inc.

Detroit Metropolitan Regional Planning Commission (1960). *Recreation in the Detroit Region.* Detroit, MI: Detroit Regional Planning Commission.

Dunn, D.R. (1980). Urban Recreation Research: An Overview. *Leisure Sciences, 3* (1), 25-28.

Ellis, G., and P. A. Witt (1984). The Measurement of Perceived Freedom in Leisure. *Journal of Leisure Research, 16* (2), 110-123.

Goodale, T. (1965). *An Analysis of Leisure Behavior and Attitudes in Selected Minneapolis Course Tracts.* Urbana-Champaign, IL: University of Illinois, Department of Recreation and Municipal Park Administration.

Graefe, A.R., R. B. Ditton, J. W. Roggenbuck, and R. Schreyer (1981). Notes on the Stability of the Factor Structure of Leisure Meanings. *Leisure Sciences, 4* (1), 51-66.

Gunter, B.G. (1987). The Leisure Experience: Selected Properties. *Journal of Leisure Research, 19* (2), 115-130.

Hammitt, W.E. (1980). Outdoor Recreation: Is it a Multi-Phase Experience? *Journal of Leisure Research, 12* (2), 107-115.

Hammitt, W.E., and C. D. McDonald (1982). Response Bias and the Need for Extensive Mail Questionnaire Follow-Ups among Selected Recreation Samples. *Journal of Leisure Research, 14* (3), 207-216.

Harper, W. (1981). The Experience of Leisure. *Leisure Sciences, 4* (2), 113-126.

Harper, W. (1986). Freedom in the Experience of Leisure. *Leisure Sciences, 8* (2), 115-130.

Hawes, D.K. (1978). Satisfactions Derived from Leisure-Time Pursuits: An Exploratory Nationwide Survey. *Journal of Leisure Research, 10* (4), 247-264.

Haynes, R. (1913). *Recreation Survey: Detroit, Michigan.* Boston, MA: Playground Association of America.

Haynes, R. (1931). After College What? A Study of Physical Recreational Activities of Some Stephens' College Graduates. *Research Quarterly, 2,* 214-216.

Henkel, D. (1967). *Assessment of Effects of Children's Drama Upon Participants in a Public Recreation Department Setting.* Urbana-Champaign, IL: University of Illinois, Department of Recreation and Municipal Park Administration.

Heywood, L.A. (1978). Perceived Recreative Experience and the Relief of Tension. *Journal of Leisure Research, 10* (2), 86-97.

Holbrook, M.B. (1980). Representing Patterns of Association Among Leisure Activities: A Comparison of Two Techniques. *Journal of Leisure Research, 12* (3), 242-256.

Holland, S.M., A.J. Fedler, and R. B. Ditton (1986). The Group Representative Bias: Another Look. *Leisure Sciences, 8* (1), 79-92.

Iso-Ahola, S. (1979). Some Social Psychological Determinants of Perceptions of Leisure: Preliminary Evidence. *Leisure Sciences, 2* (3&4), 305-314.

Iso-Ahola, S. (1979). Basic Dimension of Definitions of Leisure. *Journal of Leisure Research, 11* (1), 15-27. (b).

Iso-Ahola, S. (1986). A Theory of Substitutability of Leisure Behavior. *Leisure Sciences, 8* (4), 367-390.

Johnson, D., and D. R. Field (1981). Applied and Basic Social Science Research: A Difference in Social Context. *Leisure Sciences, 4* (3), 269-280.

Kelly, J.R. (1978). A Revised Paradigm of Leisure Choices. *Leisure Sciences, 1* (4), 345-364.

Kelly, J.R. (1980). Outdoor Recreation Participation: A Comparative Analysis. *Leisure Sciences, 3* (2), 129-154.

Kelly, J.R. and M. W. Steinkamp. (1987). Later-Life Satisfaction: Does Leisure Contribute? *Leisure Sciences, 9* (3), 189-200.

Knapp, R. and C. Hartsoe (1979). *Play for America: The National Recreation Association, 1906-1965.* Arlington, VA: National Recreation and Park Association.

Kraus, R. (1984). *Recreation and Leisure in Modern Society, 3rd ed.* Chicago, IL: Scott, Foresman & Co.

Kreimer, A. (1977). Environmental Preferences: A Critical Analysis of Some Research Methodologies. *Journal of Leisure Research, 9* (2), 88-97.

Larabee, E. and R. Meyersohn (1958). *Mass Leisure*. Glencoe, IL: Free Press.

Lehman, H.C., and P. A. Witty (1927). *The Psychology of Play Activities*. New York: A.S. Barnes and Company.

Levine, R.L. and J. E. Hunter (1983). Regression Methodology: Correlation, Meta-Analysis, Confidence Intervals, and Reliability. *Journal of Leisure Research, 15* (4), 323-343.

May, H.L., and D. Petgen (1928). New York: A.S. Barnes and Company.

Meyersohn, R. (1969). The Sociology of Leisure in the United States: Introduction and Bibliography. *Journal of Leisure Research, 1* (1), 53-68.

Miller, N.P., E. J. Staley, et al. (1966). *A Behavioral Approach to Evaluating the Effectiveness of Recreation and Youth Services Programs*. Los Angeles, CA: Recreation and Youth Service Planning Council.

Mills, A.S. (1985). Participation Motivations for Outdoor Recreation: A Test of Maslow's Theory. *Journal of Leisure Research, 17* (3), 184-199.

Mills, A.S., R. W. Hodgson, J. G. McNeely Jr., and R. F. Masse (1981). An Improved Visitor Sampling Method for Ski Resorts and Similar Settings. *Journal of Leisure Research, 13* (3), 219-231.

Moeller, G.H., M. A. Mescher, T. A. More, and E. L. Shafer (1980). The Informal Interview as a Technique for Recreation Research. *Journal of Leisure Research, 12* (2), 174-182.

Morris, Courtney Ruth. Personal Communication, April 28, 1986.

Nash, J.B. (1927). *The Organization and Administration of Playgrounds and Recreation*. New York: A.S. Barnes and Company.

National Advisory Council on Regional Planning (1959). *User Resource Recreation Planning Method*. Washington, D.C.: Resources for the Future, Inc.

National Recreation and Park Association (1964). *A Self Study Relating to Public Recreation Programs in Topeka, Kansas*. Arlington, VA: National Recreation and Park Association.

National Recreation and Park Association (1965). *Evaluation of Community Recreation: A Guide to Evaluation with Standards and Evaluative Criteria*. Arlington, VA: National Recreation and Park Association Great Lakes Standards Committee.

National Recreation Association (1925). *Normal Course in Play*. New York: National Recreation Association.

National Recreation Association (1934). *The Leisure Hours of 5,000 People*. New York: National Recreation Association.

National Recreation Association (1949). *Proceedings of the 31st National Recreation Congress*. New York: National Recreation Association.

Noe, F.P. (1987). Measurement Specification and Leisure Satisfaction. *Leisure Sciences, 9* (3), 163-172.

Norman, W. (1966). *Statistical Report of Informal Uses of Outdoor Park Area in the Park District of Oak Park*. Oak Park, IL: Park District of Oak Park.

Oderwald, R.G., J. D. Wellman, and G. J. Buhyoff (1980). Multi-Stage Sampling of Recreationist: A Methodological Note on Unequal Probability Sampling. *Leisure Sciences, 3* (2), 213-217.

Oliviera, R.A., L. M. Arthur and A. C. Papastavrou (1983). A Distributed Lag Approach to Forecasting Wilderness Use. *Journal of Leisure Research, 15* (1), 52-64.

Parker, A. (1967). *A Study of the Effect of Recreation Upon the Institutionalized Aged.* Washington, D.C.: U.S. Public Health Department.

Perdue, R.R., and R. B. Ditton (1983). Sampling from Registration Files: The Problem of Duplicate Listings. *Journal of Leisure Research, 15* (2), 95-99.

Peterson, G.L., and D. J. Styes (1986). Evaluating Goodness of Fit in Nonlinear Recreation Demand Models. *Leisure Sciences, 8* (2), 131-148.

Ragheb, M. G., and J. G. Beard (1982). Measuring Leisure Attitude. *Journal of Leisure Research, 14* (2), 155-167.

Rainwater, C. A. (1922). *The Play Movement in the United States.* Chicago, IL: University of Chicago Press.

Recreation and Youth Services Planning Council (1957). *Differentiating Communities in Los Angeles County.* Los Angeles, CA: Recreation and Youth Services Planning Council.

Recreation and Youth Services Planning Council (1958). *Guide for Planning Leisure Time Services.* Los Angeles, CA: Recreation and Youth Services Planning Council.

Recreation and Youth Services Planning Council. (1960). *Youth Project Yardstick Measuring Youth Services Needs.* Los Angeles, CA: Recreation and Youth Services Planning Council.

Riis, J. (1980). *How the Other Half Lives.* New York: C. Scribner's Sons.

Roadburg, A. (1983). Freedom and Enjoyment: Disentangling Perceived Leisure. *Journal of Leisure Research, 15* (1), 15-26.

Rosenthal, D., M. Teague, P. Retish, J. West, and R. Vessell (1983). The Relationship Between Work Environment Attributes and Burnout. *Journal of Leisure Research, 15* (2), 125-135.

Sapora, A. V. (1954). *A Survey of the Rockford, Illinois Park District.* Rockford, IL: Community Welfare Council.

Sapora, A. V., and H. E. Kenney (1960). *A Study of the Present Status, Future Needs, and Recommended Standards Regarding Space Used for Health, Physical Education, Physical Recreation, and Athletics.* Champaign, IL: Stipes Publishing.

Sessoms, H. D. (1965). *Measuring Outcomes in Terms of Socialization and Mental Health of the Individual.* Recreation Research, November.

Shaw, S. M. (1985). The Meaning of Leisure in Everyday Life. *Leisure Sciences, 7* (1), 1-24.

Shaw, S. M. (1986). Leisure, Recreation, or Free Time? Measuring Time Usage. *Journal of Leisure Research, 18* (3), 177-189.

Smith, S. L. J. (1985). An Alternative Perspective on the Nature of Recreation and Leisure Studies: A Personal Response to Rabel Burdge. *Journal of Leisure Research, 17* (2), 155-160.

Snepenger, D. J., and J. L. Crompton (1984). Leisure Activity Participation Models and the Level of Discourse Theory. *Journal of Leisure Research, 16* (1), 22-33.

Snepenger, D. J., and J. L. Crompton (1985). A Review of Leisure Participation Models Based on the Level of Discourse Taxonomy. *Leisure Sciences, 7* (4), 443-466.

Staley, S. C. (1950). *Physical Education and Recreation.* (mimeographed paper).

Steiner, J. F. (1933). *Americans at Play: Recent Trends in Recreation and Leisure Time Activities.* New York: McGraw-Hill.

Stevens, J. B. (1966). Recreation Benefits from Water Pollution Control. *Water Resources Research, 2* (2), 167.

Stover, R. G., and A. P. Garbin (1982). Explanations of Leisure Behavior: An Analysis. *Journal of Leisure Research, 14* (2), 91-99.

Stynes, D. J., and G. L. Peterson (1984). A Review of Logit Models with Implications for Modeling Recreation Choices. *Journal of Leisure Research, 16* (4), 295-310.

Tate, U. S. (1984). Convergent and Discriminant Validity of Measures of Job, Leisure, Dyadic, and General Life Satisfaction by Causal Modeling Methodology. *Journal of Leisure Research, 16* (3), 250-254.

Tinsley, H. E. A. (1983). Application of Multivariate Analysis Procedures in Leisure Research. *Journal of Leisure Research, 15* (4), 311-322.

Tinsley, H. E. A., and R. A. Kass (1978). Leisure Activities and Need Satisfaction: A Replication and Extension. *Journal of Leisure Research, 10* (3), 191-202.

Tinsley, H. E. A., and R. A. Kass (1979). The Latent Structure of the Need Satisfying Properties of Leisure Activities. *Journal of Leisure Research, 11* (4), 278-291.

Tinsley, H. E. A., and D. J. Tinsley (1986). A Theory of the Attributes, Benefits, and Causes of Leisure Experience. *Leisure Sciences, 8* (1), 1-46.

Tinsley, H. E. A., S. L. Colbs, J. D. Teaff, and N. Kaufman. The Relationship of Age, Gender, Health and Economic Status to the Psychological Benefits Older Persons Report from Participation in Leisure Activities. *Leisure Sciences, 9* (1), 53-65.

Trafton, R.S., and H. E. A. Tinsley (1980). An Investigation of the Construct Validity of Measures of Job, Leisure, Dyadic and General Life Satisfaction. *Journal of Leisure Research, 12* (1), 34-44.

Tyre, G. L., and C. D. Siderelis, C. D. (1979). Instant-Count Sampling: A Technique for Estimating Recreation Use in Municipal Settings. *Leisure Sciences, 2* (2), 173-180.

Ulrich, R. A., and D. L. Addoms (1981). Psychological and Recreational Benefits of a Residential Park. *Journal of Leisure Research, 13* (1), 43-65.

Um, S., and J. L. Crompton (1986). The Importance of Testing for a Significant Difference Between Two Pearson Product-Moment Correlation Coefficients. *Journal of Leisure Research, 18* (3), 206-209.

UNESCO (1962). *Evaluation of the Forms and Needs of Leisure.* New York: UNESCO Publications Center.

United Community Service (1963). *A Study of Principles, Policies, and Planning Criteria for Group Services.* Detroit, MI: United Community Service.

United States Government (1941). *Park Use Studies and Demonstrations.* Washington, D. C.: State Government Printing Office.

Van Der Smissen, B. (1965). *Effects of Recreation on Individuals and Society.* Recreation Research, November.

Van Doren, C. S. (1972). Recent Dissertations and Theses in Leisure Recreation. *Journal of Leisure Research, 4* (3), 245-249.

Van Doren, C., S., and D. S. Solan (1979). Listing of Dissertations and Theses in Leisure and Recreation: August 1975 to August 1977. *Journal of Leisure Research, 11* (3), 219-244.

Wade, M. G. (1985). *Constraints on Leisure.* Springfield, IL: Charles C. Thomas.

Washington State Recreational and Cultural Resources (1946). *Recreation for All.* State of Washington: Recreational and Cultural Resources.

Weblen, T. (1989). *The Theory of the Leisure Class.* New York: Mentor Books.

Wellman, J. D., E. G. Hawk, J. W. Roggenbuck, and G. J. Buhyoff (1980). Mailed Questionnaire Surveys and the Reluctant Respondent: An Empirical Examination of Differences Between Early and Late Respondents. *Journal of Leisure Research, 12* (2), 164-173.

Westchester County of New York Recreation Commission (1961). *A Study of Recreation Lands and Facilities.* Westchester County, NY: Westchester County Recreation Commission.

Wingo, L. (1964). Recreation and Urban Development. *Annals of the American Academy of Political Science, March.*

Young, R. A. and A. T. Kent (1985). Using the Theory of Reasoned Action to Improve the Understanding of Recreation Behavior. *Journal of Leisure Research, 17* (2), 90-106.

Yu, J. -M. (1980). The Empirical Development of Typology for Describing Leisure Behavior on the Basis of Participation Patterns. *Journal of Leisure Research, 12* (4), 309-320.

Yu, J. -M. (1980). A Leisure Demand Projection Model. *Leisure Sciences,* 4 (2), 127-142.

History and Philosophy of Leisure

Past, Present, and Future Research

John L. Hemingway
Department of Recreation
———————— Washington State University ————————

John R. Kelly
Department of Leisure Studies
———————— University of Illinois ————————

In the first edition of this essay, the author noted the absence, from a rigorous perspective, of genuine historical or philosophical work generated from within leisure studies. Instead, he suggested, there has been uncritical borrowing from a narrow selection of books and the repetition of often unfounded clichés, which have in turn been borrowed again. Attention was called to several contemporary projects in both history and philosophy related to leisure as worth the risk of serious scholarly engagement. It remains the authors' contention that this judgment still holds, with the proviso that there are now additional projects underway, both outside and within leisure studies, that are sufficiently rigorous to suggest the possibility that such work can become part of the field's intellectual horizon. Whether this actually occurs depends on the field's openness to diverse scholarly inquiry and willingness to commit adequate intellectual resources.

The analysis proceeds in three segments: (1) The past or Formative Period; (2) the Contemporary Period; and (3) the Future. These are summarized briefly here.

I. *The Formative Period: Living on Borrowed Courage*

In the early formative period from the end of the Civil War to World War II, the problem was one of identification. The developing recreation movement required some identified intellectual bases for action. A variety of historical and contemporary sources were gathered to develop a rationale for social action. During the 1950s and 1960s, a consensus was formed and repeated in textbooks and articles. That consensus, usually referred to inappropriately as "philosophy," included four elements: (1) The evangelical writings of movement leaders; (2) appropriated European sources, especially Pieper and Huizinga; (3) the "bridge" books of de Grazia and Dulles; and (4) the derived consensus repeated in the texts.

II. *The Contemporary Period*

The 1970s and early 1980s era was revisionist. A second generation of books was based on the assumption that there existed a research base for the field. This was taken to be the result of the new social science focus, and history and philosophy received less and less attention in textbooks.

Outside the field, three philosophical approaches to leisure appeared. (1) Critical Theory, stemming from the Institute for Social Research (popularly known as the Frankfurt School), and neo-Marxist scholarship argued that leisure is the product of a particular social system. Controlling social forces shape the nature of both public and market-provided leisure opportunities and of supporting value systems. (2) Existential European philosophies stressed the significance of play in the creation of self, culture, and society. Play and freedom are interwoven in action approaches to leisure. (3) A variety of American efforts to reconceptualize leisure emerged, often incorporating countercultural critiques of Western dualisms and materialism. As noted below, there is continuing activity in Critical Theory and Existentialism, while North American efforts have shifted direction to engage some of the themes raised on the Continent. One important development is the recognition that rigorous study of leisure requires a blending of historical and philosophical perspectives.

In historical projects, leisure became increasingly acknowledged by social and cultural historians as an important dimension of life. Most relevant historical work has been based on social class analysis and focused on working class leisure. Community studies challenged many of the old myths about recreation behaviors and provisions. Leisure, often under other labels, also emerged as significant among historians of culture. Both narrative and quantitative studies of "ordinary people" continue to analyze leisure as one element in cultural and social history. Historical scholarship from within leisure studies has been enriched by several narrative histories as well as critical studies of specific aspects of the development of leisure.

III. Leisure History and Philosophy in the Future

If the study of leisure is to be developed into a recognized field of intellectual endeavor, the new work emerging must be sustained and expanded. Borrowing from "pop" fads and oversimplifying materials from other fields must be replaced by genuine scholarship. From one perspective, the issue revolves around resources. Will we invest in historical and philosophical work? We have begun to engage in dialogue with social and behavioral scientists. At the least we can support the time and effort required for such dialogue with historians and philosophers. In time, leisure studies may even enter the same community of knowledge creation as those who *do* history and philosophy.

Critical Summary

Both history and philosophy are ancient disciplines that have developed distinctive methods and metaphors to guide their modes of inquiry. Both are filled with contention and conflict, as well as replete with complex and esoteric concepts and formulas. Like any disciplines, they require systematic, sustained effort and preparation to engage in their projects, even to begin to play in their arenas.

This effort has seldom been made in leisure studies. This could be a very short paper, recalling the meager accounts of derivative and borrowed ideas, outlining how various authors have repeated each other's ponied summaries, and lamenting the paucity of current substantial projects. There are, of course, occasional borrowed concepts that have been collected in eclectic introductory chapters of textbooks, and articles and even books repeating ancient ideas or telling "in-house" tales of the domestic recreation movement. Mostly, perhaps, there has been uncritical borrowing from the political scientist Sebastian de Grazia, who penned an essay on leisure some thirty years ago (1962).

We speak of "leisure studies" as though there was such an identified scholarly area. In social and behavioral research, we adorn our little studies with references to concepts and models from various other disciplines, usually wrenching them out of context and oversimplifying their limitations and derivations. We grasp monodimensional labels as though they could illuminate all the mysteries of complex phenomena. In historical and philosophical studies, we repeat a few old historical clichés and concepts without knowing whether they have any currency in their own fields. We not only are not *doing* history or philosophy, with very few exceptions we are not even *reading* what is current. In short, we claim the status of a scholarly realm of study without doing the work.

More recently, there have been signs the field is generating a certain number of more rigorous attempts to engage in serious historical and philosophical scholarship. But any optimism must be sharply curtailed in the light of a past lack of fresh conceptualizations grounded in contemporary history and philosophy. Most particularly, where are the critical studies that employ contemporary work in a dialogue with scholars from those disciplines? Intriguing ideas have been picked out of other contexts, then laid on leisure with a trowel. There has been too much uncritical repetition of the cliches and errors of the latest pop fads, "Future Schlock" or "Megabucks," as though these had genuine intellectual content. We repeat paperback ideas while studiously avoiding the hardcover and hard-content library. We pepper our papers with references to research insufficiently read and concepts insufficiently comprehended. And then we are annoyed when no one "out there" recognizes the significance of this field we proudly rename "leisure studies."

So much for the introductory diatribe, which remains substantively unchanged from the first edition. The paper will close on a similar note. Now, is there to be anything in between? Is there a "past, present, and future" substantial enough to support further analysis?

Our argument is simple. First, there is a past to the history and philosophy of leisure that could have been used as a springboard into deep water. Instead we have paddled around in the wading pool practicing the same strokes over and over. Second, there are indeed some exciting contemporary projects out there in the big lake of scholarly endeavor for those willing to risk some off-shore engagement. The present has its possibilities, however inarticulately expressed and inconveniently demanding. Third, the future is not waiting for us to tidy up our playrooms. The question is whether we will turn the corner into Century 21 having prepared ourselves to participate in its creation. *Will* we do and support the demanding discipline of creation, in the critical examination of the past and present as well as in the making of the future? *Are* we willing to risk our resources and ourselves to create a community of scholars who *do* the creative activity of leisure?

THE FORMATIVE PERIOD: LIVING ON BORROWED COURAGE

When does the past begin? The focus on leisure and recreation studies in North America permits concentrating on two formative periods. The first, roughly from the end of the Civil War and the rise of the industrial city to World War II, was a time of identification. The development of a recreation movement in response to industrialization required identifying some intellectual bases for action. In this period a variety of historical and contemporary sources were gathered to begin to develop a rationale for social action.

The second formative period is our immediate past, from the end of World War II until about 1970, during which themes of the previous period were enlarged and enhanced by adding the work of three philosopher-historians as well as excursions into some psychological and sociological ideas. By 1970 or so, a consensus had been formed and repeated in textbooks and journal articles that tended to duplicate each other with minor variations. This consensus is still operative for many who identify the time of their own education as contemporary.

15 2, 95 3

The Founders and Their Successors

In this critical analysis, the focus will be on how history and philosophy were developed rather than on details of their content or interrelationships. The time of the founders in the late 1880s was driven by the conditions of the working classes in the industrial city. Recreation opportunity was one element among general social concerns for the degradation and destruction of lives by the denial of essential resources. Parkland space was more oriented toward the middle classes and their presumed preferences. Recreation as opportunity for activity was directed first toward children being released from the factory. Schools developed physical activity programs. Settlement houses had more varied programs for adults.

The fundamental question was "Why?" Joseph Lee answered in terms of "play" (1929). He believed that the "battle with the slum" could be won only when play was possible. Play involved learning and discipline. It was developmental in health and emotional aims and functional in being constructive preparation for the productive adult life. Also written in the early 20th century, Luther Gulick's *A Philosophy of Play* (1920) argued that recreation would build character, especially for children whose growth required engrossment in such expressive engagement. These founders borrowed from educational theorists of their day to identify the positive dimensions of play.

Their social impact, however, was more profound than their thought as they helped consolidate diffused concern about places for children to play. In Boston at least (Hardy, 1982), the "play philosophies" were employed to undergird programs in the playgrounds established to keep working class children off the streets and in their own neighborhoods. Lee and others formulated arguments that helped gain support for recreation programs that would inculcate values functional for the political and economic elites. In Eastern cities, however, such "rational recreation" attracted relatively few working men and women who preferred the excitement of cinema, dance halls, the saloon, and the streets (Rosenzweig, 1983; Piess, 1986).

Histories are seldom written while social change is under way. Rather, social histories of this period—occasionally with leisure as a sub-theme—are only now appearing. These studies promise to revise the myths and legends that have become accepted within the parks and recreation movement as history. Within the movement, however, there are a series of significant documents that may be employed in writing the histories of this fascinating period of conflict and turmoil.

1950-1970: Building a Consensus

World War I, the Great Depression, and World War II absorbed so much intellectual energy in making history that there was little remaining for sub-themes such as leisure and recreation. The period after WWII, however, was quite different. High birth rates, economic optimism, the explosion of higher education, growth in incomes and productivity, and other positive factors opened all sorts of new interests and avenues. Within still sheltered contexts, even leisure and recreation were given a new start for what promised to be a new age.

Several sources and themes emerged: (1) the evangelical "philosophies" contained within new units for the study of leisure and recreation; (2) borrowing of European approaches to leisure and culture; (3) de Grazia and Dulles as bridges; and, (4) the derived consensus and its reproduction in textbooks. Here we can do no more than trace the themes of this period of renewal.

(1) "Philosophies" of recreation and leisure: The emerging field of leisure and recreation studies developed its own internal conceptual base in the 1950s and 1960s. The writings of Charles Brightbill (1960) exemplified this effort to explain and promote the field. Popular philosophical writings of the day (Will Durant), references from a psychiatrist (Alexander Martin), speculations about the future in an automated and cybernized world (Norbert Weiner), and other non-technical writings were compiled into an exhortation for the significance and meanings of leisure. The "evangelical" tone of such writing was based on a conviction that leisure and recreation would be increasingly central in a future with abundant time and economic resources. Brightbill and other "philosophers" of the movement gathered the fragments of knowledge then available into an argument for leisure in human and social development.

(2) European Philosopher/Historians: During this period three books were made available in English that had significant impacts on leisure studies. The first was by a German Catholic

philosopher and theologian, Josef Pieper (1952). With an introduction by T.S. Eliot in the English translation, Pieper's essay on
leisure as the basis of culture offered a Thomist-Aristotelian
analysis of the importance of leisure to cultural production.
Leisure is seen as more than retreat or inactivity, but as rising
above necessity into the celebration of meaning in festival. Pieper's
joining of leisure to cultural development and a "festival attitude" had lasting influence.

The second and most important writing was *Homo Ludens* by
the Dutch philosopher and historian Johan Huizinga (1955). An
authentic and respected scholar, Huizinga had written since the
early 1930s on the centrality of play in culture. Only when he
translated his 1944 book into English just before his death did his
writings gain recognition in America. He employed philosophical, historical, and anthropological evidence in developing his
argument that the ludic dimension of life—voluntary, non-seri-
ous, disinterested, self-contained, and ordered—is central to the
development of any culture. Play creates—in the production of
law, knowledge, the arts, philosophy, and even war. Play creates
its own realm of meaning and yet contributes to larger worlds.
Even now, leisure scholars have yet to mine all the gold from this
extraordinarily erudite work.

The third book, by Roger Caillois (1961), has been quoted in
most textbooks for its classification of play into four types. Such
schemes, whether useful for explanation or not, have an appeal
in most fields of study because they lend an aura of science in the
absence of empirical research. Caillois's typology, although too
narrowly confined to games, did suggest the variety of forms
endemic to leisure and recreation.

At the same time, references to a variety of "theories of play,"
some of which had been picked up by Lee, Gulick, and others in
the initial formation period, also appeared in various writings.
The theme of "play" with sources in both education and
anthropological literature (Ellis, 1973) retained salience through
this period until driven to a marginal position by the sociological
approaches dominant in the 1970s. With the emergence of psychological perspectives since 1975, there is renewed interest
in play as a dimension of leisure (Kelly, 1987, ch. 2).

(3) Two Bridge Books: The agenda-setting book for leisure
research in the 1960s and early 1970s was the *Work and Leisure*
volume edited by Smigel (1963). For conceptual work, however,

THE book was *Of Time, Work, and Leisure* by Sebastian de Grazia, published in 1962 and released in paperback in 1964. From 1964 on, most of the references to Greek philosophy were actually de Grazia's interpretation of Aristotle. History usually meant repeating his excursions into Greek, Roman, and Renaissance times. This engaging and well-written book did not follow the recreation party line of envisioning a glowing future for leisure. Rather, de Grazia, an intellectual elitist, distinguished between the activities of the mindless masses and leisure as a rare condition of being to be achieved by very few. Nevertheless, his book became the basis of considerable historicizing and philosophizing by those in leisure studies who did not share his elitism or pessimism. One theme, however, linked the Smigel and de Grazia volumes: concern with leisure as a *problem* for the masses unprepared for the free time that was to be bestowed on them.

At about the same time (1965), the paperback edition of Foster Dulles's earlier (1940) *A History of Recreation: America Learns to Play* became the standard historical reference for the field. This narrative was based on public documents of forms of recreation from colonial to modern times. Not an analytical social history, Dulles' book gave attention primarily to recreation events organized, advertised, and reported in print. His chronicle of events complemented the recreation movement's concern with organized activity rather than a full range of leisure.

Together, the de Grazia and Dulles books provided a bridge from the scattered references of the founding writings to the second period. They were a bridge as well to the world of scholarship outside recreation curricula. It is not surprising, then, that most early textbooks repeated their summaries. Note, however, that such developments were adventitious rather than systematic. There was little original philosophical or historical scholarship in the field. Rather, those attempting to legitimate and provide a conceptual base for the new area of study borrowed from these convenient sources. It appears that most students of leisure read only secondary sources, such as de Grazia, or tertiary summaries in textbooks.

THE CONTEMPORARY PERIOD

In this brief overview of contemporary developments, philosophy and history will be divided before being reunited in a look forward to the future. The first development to be noted is the revision of older approaches in newer texts that have incorporated some elements of the social science work of the 1960s and 1970s. The second development is the activity of a few scholars outside the field who have taken up the themes of leisure and play in their work, which offers a new set of resources and possibilities for leisure studies. This leads to a third development, the incorporation of these resources into leisure scholarship.

Revisions: 1975-1985

Max Kaplan's 1960 book, *Leisure in America: A Social Inquiry*, took a general sociological approach combined with some speculative thought. Subsequently, in *Leisure: Theory and Policy* (1975) he attempted to incorporate an even wider set of perspectives in an integrated study of leisure theory and policy. The rewritten second edition of James Murphy's *Concepts of Leisure* (1981) was similar in trying to integrate a variety of approaches. Both exemplify the shift from eclectic speculation to the inclusion of social science research-based perspectives. Neither, however, had as much impact on the field as did the new generation of textbooks.

Without depreciating the "older" philosophies of the movement, the second generation of texts was based on the assumption that there exists a research base for the field that cannot be ignored. Further, the optimism about the coming "leisure age" had been tempered by a series of economic trends and events. The issue for texts such as Godbey and Parker (1976), Kraus (1978), and Kelly (1982) had become more one of research-based knowledge than of gathering widespread ideas into a conceptual framework. It should be noted that the most referenced model for the development of a scientific field, Kuhn's paradigm shift (1970), suggests the crucial role of textbooks.

In this revision, however, history and philosophy were allotted a smaller and smaller place. With one exception (Kelly, 1982), philosophy was reduced to a ritual bow in the directions of Joseph Lee and Aristotle, and history to a few paragraphs. Sociology and psychology had become the ruling disciplines, especially in their methodological formats. The theoretical debates of the disciplines were usually ignored by students of leisure who had taken research courses without engaging in theoretical conflicts.

New Themes and Resources: Philosophy

At the same time philosophy was receiving diminished attention in North American studies of leisure, an increasing number of European scholars acknowledged leisure as a worthwhile realm of study. Their works are scattered and often classified under different headings than leisure. Nonetheless, they offer new possibilities for those willing to accept the challenge of meeting them on their own terms, including reading in their original languages.

(1) Critical Theory: The Frankfurt School has produced a series of thinkers whose critical analyses of Western culture bear directly on the nature of leisure. Beginning with Adorno's and Horkheimer's collaborative and independent critiques (1972, 1974), Critical Theory has dissected mass culture, including leisure's place in legitimizing social structures that truncate freedom and tie workers to alienating and alienated roles. This work has been extended by Jürgen Habermas in a series of untranslated essays on work, consumption, and leisure. Habermas applies the Marxian analysis of alienation in production to consumption and ties this to the eclipse of classical models of leisure (regarded as culture producing) by capitalist models of free time (regarded as culture consuming). Thus, increased amounts of free time cannot liberate workers from alienation, because the models of free time used in capitalist society are as alienating as work. Leisure is reified into a set of commodities purveyed in the market and defined as adequate reward for work that lacks engagement with real production and a social life without self-determination (Kelly, 1986). Habermas' work is closely related to an increased interest among social and political theorists in civil society, where leisure is to be recovered from market choice shaped by mass media and transformed into action creating the self and the community (Habermas, 1989).

(2) Neo-Marxism: Other neo-Marxist thinkers take somewhat different critical approaches. John Clarke and Chas Critcher (1985) employ perspectives from the Birmingham Centre of

cultural studies to analyze how leisure in Britain is a product of a particular social system rather than a gift of the Industrial Revolution. They argue that leisure studies approaches have ignored this social hegemony and have been co-opted into adopting a model in which freedom is defined as individual choices. Class and gender inequalities of opportunity and of self-definitions have been largely neglected. They offer a historical critique to the functional system-accepting approach that dominates the field. Chris Rojek (1985) has produced another critical analysis with a somewhat more complex basis. Rojek includes Marx, Weber, Freud, Foucault, Habermas, Gramsci, and Elias in his exploration of how leisure has become privatized, commercialized, and incorporated into a social program of pacification. His sometimes obscure argument suggests a number of sub-themes and analytical possibilities within the overall theme of hegemonic control through the shaping of consciousness. Finally, André Gorz's iconoclastic Marxism entails a rejection of the predominance of work. Challenging the conventional Marxist elevation of labor as creative human activity that has been alienated in capitalism, Gorz argues for the liberation from work into truly creative human activity in leisure (1985, 1989). Rather than accepting (as is being done in the current rush to embrace commercial recreation and tourism) the hegemony of economically based values, the work of these thinkers challenges us to think through these values' implications and to reclaim advocacy for the centrality of leisure itself.

(3) Existentialism: Parallel to emphasis on social forces among critical and neo-Marxist thinkers, there is a third theme which proposes that leisure may also be analyzed as self-determining action (Kelly, 1987, ch. 3). Largely European, this theme links the existentialism of Heidegger, grounded in the playfully self-creating affirmative nihilism of Nietzsche, and Sartre. It recurs in sources as diverse as the hermeneutics of Hans-Georg Gadamer (1989), the deconstructionism of Derrida (e.g., 1978), and the phenomenological existentialism of Fink (1960). Whatever their differences, thinkers working this theme stress the significance of "play" in reflexive understanding (thus recognizing that the structures of the world are constructed rather than given) and in the production of knowledge. Play both creates and is created. As such it is essential to the production of novelty

in the world (Hans, 1981). Fully aware of the profound and complex ways in which creative action is coerced and stifled, the possibility of a redetermination of the self and the world is opened through play.

(4) Until recently, little reference could be made to philosophic inquiry rising from within leisure studies. Discussions in text books were fragmentary and largely derivative. Most other work was nonrigorous, frequently drawing on counter-cultural themes that emerged in the 1960s and 1970s and which have now faded into obscurity even in California (unless they have resurfaced in Seattle). There was a brief flourish of interest in "new age" themes, but the intellectual insubtantiality of these was soon apparent. There is nonetheless some evidence of increased interest in and sophistication of philosophic work in leisure studies.

(a) Fundamental assumptions about the foundations of leisure inquiry have been questioned. Based on papers delivered to the opening session of the 1989 Symposium on Leisure Research, several essays appeared in the *Journal of Leisure Research* criticizing the moral implications of the "subjective" interpretation dominant in the social psychological analysis of leisure (Goodale, 1990; Sylvester, 1990). Hemingway (1990) extended this critique to include the epistemological foundations of empiricist social science as practiced in leisure studies, proposing instead an interpretive model based on poststructuralism. In a subsequent article, Hemingway (1993) has gone on to criticize the prevailing conception of philosophy in leisure studies as static and influenced by the same impulse towards essentialism that runs through empiricist social science. Again using poststructuralist sources, he develops a dialogical approach more consonant with the historical nature of human beings. These critical essays at least indicate some reflection on alternative approaches to inquiry freed from the corporatism of mainline academic writing. Such discussions have previously been absent from the leisure studies literature.

(b) The reinterpretation of classical sources has been applied to critical analysis of contemporary leisure and society. These reinterpretations also offer examples of the application of hermeneutic strategies available to leisure studies. Hunnicutt (1990) examines the meanings of play and leisure in Plato, with the conclusions that these represent morally superior forms of activity and that the search for knowing is best described as play. Hemingway, in two essays (1988, 1991), challenges the conventional interpretation of Aristotelian leisure as contemplation, arguing that the civil dimension to leisure has been ignored, thus losing the critical force of Aristotle's thinking when it is applied to contemporary leisure. The narcissistic, individualist tendencies in this leisure emerge when contrasted with an ethically more powerful communitarian interpretation.

(c) Two volumes of essays suggest greater awareness of the ethical dimension to leisure. Sylvester, et al. (1987) examine a variety of issues in the justification and provision of therapeutic recreation services. Fain (1991) collects essays from an interdisciplinary, international symposium on leisure and ethics, illustrating the variety of perspectives from which the topic can be approached. Although uneven in quality, both volumes contain essays that make contributions to what, it is to be hoped, is an expanding philosophical discussion of leisure.

There is considerable danger this expansion will be short lived. Interest in, and occasionally tolerance of, critical scholarship has not been the rule in leisure studies. Too much current research seems driven by the search for legitimacy, not least in the eyes of government and market sector institutions that control financial resources. There is not much funding available for critical thinking, or perhaps in any other kind of theorizing. Many in the field seem thrilled just to receive some form of attention from mainstream institutions such as government agencies, business interests, or the media. This climate, found even in our universities, does not foster or reward critical or creative scholarship.

New Themes and Resources: History

History has not been a lively option in leisure studies. Despite a common agreement that we can hardly understand where we are unless we comprehend how we arrived there, we are not *doing* much history. There are recent contributions that challenge this generalization, to which we will turn shortly. These aside, there have been only a few articles and chapters on the development of the recreation movement, its leaders, and institutions.

Coupled with the squeezing out of historical materials from our textbooks by the social science vogue, there is within leisure studies relatively little rigorous attention to historical settings.

Outside the field, however, prospects are considerably brighter. Three kinds of historical analysis are offering new insights and analysis relevant to the study of leisure. History is, after all, more than a recounting of "facts." It is the placing of those facts into an interpretive framework that yields some viable account of their connections. One such framework is that of class differences and differential social power. A second focuses on cultural development and the significance of modes of social communication. A third framework examines the steady commercialization of society, with attendant changes in forms of leisure. Employing both narrative and quantitative methodologies, historians are beginning to find important the life domain we call leisure.

(1) Social class analysis and working class leisure: There have been several historical studies of working-class leisure in Britain during various periods of the 19th and 20th centuries. Almost all take the perspective that economic elites and their surrogates in pulpits, city councils, and editors' offices regulated and shaped workers' opportunities for the benefit of dominant economic and social interests (see, e.g., Thompson, 1966, ch. 3). Leisure provisions were defined more by definitions of what would contribute to economic productivity, social stability, and a narrowly defined morality rather than by the personal and social development of workers and their households.

The same theme has been taken up in a few North American studies. One examines conflicts over leisure in Worcester, Massachusetts, from 1870 to 1920, including celebrations, saloons, entertainments, parks, and movies (Rosenzweig, 1983). Leisure is identified as an arena of class struggle, with within-class ethnic and gender divisions exploited to control activity. The connection between class politics and leisure in industrializing Cincinnati from 1788 to 1890 demonstrates how recreation opportunities and restrictions were shaped by the dominant economic groups (Ross, 1985).

An older classic study of the strife-ridden mill town of Homestead was written by a woman historian (Byington, 1975). First published in 1910, it focuses on household life, with leisure as one dimension of common life. An exciting recent study of the leisure of working women in New York from 1880 to 1920 examines market responses to desires to "have fun" as well as on class and gender issues of domination (Piess, 1986). Piess' scholarship also demonstrates the wealth of material available to the serious historian of leisure. A community history of Boston also discusses the industrializing period from 1865 to 1915, indicating how the upper classes developed a recreational system to create working class leisure according to the former's values (Hardy, 1982). Joseph Lee is seen here as one reformer who promoted supervised recreation to instill values of social compliance in lower class children.

Most such studies are limited in scope, both of historical periods and of what constitutes leisure. They accept certain theoretical premises about how the American social system has operated. Yet they are a beginning toward real histories of leisure—studies that are more than self-congratulating narratives by and for those who are lodged in the system.

(2) Cultural history: Leisure is, after all, so much more than parks and playgrounds or theaters and sports arenas. One important movement in historical studies has been to take a look at "ordinary people." Historians are using all sorts of documents from diaries to public records, to examine just how people lived and related to each other, how they worked and played, loved and fought. There is now a vast realm of study containing a variety of leisure themes without necessarily mentioning leisure or recreation in titles, chapter headings, or even indices. Such studies, often of a single community or region, are about schools and churches, bars and halls, clubs and families, children and adults. There is ample material available here for more inclusive and comprehensive histories of leisure, both from secondary analysis and from primary documentation now increasingly accessible. The problem here is that leisure studies does not support scholars engaged in the demanding task of examining cultural history.

(3) Closely related to the foregoing is the historical study of the commercialization of society. Bringing together economic history and the study of popular culture, this work illustrates shifts in leisure as industrialization accelerated. Leisure was progressively redefined to support the hegemony of dominant

interests. The literature on commercialization is well developed in Europe. British historian J.H. Plumb's essay in McKendrick, Brewer, and Plumb (1982) on the commercialization of leisure is frequently cited. A North American example of such work is the volume edited by Butsch (1990), in which American scholars examine specific aspects of the commercialization process. There are strong connections between studies of commercialization and the Critical Theory and Neo-Marxist approaches to philosophical inquiry noted above. Indeed, these efforts frequently cross over into each other.

(4) We noted above that recent contributions suggest historical study remains possible within a multidisciplinary leisure studies perspective. Hunnicutt's narrative of the end of the shorter hours movement in American labor, *Work Without End* (1988), makes an original contribution, synthesizing many themes in 20th century U.S. labor history. Hunnicutt analyzes the eclipse of demands for increased free time in favor of full employment and the development of advertising under the guise of the "new economic gospel of consumption," demonstrating the vulnerability of leisure to calculated political and economic decisions. It also raises the question why the public debate on leisure and society, marked during the 1920s and 1930s, has faded from memory. A Harvard economist, rather than a leisure studies scholar, has addressed the issue most forcefully in recent discussion (Schor, 1991).

Cross's *A Social History of Leisure Since 1600* (1990) attempts to distill themes from the social history of leisure. In doing so, Cross illustrates the influences working on the historical nature of leisure. These are too often absent in leisure studies, where the ahistorical nature of empiricist social science tends to isolate leisure from the historical forces shaping it. The field mistakes historically developed forms of leisure and distributions of time as somehow naturally occurring, rather than as the products of human action. Both Hunnicutt's and Cross's books demonstrate the intellectual emptiness of this view.

Finally, Stormann has, in two essays (1991, 1993), subjected the field's received version of its evolution to critical analysis. Drawing on approaches and works discussed earlier, Stormann demonstrates that the recreation movement and its leaders were not ideologically disinterested and that they identified with the dominant social, economic, and political forces in society. Couched in the language of reform, the recreation movement functioned to reinforce hegemonic cultural values rather than to liberate human potential. Stormann's analytic framework is well elaborated and his argument suggests the possible need for a fundamental reassessment of the field's roots. Perhaps the recent spate of interest in commercial recreation and entrepreneurship are more deeply grounded in the field's history than has been realized.

LEISURE HISTORY AND PHILOSOPHY IN THE FUTURE

Philosophically and historically based leisure inquiry is occurring, within and outside the leisure studies field. There are some indications its presence within the field has increased slightly. But what is ahead for such work? A cynical response is that it will go on without us. There will be increasing recognition by historians, philosophers, social and behavioral scientists, and students of popular culture of the significance of nonwork domains in human life. And a little late and generally a dollar short, leisure studies will borrow from that work, pretending to be current in its scholarship.

What about the field of leisure studies? Are we always to be derivative, always latching on to pop fads and seldom in touch with substantive issues in either society or scholarship? Are we always to borrow from and never contribute to the creation of knowledge, to theory-building and explanation-seeking?

There have been a number of attempts to open the range of theoretical possibilities for the field, to which the authors have tried to contribute (Kelly, 1987; Hemingway, 1990). It is central to these attempts that no issue be presented as closed or resolved. The difficulty is that most people are more comfortable with answers rather than questions. Slogans, it seems, sell better than analysis, especially dialectically inspired analysis that consciously avoids resolution. Yet it is questioning, rather than answering, that advances inquiry.

A more troubling issue must be raised here, one beyond identifying issues and questions to be addressed. That is something in which we can all join, *provided* we really believe in the field of leisure studies. But *are* we committed to the integrity and development of the serious study of leisure in many disciplines, using many metaphors of explanation? If leisure studies is to succeed as a scholarly area, then it will necessarily support and promote scholars from all relevant disciplinary perspectives and will in fact strive to break down disciplinary barriers. History and philosophy, however, are perhaps the two most self-evidently central disciplines for which we seem now to have little time or support.

Of course we should be engaged in dialogue with the practitioners of history and philosophy as we are beginning to engage psychologists, economists, and sociologists. *Of course* we need to listen, read, and learn. That is the beginning, however, not the goal.

If we are serious abut the integrity of the field, then we will be nurturing those who *do* history and philosophy. Our degree programs will then go beyond *training* in professional techniques to embrace *education* in the dilemmas and underlying issues of leisure in society and culture, past, present, and future. Our programs would then include prerequisite immersion in the history and philosophy of the field and its subject, not just a course or two to satisfy vocationally driven accreditation standards. It is a question of investment: will we invest in the support of scholars, or will we continue to advertise teaching positions defined by lists of courses to be taught? Will we give up the pretense that our repetitious litanies about Greece and the Renaissance constitute philosophy, or that our cautionary tales about Rome and the Puritans are history? Most importantly, will we take the risks of being scholars ourselves? For leisure studies to become a fully authentic field of inquiry, we must put resources—faculty time and department money—into scholarship. Then in time we will find that we can do history and become historians, do philosophy and become philosophers. Not all of us, to be sure, but enough so that we open ourselves to that exciting human world still all around us, learn from it and even join it. Then, and only then, will we become full members of that community of scholars who create knowledge and understanding.

BIBLIOGRAPHY

Brightbill, Charles K. (1960). *The Challenge of Leisure*. Englewood Cliffs, NJ: Prentice-Hall.

Butsch, R. (Ed.). (1990). *For Fun and Profit: The Transformation of Leisure into Consumption*. Philadelphia: Temple University Press.

Byington, Margaret. (1975, 1910). *Homestead: The Households of a Mill Town*. Pittsburgh: University of Pittsburgh Center for International Studies.

Caillois, Roger. (1961). *Man, Play, and Games*. London: Thames & Hudson.

Clarke, John and Chas Critcher. (1985). *The Devil Makes Work: Leisure in Capitalist Britain*. Urbana, IL: University of Illinois Press.

Cross, Gary. (1990). *A Social History of Leisure Since 1600*. State College, PA: Venture Publishing.

de Grazia, Sebastian. (1964). *Of Time, Work, and Leisure*. New York: Doubleday/Anchor.

Derrida, Jacques. (1978). Structure, Sign, and Play in the Discourse of the Human Sciences. In *Writing and Difference*, pp. 278-293. (Trans. A. Bass). Chicago: University of Chicago Press.

Dulles, Foster R. (1965). *A History of Recreation: America Learns to Play*. (2nd ed.). New York: Appleton-Century-Crofts.

Ellis, Michael J. (1973). *Why People Play*. Englewood Cliffs, NJ: Prentice-Hall.

Fain, Gerald S. (Ed.). (1991). *Leisure and Ethics: Reflections on the Philosophy of Leisure*. Reston, VA: American Association for Leisure and Recreation.

Fink, Eugen. (1960). *Spiel als Weltsymbol*. Stuttgart: W. Kohlhammer.

Gadamer, Hans-Georg. (1989). *Truth and Method*. (2nd rev. ed.). (J. Weinsheimer & D.G. Marshall, Trans.). New York: Crossroad Publishing.

Godbey, Geoffrey and Stanley Parker. (1976). *Leisure Studies and Services*. Philadelphia: W.B. Saunders.

Goodale, Thomas L. (1990). Perceived Freedom as Leisure's Antithesis. *Journal of Leisure Research, 22*, 296-302.

Gorz, André. (1985). *Paths to Paradise: On the Liberation from Work*. (M. Imrie, Trans.). Boston: South End Press.

Gorz, André. (1989). *Critique of Economic Reason*. (G. Handyside & C. Turner, Trans.). New York: Verso Press.

Gulick, Luther H. (1920). *A Philosophy of Play*. New York: Schirmer Books.

Habermas, Jürgen. (1989). *The Structural Transformation of the Public Sphere: An Inquiry into a Category of Bourgeois Society*. (T. Burger & F. Lawrence, Trans.). Cambridge, MA: MIT Press.

Hans, James S. (1981). *The Play of the World.* Amherst, MA: University of Massachusetts Press.

Hardy, Stephen. (1982). *How Boston Played.* Boston: Northeastern University Press.

Hemingway, J.L. (1988). Leisure and Civility: Reflections on a Greek Ideal. *Leisure Sciences, 10,* 179-191.

Hemingway, J. L. (1990). Opening Windows on an Interpretive Leisure Studies. *Journal of Leisure Research, 22,* 303-308.

Hemingway, J.L. (1991). Leisure and Democracy: Incompatible Ideals? In G.S. Fain (Ed.), *Leisure and Ethics: Reflections on the Philosophy of Leisure* (pp. 59-81). Reston, VA: American Association for Leisure and Recreation.

Hemingway, J.L. (1993). Recovering the World: Varieties of Philosophical Experience. *Schole, 8,* 1-23.

Horkheimer, Max. (1974). *Critique of Instrumental Reason.* (M.J. O'Connell, Trans.). New York: Seabury Press.

Horkeimer, Max and Theodor W. Adorno. (1972). *Dialectic of Enlightenment.* (J. Cumming, Trans.). New York: Seabury Press.

Huizinga, Johan. (1955). *Homo Ludens: A Study of the Play Element in Culture.* Boston: Beacon Press.

Hunnicutt, Benjamin Kline. (1988). *Work Without End: Abandoning Shorter Hours for the Right to Work.* Philadelphia: Temple University Press.

Hunnicutt, Benjamin Kline. (1990). Leisure and Play in Plato's Teaching and Philosophy of Leisure. *Leisure Sciences, 12,* 211-227.

Kaplan, Max. (1960). *Leisure in America: A Social Inquiry.* New York: John Wiley.

Kaplan, Max. (1975). *Leisure: Theory and Policy.* New York: John Wiley.

Kelly, John R. (1982). *Leisure.* Englewood Cliffs, NJ: Prentice-Hall.

Kelly, John R. (1986). Commodification of Leisure: Trend or Tract? *Loisir et Societé* (9.2) (455-476).

Kelly, John R. (1987). *Freedom to Be: A New Sociology of Leisure.* New York: Macmillan.

Kraus, Richard. (1978). *Recreation and Leisure in Modern Society.* (2nd ed.). Santa Monica, CA: Goodyear.

Kuhn, Thomas. (1970). *The Structure of Scientific Revolutions.* Chicago: University of Chicago Press.

Lee, Joseph. (1929). *Play in Education.* (2nd ed.). New York: Macmillan.

McKendrick, N., J. Brewer, and J. Plumb. (1982). *The Birth of a Consumer Society: The Commercialization of Eighteenth-Century England.* Bloomington, IN: Indiana University Press.

Murphy, James F. (1981). *Concepts of Leisure.* (2nd ed.). Englewood Cliffs, NJ: Prentice-Hall.

Pieper, Josef. (1952). *Leisure, the Basis of Culture.* (A. Dru, Trans.). New York: Pantheon.

Piess, Kathy. (1986). *Cheap Amusements: Working Women and Leisure in Turn-of-the-Century New York.* Philadelphia: Temple University Press.

Rojek, Chris. (1985). *Capitalism and Leisure Theory.* London: Tavistock.

Rosenzweig, Roy. (1983). *Eight Hours for What We Will: Workers and Leisure in an Industrial City, 1870-1920.* New York: Cambridge University Press.

Ross, Steven J. (1985). *Workers on the Edge: Work, Leisure, and Politics in Industrializing Cincinnati, 1788-1890.* New York: Columbia University Press.

Schor, Juliet B. (1991). *The Overworked American: The Unexpected Decline of Leisure.* New York: Basic Books.

Smigel, Erwin. (1963). *Work and Leisure: A Contemporary Social Problem.* New Haven: College and University Press.

Stormann, Wayne F. (1991). The Ideology of the American Urban Parks and Recreation Movement: Past and Future. *Leisure Sciences, 13,* 137-151.

Stormann, Wayne F. (1993). The Recreation Profession, Capital, and Democracy. *Leisure Sciences, 15,* 49-66.

Sylvester, C., Hemingway, J.L., Howe-Murphy, C., Mobily, K., and Shank, P., (Eds.). (1987). *Philosophy of Therapeutic Recreation: Ideas and Issues.* Arlington, VA: National Recreation and Park Association.

Sylvester, Charles D. (1990). Interpretation and Leisure Science: A Hermeneutical Example of Past and Present Oracles. *Journal of Leisure Research, 22,* 290-295.

Thompson, E.P. (1966). *The Making of the English Working Class.* New York: Vintage Books.

The Anthropology of Leisure

Past, Present, and Future Research

Garry E. Chick
Department of Leisure Studies
University of Illinois

INTRODUCTION

Lewis Henry Morgan's *League of the Iroquois* (1952, orig. 1851) was probably the first modern ethnography. If we mark the beginning of the contemporary era of anthropology with its publication, the discipline is just a decade shy of being a century and a half old. In those 140 years, anthropological interest in leisure, recreation, play, and related concepts has waxed and waned but it has never occupied more than a tiny corner in the discipline (Chick & Donlon, 1992). The level of interest in leisure at any particular time has largely depended upon the prevailing theoretical orientation toward culture. Theoretical orientations in anthropology have typically focused on aspects of production and reproduction, such as subsistence, economics, politics, kinship and other aspects of social organization that presumably play a significant role in determining the structure and content of culture. To the extent that leisure has been evaluated by anthropologists, it has generally been either as a part of what is termed expressive culture, which includes play, games, the plastic and graphic arts, music, dance, folk tales, riddles, and the like, or as part of time budget studies. In the latter, unfortunately, it has generally been regarded as a residual.

For their part, leisure researchers have basically ignored anthropological and cross-cultural data and theory. The reasons for this are not entirely clear but a consistent thread seems to be that the field of leisure studies has maintained a western chauvinistic and ethnocentric character (Chick, 1985; see also Allison, 1988). From such a perspective there is little point in attempting to study leisure outside of the western context simply because it is assumed not to exist in other times and places. When writing about preliterate cultures, leisure theorists have typically indicated either that the concepts of leisure and/or recreation are unknown (e.g., Nash, 1960) or that work and non-work are so intertwined or confused in the rhythms of daily life that they are not distinguished (e.g., Parker, 1983). But, for the most part, preliterate cultures simply have been treated as irrelevant. Goodale and Godbey (1988), for example, sought to explicate the evolution of leisure but they began with the ancient Greeks and coursed through the history of western civilization. They incorporated essentially no information about preliterate cultures, thus fixing the origin of leisure in both time and space. It may be that the ethnocentrism in leisure studies results from, or at least reflects, de Grazia's (1962, p. 9) elitist characterization, ". . . leisure cannot exist where people don't know what it is." Knowing what leisure is, however, has been no small problem and perspectives from the four subfields of anthropology (i.e., anthropological linguistics, archaeology, cultural anthropology, and physical anthropology) may be helpful in this regard. First, the anthropological conceptions of culture and of leisure will be discussed briefly.

CULTURE AND LEISURE—ANTHROPOLOGICAL USAGES

Culture

As might be expected, there is no universally accepted definition of culture despite the obvious utility of having one. Many current definitions, however, reflect the idea that culture is a system of information (see e. g., Roberts, 1964; D'Andrade, 1981; Romney, Weller, & Batchelder, 1986). The information that is more or less shared by a group constitutes their culture. Culture as information may be stored in the heads of individuals, in artifacts or information storage devices (i.e., books, computers).

It may be generated or lost, or it may remain relatively static for long periods of time. Cultural change reflects alterations of, additions to, or deletions from pools of shared information which may be followed by changes in culturally appropriate behavior (Chick, 1986).

Cultural evolution is generally held to involve change from simpler to more complex forms and, as such, is typically postdicted by comparing roughly contemporary cultures that differ in complexity (Jorgensen, 1979). Care must be taken to recognize the dangers inherent in this technique, however. First, there is no necessary directionality in cultural evolution—there are instances of cultures changing in the direction of less complexity. Familiar examples include the culture loss after the collapse of the Roman Empire or that which occurred in much of Europe due to the ravages of the Black Plague (McNeill, 1976). Second, the concept of cultural complexity itself is problematic. During the last 30 years at least seven different indices of cultural complexity have been developed and tested (Levinson & Malone, 1980). Measures of social stratification, political integration, and subsistence type, including technological development and specialization, are typically used to construct these indices. The problem is that technology is the hallmark of western culture and it is questionable whether it should be used as a benchmark for others. Wonderfully complex cultural forms, such as aboriginal Australian kinship and marriage systems (see Radcliffe-Brown, 1913) are disregarded in measures of cultural complexity, betraying the ethnocentric nature of these indices. Finally, to assume that contemporary cultures that vary in terms of complexity represent different evolutionary stages of culture disregards that fact that the environmental and social contexts in which contemporary cultures find themselves may be quite unlike those of past cultures. Cultural features that appear to be appropriate today may have come about for quite different reasons in the past. Hence, caution is warranted in interpreting cross-cultural comparisons.

Leisure

When and where they have studied them, anthropologists have almost universally regarded leisure as free time and recreation as activity that takes place in the context of free time. More existential definitions have rarely been utilized. Indeed, caution is advisable when considering ethnographic descriptions where deep existential or symbolic meanings have been ascribed to leisure pursuits, such as in Geertz's (1973) classic study of Balinese cockfighting. Anthropologists often have little more than minimal competence in native languages—and sometimes not even that—and it is difficult to see how deep symbolic meanings can be assessed with accuracy through an interpreter or by means of a lingua franca (Chick & Donlon, 1992).

The fact is that leisure and recreation have not been popular topics in anthropological research. Studies of games and play, especially children's play, have been much more common. However, even the frequency of publications about both games and play has declined in anthropology since the early part of this century (Chick, 1985; Chick & Donlon, 1992).

Given that anthropologists have typically defined leisure as free time and that time budget studies are becoming more popular in the field, one would hope that such studies would provide fertile data sources. Unfortunately, most anthropological time budget studies have lacked standard, hence comparable, formats and few have included leisure as a distinct category. The ongoing Cross-Cultural Studies in Time Allocation program (Johnson, 1992), for example, has a standard format but does not include leisure as a category. Those anthropological time budget studies relevant to leisure will be reviewed later in this paper.

LEISURE AND THE FOUR FIELDS OF ANTHROPOLOGY

Leisure and Language

The essence of de Grazia's view, noted above, seems to be that one must have the concept of leisure in order to have leisure. Further, the detailed treatments given to ancient Greek words related to leisure in various texts in the field (e.g., Arnold, 1985, pp. 10-19; Dare, Welton & Coe, 1987, pp. xvii-xviii; Kraus, 1984, pp. 41-42) imply at least that some aspects of the Greek world view either reflected or were reflected in the vocabulary of leisure. This is reminiscent of the turn of the century view of von Humboldt (1905) who hypothesized that the unique design of each language encoded a distinctive view of the world. The

anthropologist Edward Sapir (1921) elaborated this idea, arguing that ". . . the worlds in which different societies live are
distinct worlds, not merely the same worlds with different labels
attached." Sapir's student, Benjamin Lee Whorf (1956) carried
the notion even further, hypothesizing that language provides
not just a way of speaking about the world, but, indeed, a model
of the world.

The Sapir-Whorf Hypothesis, as this form of linguistic deter-
minism has come to be called, has received only equivocal and
ambiguous empirical support over the years but its truth often
seems to be taken for granted. It is now recognized, however,
that the lack of specific words or syntactic forms does not indicate
the absence of an idea, thought, concept, or understanding.
Though the old anthropological saw that dialects of the Eskimo[1]
language family have three, four, or more distinct words that
refer to different kinds of snow while English has only one is false
(Martin, 1986), the French Canadians recognized the utility of
assigning more than one generic term to a phenomenon common
in their environment and coined the term *poudrerie,* meaning
"drifting snow," from their word *poudre,* which means "pow-
der" (Taylor, 1976). Similarly, there are instances where a language has the concept, but no word for it. An example is
"gloating over another person's misfortune," a concept we know
to exist in English but for which there is no word. German, on the
other hand, has the term *Schadenfreude,* literally "shame-joy."
The numerous loan words in English, such as "chic," "touché,"
"nirvana," and so on, demonstrate that English lacks terms for
some commonly recognized concepts (Taylor, 1976).

Is it then reasonable to assume that cultures that lack a term
more or less directly translatable as leisure thus lack the concept?
Although a weak version of the Sapir-Whorf Hypothesis would
suggest that it may be easier to think about certain things in some
languages than others, concepts—and related behaviors—do not
appear to be tightly constrained by the presence or absence of
words or by differences in syntactic structures. Recent research
by Yeh (1993), for example, clearly indicates that a concept (i. e.,
hsiao yao) very similar to the Western notion of leisure has existed
for hundreds of years in China even though there is no Chinese
word that translates precisely as "leisure." We must therefore be
very careful to avoid the conclusion that the character of leisure,

or its very existence, differs among cultural groups on the basis of linguistic evidence alone.

Leisure and Archeology

The "discovery" of leisure is commonly attributed to the ancient Greeks despite the fact that there is abundant archaeological evidence of the sports, games, and other recreational activities of many past cultures (see e. g., Howell, 1971, Chick, 1984). Unfortunately, leisure researchers have tended to concentrate on the western cultural tradition using a strategy much like that of the individual who looks for lost keys under a street lamp because that is where the light is best. When we have utilized historical or archeological data we have tended to concentrate on the spectacular (e.g., the Olympics) and the lurid (e.g., the Roman games). As Kelly (1982) emphasized, we know very little about the recreation of the common folk of the past simply because theirs were not the lives that were recorded for posterity. Our lack of knowledge does not mean that leisure did not exist for the masses, however. Archeology can make contributions to the study of leisure and recreation of both elites and of the masses, but only if such contributions are recognized as important by archeologists.

Leisure and Physical Anthropology

The study of leisure has been restricted thus far to humans. We know, of course, that many animals spend a considerable amount of their time in play, especially as juveniles (see e.g., Fagen, 1981; Smith, 1982) but leisure (and recreation) have evidently not been thought of as appropriate categories for considering animal behavior. Leisure researcher Steven Smith (1985), for example, has stated that animals cannot receive pleasure through creative thought and symbolic processes. This view reflects a broader western cultural perspective that holds humans to be qualitatively distinct from the rest of the natural world. This is a position that is still favored by many (see e. g., Latto, 1986), and it relegates nonhuman animals to the category of nonconscious biological machines, a position championed by Descartes. Yet, there has never been any empirical basis for choosing the position of Descartes over that of Darwin, who argued that it is just as reasonable to claim that the human mind evolved from animal minds as to claim that human anatomical structures evolved from animal counterparts (Terrace, 1987). Indeed, the Darwinian perspective that there is a continuity between the minds of animals and humans is now ascendant (see Degler, 1991, for an extended review of this point). A recent article in *Time* magazine, for example, asked the question "Can animals think?" The answer given was strongly in the affirmative. Evidence cited included the creativity of dolphins, the symbolic capacities of chimpanzees, logical skills of sea lions, and semantic skills of a parrot (Linden, 1993). There is, in fact, a large body of evidence, both direct and inferential, that demonstrates that at least some animals exhibit consciousness, intentionality, and self-awareness and can think creatively and symbolically (see, e. g., Cheney & Seyfarth, 1990; Griffin, 1992). And, in some circumstances, they appear to enjoy it.

But even if some animals, such as primates, can experience something akin to leisure, why is that important? It is important because leisure, or leisure-like behavior, may play a significant role in the social organization of animals and in physical, social and behavioral evolution. Most evolutionists maintain that one must explain why a phenomenon (such as leisure) has evolved in the first place. Physical or behavioral characteristics that are of no advantage or, worse, disadvantageous, should never evolve. Those that lose their advantage (such as little toes or wisdom teeth) may remain so long as they are not deleterious but will be selected against if they become disadvantageous (as wisdom teeth may have). Both play and leisure appear to have some clear evolutionary disadvantages. Participation can result in injury or putting oneself at risk of predation among prey species and it appears to waste energy among all species. However, a physiological or behavioral trait will be adaptive if its long-term benefits must exceed its short-term costs (Smith, 1982). Thus, it is possible that leisure is somehow adaptive in the long haul. This question will be explored shortly.

Leisure and Culture

Numerous ethnographies of non-Western societies refer to their leisure and recreation. The Human Relations Area Files, a topically coded ethnographic data source, includes the categories "recreation," "recreation facilities," "labor and leisure," and "leisure time activities" for each of the more than 300 cultures in the file although information for each of these is not available for every culture (see Chick [1985] for a brief introduction to the use of the Human Relations Area Files).

Moreover, several authors have gone beyond merely describing leisure and recreational activities in non-Western cultures to examining the availability of free time, its use, and its interdependence with other aspects of culture. One quest is for the discovery of a lawlike relationship between leisure and cultural change or evolution. If such a relationship exists, it may be between patterns of subsistence or mode of production and leisure or between a generalized concept of cultural complexity—often taken as a measure of cultural evolution—and the availability and use of leisure. A consistent cross-cultural pattern would demand theoretical explanation. Finally, a variety of relationships between forms of expressive culture and other aspects of culture, including cultural complexity, patterns of child socialization, war, social stratification, belief systems, and forms of subsistence, have been demonstrated by cross-cultural researchers (see Levinson & Malone [1980] for a review). Leisure is expressed largely in the context of expressive culture and these piecemeal studies suggest the need for, and the possibility of, a comprehensive cultural theory of leisure.

LEISURE AND CULTURE CHANGE

Early anthropological interest in leisure and recreation was primarily descriptive. Morgan (1851), for example, described the games of the Iroquois, dividing them into athletic games and games of chance. Edward Burnett Tylor (1881), in his text *Anthropology*, included a chapter on the "Arts of Pleasure" which described play and various games, musical, and artistic activities. Tylor also was interested in the evolution and diffusion of culture, both prominent theoretical interests at that time. In 1879 he published an article wherein he attempted to demonstrate that the Aztec game *patolli* was derived from the game *pachisi*, as played in India and, hence, that Mesoamerican civilization was influenced by Asian civilization.

The concept of cultural evolution itself is very old and an evolutionary classification of societies was presented as early as 1748 by Montesquieu (Harris, 1968). The idea that leisure, or surplus time, contributes to cultural change and evolution has been traced to Rousseau (1967, orig. 1755) and Mill (1920, orig. 1848) by Just (1980). More generally, the concept of economic surplus dates directly to Ricardo's (1933, orig. 1817) *Principles of Political Economy and Taxation*. Some anthropologists and archaeologists, including Boas (1940) and Childe (1951) regarded economic surplus as a prime mover in cultural evolution. Boas (1940) stated this most clearly:

> ... a surplus of food supply is liable to bring about an increase of leisure, which gives opportunities for occupations which are not absolutely necessary for the needs of life. In turn the increase of population and of leisure, which may be applied to new inventions, give rise to a greater food supply and to further increase in the amount of leisure, so that a cumulative effect results (p. 285).

This "Surplus Theory" or positions close to it forms the theoretical basis for discussions of prehistoric leisure (see e.g., Shivers, 1981) or leisure and culture (see e.g., Ibrahim, 1991) that appear in the leisure studies literature.

Unfortunately, the Surplus Theory is dead wrong. Evidence that has accumulated since the late 1950s refutes the notions that hunter-gatherers have little or no free time, that sedentary agriculture provides a better and more dependable supply of food than food collecting, that sedentary agriculture results in more leisure, or that any increase in leisure is devoted to cultural development (Harris, 1975; Just, 1980; Chick, 1986). Indeed, Harris (1975) and Sahlins (1968) have claimed that agriculture is a more time consuming subsistence method than food collection and that the intensification of cultivation (that is, the requirement of greater productivity per farmer in order to support denser populations) results in even less free time. In disputing the role of leisure in cultural evolution, Elman Service (1958) indicated in his description of the Arunta, an aboriginal hunter-gatherer group in Australia, that "the condition of the Arunta illustrates very well that it is not 'leisure' which is responsible for cultural development, but quite the contrary. The Arunta ... are literally one of the most leisured people in the world" (p. 10).

Just (1980) has argued that hunter-gatherers do not possess "true" leisure but, instead, forced idleness. From an economic perspective, free time has little or no relative value for them because of its abundance. In modern "time famine" cultures (Linder, 1970), however, time is valuable due to its scarcity and, thus, is to be used wisely. From this perspective, Just (1980) hypothesized that technological efforts would be aimed at increasing valued free time. He argued that relatively scarce, rather than abundant, leisure may therefore be instrumental in cultural evolution.

Other studies have suggested that the monotonic relationships between cultural evolution and free time suggested either by the Surplus Theory or Just's (1980) time scarcity hypothesis are overly simple and fail to accord with available evidence (Burch, 1970; Johnson, 1978; Munroe et al., 1983). Munroe et al. (1983) compared productive labor inputs (i.e., a summation of time spent in food preparation, garden labor, chores, animal care, and wage labor) of women among five cultural groups. Two of these groups were primarily from food collectors (the !Kung San of the Kalahari Desert of west Africa and the Machiguenga of the western Amazon), three were primarily horticulturalists and herders (the Canchino of southern Peru, the Kikuyu of central Kenya, and the Logoli of western Kenya), and the final group was a sample of American women from suburban Los Angeles County. Munroe et al. (1983) found that the labor inputs for women in the three horticultural societies (the Canchino, Kikuyu, and Logoli) were much higher than for either the hunter-gatherers or the American sample. They concluded that "labor input (measured in time) may be moderate at a low techno-economic level, rise sharply with medium techno-economic complexity, and fall back again to moderate intensity at high techno-economic levels" (Munroe et al., 1983, p. 363). Both Johnson (1978) and Burch (1970) reached similar conclusions.

A final perspective might be called the null model. Research by Hawkes and O'Connell (1981) and Hill, Kaplan, Hawkes, and Hurtado (1985) has suggested that the amount of time devoted either to work or to leisure is not related to cultural complexity. Their perspective reflects sort of a Parkinson's Law of subsistence: when the time spent traveling to food sources, bringing it to camp, processing it, and in miscellaneous other activities, is added up, hunter-gatherers spend roughly the same amount of time in productive effort as subsistence horticulturalists (Hill et al., 1985; see Chick, 1986, for a detailed review of each of these perspectives).

Based on the views of Munroe et al. (1983), Johnson (1978), Harris (1975), Just (1980), and Burch (1970), Chick (1986) hypothesized that if a sample of cultures was plotted based on a measure of cultural complexity on the x-axis and their available leisure time on the y-axis, the result would be best fit by a curve resembling a reversed J. Societies at low levels of cultural complexity would have the most free time followed by societies at high levels of cultural complexity. Those at moderate levels of cultural complexity would have the least free time. Two related hypotheses were also offered. Children can be cheap sources of labor if they are net producers rather than net consumers. Hence, if adult labor input for subsistence is very high, efforts may be made to augment the labor pool with child labor. In this case, societies at low and at high levels of cultural complexity should have relatively low fertility and relatively extended periods of childhood and adolescence (where children and adolescents provide little or no productive labor). On the other hand, societies at moderate levels of cultural complexity should have large families and children should begin productive labor at an early age.

These hypotheses were tested using data from the Human Relations Area Files (Chick, 1991, 1992). One hundred and eighty-six societies from the Standard Cross Cultural Sample (Murdock & White, 1969) were coded for hours of productive labor per day (for adult males), the number of children who reach the age of productive labor per female, and the age at which children become economically productive. Codes for cultural complexity were taken from Murdock and Provost (1973). Polynomial regression was used to assess the curvilinear nature of the lines of best fit for the data. Results were suggestive but not conclusive. The relationship between cultural complexity and the amount of free time available was fit best by a curve but rather than being distinctly parabolic it was rather flat. The data could be described nearly as well by a straight line that showed that productive labor increases with cultural complexity, much as suggested by Harris (1975) and Just (1980). So the first hypothesis was rejected. Indeed, recent evidence (e. g., Shott, 1991) suggests that early estimates of hunter-gatherer free time were generous in the extreme.

On the other hand, the second and third hypotheses were supported. The number of children reaching the age of economic productivity and cultural complexity had a distinct inverted U relationship as hypothesized. The plot of age at which children become economically productive (Chick, 1991, 1992) and cultural complexity was best fit by a U-shaped curve. Given that relevant data in the HRAF are often nonexistent, vague, or contradictory, cross-cultural studies of this type are best viewed as exploratory. Currently efforts are underway to refine the coding to reduce measurement error. Finally, this essentially economic analysis does not account for the meanings ascribed to work or leisure, or how children are viewed or treated (Chick, 1991) nor does it account for the kinds of activities that take place during leisure.

Intracultural rather than cross cultural aspects of leisure and culture change have been examined in other studies. Heider (1977), for example, found that the Dani, a highland New Guinea tribal group altered a game that was introduced into their community from Java so that it accorded better with their own cultural values. Since they lacked a cultural emphasis on competition, had no system of counting or numbers, and had a "casual" attitude toward regulations, they transformed the game such that competition, scorekeeping, and adherence to the rules were largely eliminated.

As a final example, a collateral aspect of the festival system in rural Mesoamerica is that it provides community-wide recreational opportunities during the festivals. Chick (1991) found that the festival system, in general, and its ancillary function as a provider of community recreation has declined in rural villages as they have become acculturated to modern Mexican society. Villagers increasingly look to the outside for recreational opportunities that are better in accord with the cultural mainstream.

LEISURE AND ADAPTATION

The modern theory of evolution holds that the purpose of both the physiological and behavioral characteristics of an organism is to maximize the survival and reproduction of the organism's genetic material. A perspective that may shed some explanatory light on the way in which leisure is spent involves whether or not leisure has any adaptive character that contributes to this maximization. Adaptation is both genetic and cultural and it occurs when traits are selected for by the environment. Physiological, morphological, or behavioral variations among members of a species that enhance the chance for some individuals, over others, to survive and reproduce offspring that also survive and reproduce are thus adaptive. The question is, then: Does leisure, in any guise, confer such a selective advantage?

The adaptive values of play have been considered in both animals and humans (e.g., Fagen, 1981; Smith, 1982) but the study of leisure has been restricted to humans (and, as I have argued above, almost exclusively to members of western cultures). Observation of some animals, such as dogs, monkeys, or apes, suggests that they often engage in activities that seem to be distinct from play but that are neither primarily productive nor reproductive in nature. Ethological studies of primates indicate that grooming or idle play of adults with infants exhibits certain leisure-like qualities (see e. g., Altmann, 1980). Dog owners are aware of the leisurely qualities of the chewing of a bone, real, rawhide, or nylon, by their pet (Chick & Barnett, 1987). Any instrumental value of such activities, such as teeth cleaning, appears to be completely incidental.

Grooming among baboons or gorillas, for example, does serve to remove parasites but, more importantly, it affirms social hierarchy. Further, it is apparently pleasurable, though it is not play. We recognize instrumental functions for human leisure—social interaction, learning, physical fitness, etc.—so there should be no reason that animals, especially those most closely related to us, cannot also have leisure-like experiences that have utilitarian aspects. A significant part of the learning of social behavior among social animals, including primates, takes place in the context of play and leisure-like activities. Critical learning about social hierarchy and the ability to predict the behavior of others occurs in the rough-and-tumble play of infants and juveniles, the casual play of infants, juveniles, and adults, and in social leisure activities such a grooming among monkeys and apes. Wilson (1975) has claimed that such social behavior has a calculable evolutionary advantage.

Leisure may also have adaptive features among humans. Rubin, Flowers, and Gross (1986) used time-allocation data from four native groups living in Brazil to examine the adaptive significance of leisure. The four groups are all village units, are linguistically and culturally similar, and reside in similar habitats in central Brazil. They differ in terms of their length and degree of contact with western (Brazilian) society and in the degree of habitat degradation where they live. All four groups are primarily slash-and-burn horticulturalists but augment their subsistence by hunting and fishing. Two of the groups, the Kanela and the Bororo, live in substantially degraded habitats. That is, the soil nutrient levels and the forest biomass are substantially below those where the other two groups, the Xavante and the Mekranoti, live. Rubin et al. (1986) found that the composition of work differs among the groups but that the total work input (in time) varies little. Therefore, they chose to look for evidence of adaptation outside of productive work. They defined leisure "as activities that make no direct contribution to production or reproduction. This includes lying down, staring off into space, ceremonies, games, sports and athletic events, singing, sleeping between the hours of 6 a. m. and 8 p. m. and so on" (p. 526). They hypothesized that a comparison of leisure among the four groups might reveal adaptive processes that occur through the adjustment of consumption patterns. Further, people may conserve energy in both consumption as well as production. Some leisure activities can be categorized as "high energy cost," such as vigorous play or dancing, while others, including sitting quietly or sleeping, are "low energy cost." The choice of low over high energy cost leisure activities would have the same net effect on energy availability as an increase in productivity. Hence, Rubin et al. (1986) hypothesized that "as the rate of return on subsistence activity goes down, the proportion of low-cost leisure activities goes up" (p. 526).

Their time-allocation data supported this hypothesis. The four groups can be divided into two pairs. Both the Xavante and the Mekranoti produce more than the minimum of necessary calories because of their abundant resources. The Kanela and the Bororo, on the other hand, must work longer at certain activities in order to produce similar amounts of food, due to their degraded environment. But they do so by reallocating labor from certain activities to others, rather than actually spending more time in work. As Rubin et al. (1986) anticipated, the Xavante and Mekranoti spend nearly twice as much of their leisure in active pursuits (47.4% and 48.6% respectively) than the Kanela or the Bororo (25.3% and 33.4% respectively). The results are most striking for children under age 15. Kanela children spend more than twice as much time resting and sleeping as they do in active play. Bororo children also spend more time resting than playing. Xavante and Mekranoti children, on the other hand, spend significantly more time in active play than in resting. It should be pointed out that children under 15 do little productive or reproductive work in any of these societies (Rubin et al., 1986).

Rubin et al. (1986) found support for an association between the degree of habitat degradation for these four groups and the amount of energy that is spent during leisure. In particular, children seem to adjust their activity levels relative to the effort required to obtain an adequate diet from their habitat. Rubin et al. (1986) were cautious to point out that actors need not be aware of the benefits of this strategy, however. Conscious decisions could be made to intensify production but they are not, possibly because the marginal increase in yield with additional labor is not worth its energy cost. Rather than increase production, members of these societies reduce their needs. For comparison, studies of primates in degraded environments indicate that the animals spend little, if any, time in play. Instead, they choose to marshal their energy resources for the food search (Baldwin & Baldwin, 1972).

Rubin and his colleagues did not go so far as to claim that how leisure was spent enhances survival and reproduction among members of the four groups studied but such an inference is not far-fetched. Whether processes similar to those found by Rubin et al. (1983) take place in industrialized societies is not known. There are groups in America that live in what might be called

degraded environments—the inner cities or small rural communities where jobs are scarce, for example—while others live in
affluent environments. It may be that unconscious adjustments
in active versus inactive leisure are, in fact, being made based on
the degree of ease with which adequate nutrition is acquired
even in modern society. We need to look for such differences.

SUMMARY

Leisure, as free time and/or expressive activity, is clearly a
pan cultural phenomenon and, unless one accepts de Grazia's
(1962) dictum on the nature of leisure, it is likely that it is
universal in its existential sense as well. Further, Malinowski
(1931) referred to recreation as a creative element in culture and
noted that "the vanguard of progress is often found in works of
leisure" (p. 643). Kroeber (1948) suggested that important inven-
tions, including the bicycle, the automobile, and possibly even
the bow and arrow, were developed in recreational contexts with
their utilitarian values realized only later. It may be, as these
pioneers of anthropology postulated, that leisure is a nexus for
invention and cultural change. Forms of leisure may also be
adaptive responses that reflect the most basic cultural infrastruc-
tures of production and reproduction and, at an ideological level,
cultural values.

For greater understanding of the intracultural and cross
cultural aspects of leisure to come about, however, two things
must take place. First, anthropologists must recognize leisure to
be an important aspect of human (and possibly animal) behavior
and culture and they must adjust their research strategies accord-
ingly. Second, leisure researchers must break free of their paro-
chial, ethnocentric blinkers and take note of the information that
already exists about leisure and recreation in other cultures. By
doing so they can convey the message to cultural anthropologists, archeologists, and others that leisure is a phenomenon
worthy of study.

A final, and potentially controversial, point is whether leisure researchers will favor existential descriptions of leisure to
the exclusion of efforts to explain the existence and nature of the
phenomenon, favor explanation over description, or attempt to
do both. Is knowledge of the meaning of leisure to individuals

what is really important or is attempting to explain how and why individuals and groups experience leisure in the ways that they do more important? Or are these kindred goals? At this juncture, anthropology has contributed relatively little to any of these questions although the potential to do so seems to be there. Detailed ethnographies can shed light on the first question. Cross-cultural research and research that incorporates a biosocial, evolutionary posture will illuminate the second. Further, these perspectives must be viewed as complementary, rather than contradictory, as is so often the case. As anthropologist William H. Durham stated in 1978, "However culture changed and evolved and whatever meaning was given by people to their cultural attributes, the net effect of these attributes was to enhance human survival and reproduction" (quoted in Degler, 1991, p. 312). Does leisure contribute to human survival and reproduction? Some of the results from studies cited above are suggestive, at the very least.

There are a few enduring questions in social science. One of them is "How and why do cultures change?" Some of the studies reviewed above indicate that leisure may have an important role in the processes of culture change and evolution or that the way in which leisure is experienced may be an adaptive response to environmental conditions. Anthropologists have consistently been interested in culture change and adaptation but have largely ignored the possible place of leisure in these processes. Leisure researchers have, for the most part, ignored the processes altogether. For the field of leisure studies to progress and to become a legitimate area for social science inquiry, such indifference must be not be allowed to continue.

NOTE

[1]Members of those groups that have long been called "Eskimo" now prefer to be addressed by terms that refer to their particular ethnic affiliation (e.g., Aleut, Inuit). Like Martin (1986), "Eskimo" is used here because it is the term used by those who originated and by those who have perpetuated the snow words myth.

REFERENCES CITED

Allison, M. T. (1988). Breaking Boundaries and Barriers: Future Directions in Cross-Cultural Research. *Leisure Sciences, 10*, 247-259.

Altmann, J. (1980). *Baboon Mothers and Infants.* Cambridge, MA: Harvard University Press.

Arnold, S. (1985). The Dilemma of Meaning. In *Recreation and leisure: Issues in an Era of Change, 2nd Ed.* (pp. 5-22). T. L. Goodale and Peter A. Witt (Eds.), State College, PA: Venture Publishing.

Baldwin, J. D. and Baldwin, J. I. (1972). The ecology and Behavior of Squirrel Monkeys (*Saimiri oerstedi*) in a Natural Forest in Western Panama. *Folia Primatologica, 18*, 161-184.

Boas, F. (1940). *Race, Language and Culture.* New York: Macmillan.

Burch, Jr., W. R. (1970). Recreation Preferences as Culturally Determined Phenomena. In B. L. Driver (Ed.), *Elements of Outdoor Recreation Planning* (pp. 61-87). Ann Arbor, MI: University of Michigan Press.

Cheney, D. L., and R. M. Seyfarth (1990). *How Monkeys See the World.* Chicago: University of Chicago Press.

Chick, G. E. (1984). The Cross-Cultural Study of Games. In R. L. Terjung (Ed.), *Exercise and Sport Sciences Reviews, Vol. 12* (pp. 307-337). Lexington, MA: The Collamore Press.

Chick, G. E. (1985). The Cross-Cultural Analysis of Leisure Behavior. *Leisure Information Quarterly, 12*, 8-9.

Chick, G. E. (1985, October). "Anthropology and the Study of Leisure: Searching for the Missing Link." Keynote Address presented at the Symposium on Leisure Research, National Recreation and Park Association. Dallas, TX.

Chick, G. E. (1986). Leisure, Labor, and the Complexity of Culture: An Anthropological Perspective. *Journal of Leisure Research, 18*, 154-168.

Chick, G. E. (1991). Acculturation and Community Recreation in Rural Mexico. *Play & Culture, 4*, 185-193.

Chick, G. E. (1991, July). Leisure and Cultural Evolution: Tests of Several Hypotheses. Presented at the World Leisure and Recreation Association Congress, Sydney, Australia.

Chick, G. E. (1992, February). A Cross-Cultural Perspective on Leisure. Presented at the Annual Meeting of the Society for Cross-Cultural Research, Santa Fe, NM.

Chick, G. E. and L. Barnett (1987, September). The Hairy Leisure Class: A Consideration of Leisure Among Nonhuman Higher Mammals. Presented at the Leisure Research Symposium, National Recreation and Park Association Congress, New Orleans, LA.

Chick, G. E. and J. Donlon (1992). Going Out on Limb: Geertz's "Deep Play: Notes on the Balinese Cockfight" and the Anthropological Study of Play. *Play & Culture, 5,* 233-245.

Childe, V. G. (1951). *Man Makes Himself.* New York: New American Library.

D'Andrade, R. G. (1981). The Cultural Part of Cognition. *Cognitive Sciences, 5,* 179-195.

Dare, B., G. Welton and W. Coe (1987). *Concepts of Leisure in Western Thought: A Critical and Historical Analysis.* Dubuque, IA: Kendall/Hunt.

De Grazia, S. (1962). *Of Time, Work, and Leisure.* New York: Twentieth Century Fund.

Degler, C. N. (1991). *In Search of Human Nature: The Decline and Revival of Darwinism in American Social Thought.* New York: Oxford University Press.

Fagen, R. M. (1981). *Animal Play Behavior.* New York: Oxford University Press.

Geertz, C. (1973). Deep Play: Notes on the Balinese Cockfight. In C. Geertz (Ed.), *The Interpretation of Cultures* (pp. 412-453). New York: Basic Books.

Goodale, T. L. and G. C. Godbey (1988). *The Evolution of Leisure: Historical and Philosophical Perspectives.* State College, PA: Venture Publishing, Inc.

Griffin, D. R. (1992). *Animal Minds.* Chicago: The University of Chicago Press.

Harris, M. (1968). *The Rise of Anthropological Theory.* New York: Thomas Crowell.

Harris, M. (1975). *Culture, People, Nature: An Introduction to General Anthropology, 2nd Ed.* New York: Thomas Crowell.

Hawkes, K., and J. F. O'Connell (1981). Affluent Hunters? Some Comments in Light of the Alyawara Case. *American Anthropologist, 83,* 622-626.

Heider, K. (1977). From Javanese to Dani: The Translation of a Game. In P. Stevens, Jr. (Ed.) *Studies in the Anthropology of Play* (pp. 72-81). West Point, NY: Leisure Press.

Hill, K., H. Kaplan, K. Hawkes, and A. M. Hurtado (1985). Men's Time Allocation to Subsistence Work Among the Ache of Eastern Paraguay. *Human Ecology, 13,* 29-47.

Howell, M. L. (1971). Archaeological Evidence of Sports and Games in Ancient Civilizations. *Canadian Journal of the History of Sport and Physical Education, 11,* 14-30.

Ibrahim, H. (1991). *Leisure and Society: A Comparative Approach.* Dubuque, IA: Wm. C Brown.

Johnson, A. (1978). In Search of the Affluent Society. *Human Nature, 1,* 50-59.

Johnson, A. (series Ed.). (1992). *Cross-Cultural Studies in Time Allocation.* New Haven, CT: HRAF Press.

Jorgensen, J. G. (1979). Cross-Cultural Comparisons. *Annual Review of Anthropology, 8,* 309-331.

Just, P. (1980). Time and Leisure in the Elaboration of Culture. *Journal of Anthropological Research, 36,* 105-115.

Kelly, J. R. (1982). *Leisure.* Englewood Cliffs, NJ: Prentice-Hall.

Kraus, R. (1984). *Recreation and Leisure in Modern Society, 3rd Ed.* Glenview, IL: Scott, Foresman and Company.

Kroeber, A. L. (1948). *Anthropology.* New York: Harcourt, Brace.

Latto, R. (1986). The Question of Animal Consciousness. *Psychological Record, 36,* 309-314.

Levinson, D., and M. J. Malone (1980). *Toward Explaining Human Culture: A Critical Review of the Findings of Worldwide Cross-Cultural Research.* New Haven, CT: HRAF Press.

Linden, E. (1993). Can Animals Think? *Time, 141,* 12, 54-61.

Linder, S. (1970). *The Harried Leisure Class.* New York: Columbia University Press.

Malinowski, B. (1931). Culture. In E. R. A. Seligman (Ed.), *Encyclopedia of the Social Sciences, Vol. 4* (pp. 621-646). New York: Macmillan.

Martin, L. (1986). "Eskimo Words for Snow": A Case Study in the Genesis and Decay of an Anthropological Example. *American Anthropologist, 88,* 418-423.

McNeill, W. H. (1977). *Plagues and People.* Garden City, NY: Doubleday Anchor.

Mill, J. S. (1920). *Principles of Political Economy.* (first published 1848). New York: Colonial.

Morgan, L. H. (1877). *Ancient Society.* New York: Holt.

Morgan, L. H. (1962). *League of the Iroquois.* (first published 1851). New York: Corinth Books.

Munroe, R. H., R. L. Munroe, C. Michelson, A. Koel, R. Bolton, and C. Bolton (1983). Time allocation in Four Societies. *Ethnology, XXII,* 355-370.

Murdock, G. P. and C. Provost (1973). Measurement of Cultural Complexity. *Ethnology, 11,* 254-295.

Murdock, G. P. and D. R. White (1969). Standard Cross-Cultural Sample. *Ethnology, 8,* 329-369.

Nash, J. B. (1960). *Philosophy of Recreation and Leisure.* Dubuque, IA: Wm. C. Brown.

Parker, S. (1983). *Work and Leisure.* London: George Allen & Unwin, Ltd.

Radcliffe-Brown, A. R. (1913). Three Tribes of Western Australia. *Journal of the Royal Anthropological Institute, 43,* 143-194.

Ricardo, D. (1933). *Principles of Political Economy and Taxation.* (first published 1817). New York: Dutton.

Roberts, J. M. (1964). The Self-Management of Cultures. In W. H. Goodenough (Ed.), *Explorations in Cultural Anthropology* (pp. 433-454). New York: McGraw-Hill.

Romney, A. K., S. C. Weller, and W. H. Batchelder (1986). Culture as Consensus: A Theory of Culture and Informant Accuracy. *American Anthropologist, 88*, 313-338.

Rousseau, J. J. (1967). *Discourse on the Origins of Inequality.* (first published 1755). New York: Washington Square Press.

Rubin, J., N. M. Flowers and D. R. Gross. (1986). The Adaptive Dimensions of Leisure. *American Ethnologist, 13*, 524-536.

Sahlins, M. (1968). Notes on the Original Affluent Society. In R. B. Lee & I. DeVore (Eds.), *Man the Hunter* (pp. 85-89). Chicago: Aldine.

Sapir, E. (1921). *Language.* New York: Harcourt, Brace.

Service, E. R. (1958). *A Profile of Primitive Culture.* New York: Harper.

Shivers, J. S. (1981). *Leisure and Recreation Concepts: A Critical Analysis.* Boston: Allyn & Bacon.

Shott, M. J. (1991). Archaeological Implications of Revisionism in Ethnography. In P. T. Miracle, L. E. Fisher, & J. Brown (Eds.), *Foragers in Context: Long-Term, Regional and Historical Perspectives in Hunter-Gatherer Studies* (pp. 31-40). Ann Arbor: Michigan Discussions in Anthropology 10.

Smith, P. K. (1982). Does Play Matter? Functional and Evolutionary Aspects of Animal and Human Play. *The Behavioral and Brain Sciences, 5*, 139-184.

Smith, S. L. J. (1985). On the Biological Basis of Pleasure. Some Implications for Leisure Policy. In T. L. Goodale & P. A. Witt (Eds.), *Recreation and Leisure: Issues in an Era of Change, Revised Edition* (pp. 56-68). State College, PA: Venture Publishing.

Taylor, I. (1976). *Introduction to Psycholinguistics.* New York: Holt, Rinehart and Winston.

Terrace, H. S. (1987). Thoughts without Words. In C. Blakemore & S. Greenfield (Eds.), *Mindwaves: Thoughts on Intelligence, Identity, and Consciousness* (pp. 123-137). Oxford: Basil Blackwell.

Tylor, E. B. (1879). On the Game of Patolli in Ancient Mexico and Its Probable Asiatic Origin. *Journal of the Royal Anthropological Institute of Great Britain and Ireland, 8*, 116-131.

Tylor, E. B. (1965). *Anthropology.* (first published 1881). Ann Arbor: University of Michigan Press.

von Humboldt, W. (1905). *Uber das Vergleichende Sprachstudium in Beziehung auf die Verschiedenen Epochen der Sprachentwicklung: Gesammele Schriften, Vol. 4.* Berlin: Koniglich-Preussiche Akademie der Wissenschaften.

Whorf, B. L. (1956). *Language, Thought and Reality: Selected Writings of B. L. Whorf.* J. B. Carroll (Ed.), Cambridge, MA and New York: MIT Press and John Wiley & Sons.

Wilson, E. O. (1975). *Sociobiology: The New Synthesis.* Cambridge, MA: Harvard University Press.

Yeh, C.K. (1993). *Hsiao yao: The Chinese Way of Leisure.* Unpublished Ph.D. dissertation, University of Illinois, Urbana.

The Social Psychology of Leisure

Past, Present, and Future Research

Seppo E. Iso-Ahola
College of Health and Human Performance
——————— University of Maryland ———————

INTRODUCTION

The first Psychology/Social Psychology of Leisure session as part of the National Recreation and Park Association's Leisure Research Symposium was held in Miami in 1978. During the 1977 Las Vegas Leisure Research Symposium, I asked Lynn Barnett (Chairperson of the 1978 Leisure Research Symposium) if she accepted my offer to organize the Social Psychology/Psychology session for the following year's Symposium. She enthusiastically supported the session's inclusion, and so was the Social Psychology/Psychology of Leisure session conceived and a year later in Miami born. Ten papers were accepted for the inaugural presentations, and 118 scholarly papers altogether were presented in this session by 1988 (including 1988). It should be noted at the outset that these papers as well as "the vast majority of psychological work in leisure have been in the social psychological areas of the discipline" (Ingham, 1986, p. 255). In his review of the psychological research, Mannell (1984) came to the same conclusion. Thus, it is more appropriate to talk about the social psychology of leisure than the psychology of leisure when reviewing past, present and future research here.

Although the total number of research papers presented in the Social Psychology/Psychology session is not high by comparison to other disciplines outside leisure studies, it is significant within our field for two reasons: (1) through its continuous contributions, the social psychology/psychology of leisure studies constitutes a formal and legitimate scientific enterprise to explain leisure behavior, and (2) the number and quality of papers presented in this session compare favorably to other basic disciplines' attempts to explain leisure behavior. In fact, the Social Psychology/Psychology of Leisure session seems to draw more submissions and interest from leisure researchers than other disciplines such as sociology, geography, economics and philosophy.

Perhaps more significant is the fact that psychological papers presented in the Symposium are not limited to the Social Psychology/Psychology session. When looking at the papers presented in the entire symposium, the psychologization of other sessions is evident. Studies focusing on psychological variables have been reported in most of the other sessions, from Therapeutic Recreation and Human Development to Management and Sociology. It is not surprising that this psychologization has occurred with such allied areas as therapeutic recreation and human development, but what is surprising is that the psychologization has spread to seemingly unrelated fields like sociology, resource planning and management. This, of course, is exciting and represents a very positive development. Needless to say, it also says something about the perceived power of psychological variables to explain leisure behavior. In short, a psychological/social psychological analysis has become an integral part of the Leisure Research Symposium not only because of the formal session in which psychological papers are reported, but also because of the application of psychological analysis to other areas of leisure studies. To have an avenue for reporting social psychological findings about leisure on a consistent, continuous and successful basis is perhaps the most significant achievement in the development of new knowledge in this field.

It should not be forgotten that the NRPA's Leisure Research Symposium is not the only outlet for reporting psychological papers. The Canadian Congress on Leisure Research, which is held every three years, has become an increasingly important place for leisure psychologists to share their findings. As an example of this importance, it is the second Canadian Congress where Mannell (1978a) first reported his innovative laboratory experiments on antecedents and consequences of leisure experiences. Although this Congress does not formally have its own psychology of leisure session, many of the papers reported in the Congress are clearly psychological studies of leisure.

Past Accomplishments

The establishment of the Leisure Research Symposium (and the Psychology/Social Psychology session) has to be viewed in an historic light and as a response to a rapidly growing interest in leisure research. The initiation of the *Journal of Leisure Research* in 1969 was the most significant milestone in this respect. For the first time it was possible to publish psychological papers on leisure behavior in a journal that was openly looking for such papers. Neulinger and Breit's (1969) attitude dimensions study and Witt and Bishop's (1970) situational antecedents paper were trend setting and served as an invitation for others to follow. Although psychological papers were slow in coming mainly because of a lack of interested and competent researchers, the growth nevertheless was steady. One of the major contributions to this literature was Bishop and Witt's (1970) experiment on sources of behavioral variance during leisure time. Besides its informativeness, the study was significant for its publication in the prestigious *Journal of Personality and Social Psychology* — still one of the few leisure-related studies published in prestigious non-leisure journals by leisure researchers.

Despite the progress, the publication of Neulinger's *Psychology of Leisure* in 1974 was surprising in light of the relatively little research published on leisure. His text, however, was an important milestone and stimulant, giving a major boost for other scholars to pursue research on the psychological aspects of leisure behavior. Neulinger's text was also important because of the three-factor model of leisure presented in it. The model was later used as a basis for much of the empirical research on subjective definitions of leisure (e.g., Iso-Ahola, 1979a, b; Shaw, 1985a, 1986; Roadburg, 1983; Mannell, 1978a, b; Mannell & Bradley, 1986). In considerable support of Neulinger's model, research has shown the importance of various dimensions of intrinsic motivation to definitions of leisure. The volume of this research and the consistency of the findings speak strongly against Sessoms' (1986, p. 110) claim that "we are no closer to resolving the issue of definition (of leisure) than we were 25 years ago."

Following Neulinger's book, psychological research publications became more frequent and provided the impetus for this author to review the vast but scattered literature on the social psychology of leisure and recreation (Iso-Ahola, 1980a). The book was more of a review of the existing literature than a text to be used in introductory recreation classes, and it clearly focused on the social psychological aspects of leisure behavior as opposed to a purely psychological analysis of leisure. In the same year, two edited books were published, one on social psychological perspectives of leisure (Iso-Ahola, 1980b) and the other on psychological aspects (Ibrahim & Crandall, 1980). All of this publication activity in the span of six years lent considerable credence to the psychology/social psychology of leisure as a subfield of leisure studies and as noted earlier, has made it a formidable force among the basic disciplines' attempts to explain leisure behavior.

Although no new texts have been published since 1980, two concerted efforts have been put forth. In 1984, Quellet edited a special issue of *Society and Leisure* on the "psychological studies of the leisure experience" and in the same year, Stringer edited a special issue of *Annals of Tourism Research* on "the social psychology of tourism." The former is a collection of varied articles ranging from conceptualizations of, and individual differences in leisure to psychological intervention in leisure. The latter, on the other hand, focuses not only on one particular leisure behavior (tourism) but also on specific social psychological phenomena or aspects of this leisure behavior, such as tourist-guide interactions. It should also be mentioned that most of the articles included in Wade's (1985) edited text on constraints to leisure contain psychological and social psychological analyses of constraints to leisure behavior and experiences. The same is true of the special issue of *Journal of Leisure Research* on leisure constraints edited by Jackson (1991) and on benefits of leisure edited by Driver (1990). These developments have made important contributions to the overall psychological literature on leisure and in doing so, have maintained the momentum and thrust of the psychological analysis initiated in the 1970s.

In addition to the above major milestones, other contributions have been critical to the emergence of the social psychological/psychological field of leisure. Perhaps the most important of these is the publication of leisure (or leisure related) studies by non-leisure researchers in non-leisure journals or books. Included in this category are Brooks and Elliott's (1971) study on prediction of psychological adjustment at age thirty from leisure activities and satisfactions in childhood; Campbell's et al. (1976) research on the quality of American life and London's et al. (1977a) study on the contribution of job and leisure satisfaction to quality of life; Lepper's et al. (1973) experiments on undermining children's intrinsic interest with extrinsic rewards; Harackiewiczs' et al. (1985) studies on rewarding pinball wizardry, and Deci's (1975) work on intrinsic motivation in general; Cialdini's et al. (1976) experiments on "basking in reflected glory" to explain spectator sports; DeCarlo's (1974) study on recreation participation and successful aging; Copp's (1975) qualitative piece on why hunters like to hunt; Ivancevich and Lyon's (1977) field experiment on the effects of the shortened work week; Langer and Rodin's (1976) and Schulz's (1976) field experiments on the effects of choice and enhanced personal responsibility for the aged; Orthner's (1975) study on leisure activity patterns and marital satisfaction and Crawford and Huston's (1993) study on the restrictive and facilitative effects of parenthood on spouses' leisure activity; Rosenhan's (1973) qualitative study on being sane in insane places; Reich and Zautra's (1981) experiment on the effects of perceived personal causation in leisure behaviors on psychological well-being; Kobasa's work (1979) on stressful life events, personality and health; Brown's (1991) experiment on stress-buffering effects of fitness; Haworth and Hill's (1992) research on work, leisure and psychological well-being; Marsh's et al. (1986a,b) studies on the effects of participation in an Outward Bound program on multidimensional self-concepts; Lounsbury and Hoopes' (1986) study on the effects of vacations on job satisfaction and productivity and Rubenstein's (1980) survey on psychological factors in vacation behavior; Crouter's et al., (1989) study on the influence of work-induced psychological states on leisure behavior at home; Gilovich's (1983) experiments on causes of persistence in gambling as a leisure activity; O'Brien's (1981) study on leisure attributes and retirement satisfaction; Kabanoff's (1980) review of research on the relationship between work and non-work; Forgas and Moylan's (1987) work on the effects of movie-induced moods on social judgements; Larsen and Kasimatis' (1990) study on individual differences in entrainment of mood to the weekly calendar and Stone's (1985) data on the "Blue Monday" phenomenon; Tangney and Feshbach's (1988) study on children's TV viewing habits and Schutte et al.'s (1988) work on effects of playing video games on children's aggressive and other behaviors.

Although the above list is not comprehensive by any means, it is clear that non-leisure researchers have made many important contributions to the social psychology/psychology of leisure. One of these "outsiders" was left out of the above listing on purpose because his work deserves a special recognition. Csikszentmihalyi's (1975, 1982, 1988, 1990) extensive research on antecedents and consequences of "flow" has undoubtedly had more impact on the psychological explanation of leisure behavior than the works of other non-leisure researchers. Particularly important was the publication of his empirical study with LeFevre on optimal experiences in work and leisure in *Journal of Personality and Social Psychology* in 1989. The concept of "flow" has been embraced as a core construct in leisure behavior, although some criticism of it has surfaced (Samdahl, 1986). Csikszentmihalyi's work has stimulated a lot of research in the field (e.g., Larson, et al. 1985; Mannell, 1978a, b, 1980; Mannell & Bradley, 1986; Mannell et al., 1988) and continues to be a rich source for new studies and explanations of leisure.

His work is also important because some of it has been done as a response to invitations and requests made by leisure researchers. In other words, leisure researchers (e.g., mainly Kleiber and Mannell) have succeeded in channeling some of this creative psychologist's energies into studying leisure. Unfortunately, such coups are rare (other notable psychologists studying leisure are Haworth, Lounsbury and Tinsley) and suggest that this is an important strategy of increasing the body of knowledge in the field. That social psychologists are beginning to understand the importance of leisure is demonstrated by Argyle's (1992) recent work. This famous European social psychologist included one full chapter on leisure in his best-selling text, "The Social Psychology of Everyday Life." Of course, it is not surprising that psychologists generally are not interested in studying leisure. Ingham (1986) reported that only 13 of a total of 862 psychologists on the staff in the United Kingdom University or Polytechnic Psychology departments indicated "leisure" or "sport" as one of their main research interests. In contrast, 72 listed "work" or "occupation" as one of their primary research topics. Although a similar survey has not been reported in North America, it is safe to say that the proportional difference in the number of leisure and work psychologists is even greater in North America.

On the other side of the coin are contributions made by leisure psychologists through publications in non-leisure journals and books. Although such reports are relatively rare, they nevertheless exist. As mentioned earlier, Bishop and Witt's (1970) study on the effects of personality and situational factors on leisure behavior is an important and classic contribution to the literature. Similarly, Bishop and Chace's (1971) experiment on the effects of parents' cognitive style and their children's home play environment on their creativity is another classic contribution. Wankel and Thompson's (1977) field experiment on the effects of self-persuasion motivation techniques on the attendance at a recreation exercise club is also an important study published in a prestigious social psychology journal. The same is true of a field study on little league players' causal attributions of success and failure (Iso-Ahola, 1977). More recent efforts include Knopf's (1983) chapter on motivation in outdoor recreation settings, Kleiber's (1985) chapter on leisure resources, Bradley and Mannell's (1984) experiment on intrinsic motivation and Iso-Ahola and Weissinger's (1987) field study on the relationship between leisure and boredom. Such publications are important not only because of their contributions to the body of knowledge, but above all, because of the visibility and interest they are likely to generate among some psychologists and social psychologists.

WHAT DO WE KNOW?

Besides examining how (and by whom) the past contributions have been made it is also important to ask:

What is the content and substance of the reported research? Where is our body of knowledge good and in what areas is it lacking? Many of the answers to these questions can be found in Ingham's (1986, 1987) two-part review of the psychological contributions to the study of leisure, and a reader is referred to these sources for a more detailed analysis of content areas covered.

While many different topics have been studied, even to the extent that the coverage may have been haphazard (Ingham, 1986), considerable knowledge has been created in some areas. One of the most basic social influence processes includes the effects of social agents (e.g., parents) on leisure participation and other variables, and this has been investigated by Hoff and Ellis (1992) and Hultsman (1993). The most researched areas include motivation and needs, satisfaction, attitude, subjective definitions and leisure experiences, personality and individual differences, and crowding and social carrying capacity. Based upon numerous factor analytic studies (e.g., Clough et al., 1989; Ewert, 1985; London et al., 1977b; Mills, 1985; Tinsley et al., 1977; Tinsley & Kass, 1978; Williams et al., 1990), we know the basic dimensions of leisure motives and needs. The importance of informal social interaction in leisure situations has been demonstrated (Samdahl, 1992), and the negative relationship between intrinsic motivation and leisure boredom has been established (Iso-Ahola & Weissinger, 1987; Weissinger et al., 1992). There are psychometrically respectable measures of leisure motivation (Beard & Ragheb, 1983; Weissinger, 1985), and a two-dimensional theory of leisure motivation has been proposed (Iso-Ahola, 1984, 1989). We also know that leisure motives and needs are dynamic and temporary in nature, varying as a function of a particular leisure experience (Hull et al., 1992; Iso-Ahola & Allen, 1982; Manfredo, 1984; Stewart, 1992) and that leisure motivation and satisfaction are empirically related (Dunn Ross & Iso-Ahola, 1991). But many intuitively obvious and important questions have not been raised, nor answered, such as: How are leisure motives and needs acquired? How systematically or haphazardly are motives used in decision-making regarding leisure participation? How important are leisure motives to actual leisure engagements? How important is it to be cognitively aware of one's leisure motives and needs and how important is such awareness to leisure satisfaction?

In a similar vein, we know the basic dimensions and determinants of leisure satisfaction (e.g., Francken & Van Raaij, 1981; Hawes, 1978; Haworth, 1983; Iso-Ahola et al., 1982; Lounsbury &

Hoopes, 1985; Riddick, 1986; Vaske et al., 1982), and there exist reliable and valid tests of leisure satisfaction (Beard & Ragheb, 1980; Noe, 1987; Pierce, 1980). Mannell (1989) has advanced a theoretical model of leisure satisfaction, in which he distinguishes between appraisal-satisfaction and need-satisfaction. We also know about the relatively superior contribution of leisure satisfaction to perceived quality of life (London et al., 1977a) and of the positive effect of satisfying leisure participation on life satisfaction (Riddick & Daniel, 1984; Russell, 1987). We have some understanding of the interrelationships among leisure participation, leisure satisfaction and leisure attitudes (Ragheb, 1980) and of the relationship between leisure attitudes and actual leisure behaviors (Ajzen & Driver 1991; Madden et al., 1992; Manfredo et al., 1992; Young & Kent, 1985). The cognitive dissonance theory has been used as a basis of understanding attitudes and attitude changes in recreation behavior (Vingerhoets & Buunk, 1987). Studies have also helped us understand the relationship between leisure attitudes and work attitudes (Iso-Ahola & Buttimer, 1982) and between leisure attitudes and the perceived control of life's circumstances (Kleiber & Crandall, 1981).

As mentioned earlier, a considerable body of knowledge has been accumulated on the role of perceived freedom in subjective definitions of leisure (e.g., Iso-Ahola, 1979a, b; Mannell, 1978a, b; Mannell & Bradley, 1986; Neulinger, 1974; Roadburg, 1983; Shaw, 1985a, 1986) and in leisure experiences (Csikszentmihalyi 1982; Csikszentmihalyi & Graef, 1979; Graef et al., 1983; Harper, 1981, 1986; Kleiber et al., 1986; Mannell, 1980). These studies have shown the general nature and the central characteristics of a leisure experience, and this line of research has been extended to different populations (e.g., Larson et al.,1985) and different activities (Brown & Haas, 1980; Hautaluoma & Brown, 1978; Iso-Ahola, 1983; Mannell & Iso-Ahola, 1987). A different dimension of leisure experience is revealed by the perceived nature of meaningful activities, how seriously people take leisure, and how committed they are to leisure (Haworth, 1984; Mannell, 1993; McIntyre, 1989; McIntyre & Pigram, 1992; Stebbins, 1993; Yair, 1990).

Following the social psychological tradition, researchers have explored the relationship between leisure and individual differences. Bishop and Witt (1970) and Witt and Bishop (1970) were the first to demonstrate that personality and situational factors account independently as well as interactively for leisure behaviors. Which of the many personality traits would then relate significantly to leisure? With few exceptions, fortunately, leisure researchers have not fallen into a trap of correlating countless and theoretically meaningless personality traits and leisure behaviors in which persons engage actively (Driver & Knopf, 1977). Instead, some of the theoretically strong and meaningful personality factors should be and have been investigated in relation to leisure. Most notably, these include locus of control (Kleiber & Crandall, 1981), Type A-B personality (Becker & Byrne, 1984; Iso-Ahola & Weissinger, 1985; Tang, 1986), sensation seeking (Zuckerman, 1979), and introversion-extraversion (Eysenck, 1981). In addition, Mannell (1984b) has developed a measure of a leisure-related personality characteristic, called self-as-entertainer. Such an approach is recommendable because it starts with leisure-specific personality rather than borrowing general trait measures from social psychology. In a similar vein, Weissinger (1985) has created a measure of intrinsic leisure motivation as a personality disposition, and the relationship of this personality characteristic to psychological and physical health has been discussed (Weissinger, & Iso-Ahola, 1984). Finally, the effects of leisure participation on self-concept (Iso-Ahola, et al., 1989; Koocher, 1971; Marsh et al., 1986a, b; McDonald & Howe, 1989) and psychological adjustment (Bishop, 1973; Brooks & Elliot, 1971) have been explored.

Another important individual difference variable concerns the effect of gender and sex roles on leisure behavior. Many studies have shown clear sex differences in leisure cognitions, motives, and behaviors (Hirschman, 1984; Kleiber & Kane, 1984). It appears, however, that it is the sex roles rather than gender per se that explains the differences and inequalities in men's and women's leisure (Henderson, 1990; Rohrbaugh, 1979; Shank, 1986; Shaw, 1985b, 1992). It is interesting to know, for example, that wives have, on the average, over two hours less free time on weekends than their husbands do, mainly because of their household activities, the needs of their children and the demands of their husbands' employment (Shaw, 1985b). Such inequalities have led some (e.g., Dempsey, 1990) to argue that men often achieve their leisure at the expense of women and use their "superior powers" to exclude women from much of leisure activity. There is evidence (Bird & Fremont, 1991) demonstrating that men's health benefits on passive leisure are nearly twice as high as women's, whereas women's returns on active leisure are higher than men's.

Applications of Psychological Concepts

In addition to the above areas of considerable psychological knowledge on leisure, there are several areas of leisure studies where basic psychological knowledge has been successfully applied. One of these deals with the application of social psychology to outdoor recreation and resource management (Driver, 1972; Driver & Tocher, 1970). Most of this research can be placed under the heading "social carrying capacity" (Shelby & Heberlein, 1986). In general, social carrying capacity refers to the level of recreational use of outdoor recreation settings that can be sustained without undercutting the quality of leisure experiences. The research literature on this topic is vast and impressive, leading to a special issue of *Leisure Sciences* in 1984 on social carrying capacity and an integration and synthesis of twenty years of research (Graefe et al., 1984). As might be expected, one of the most frequently studied phenomena of social carrying capacity includes perceptions of crowding and encounter norms and their effects on recreation experiences (e.g., Andereck & Becker, 1993; Ditton et al., 1983; Hammitt & Patterson, 1991; Kuentzel & Heberlein, 1992; Manning, 1985; Shelby et al., 1983, 1989; Schreyer & Roggenbuck, 1978; Vaske et al., 1986; Williams et al., 1991). Related to this is a long line of research on the effects of past experience on recreation choices and behaviors (Hammitt et al., 1989; Kuentzel & McDonald, 1992; Schreyer et al., 1984; Watson et al., 1991).

Another area to which social psychology has successfully been applied concerns therapeutic recreation and leisure counseling. Although the research literature as a whole is not vast (Iso-Ahola, 1988), it nevertheless has some notable achievements and includes promising experimentation. One of the success stories is Witt and Ellis' (1984) and Ellis and Witt's (1986) development of the "Leisure Diagnostic Battery." This set of measurements was designed to assess disabled children's and adults' leisure functioning from various psychological perspectives. It is strongly grounded in theory and meets the psychometric standards set for test construction. Besides being a useful set of tools for researchers and practitioners in the field, this instrument package serves as an excellent model of test construction for leisure researchers in general.

Other instruments useful for therapeutic recreators include the Leisure Boredom Scale (Iso-Ahola & Weissinger, 1990), Leisure Experience Battery for Adolescents (Caldwell et al., 1992), and Brief Leisure Rating Scale (Ellis & Niles, 1985). Although this latter instrument needs more psychometric work, it is well grounded in social psychological theory and measures the central concepts in therapeutic recreation and leisure counseling, namely learned helplessness and perceived control. It has been shown theoretically that therapeutic recreation revolves around these concepts (Iso-Ahola et al., 1980) and that a social psychological approach to leisure has important implications for leisure counseling (Iso-Ahola, 1984) and therapeutic recreation programming (Savell, 1986).

In addition to the successful work on test construction, the reported research includes some promising experimentation. It appears that researchers are finally beginning to address some of the fundamental questions about therapeutic recreation and leisure counseling. Such questions include: Are therapeutic recreation programs indeed as therapeutic and psychologically beneficial as they have been assumed to be? If they are, what is it about these programs that promotes psychologically successful outcomes? Backman and Mannell's (1986), Searle and Mahon's (1993), Shary and Iso-Ahola's, (1989) and Wolfe and Riddick's (1984) experiments on the effects of leisure counseling, leisure education, and intervention programs on selected social-psychological variables are examples of studies that begin to answer such fundamental questions. Similarly, Schleien et al. (1990) reported data on the effects of social level of activity on play behavior of children with autism. Finally, Dattilo and Barnett's (1985) experiment based upon a single-subject design is important as a methodological application of experimental research to severely disabled persons and as an illuminating study on the role of choice in defining a leisure experience among severely disabled individuals. It should also be mentioned that to better understand the effectiveness of therapeutic recreation interventions, individual differences have to be considered in future research (Ellis & Yessick, 1989).

Another area of the successful application of social psychology to leisure is concerned with youth sports. Studies have addressed, among other things, factors underlying enjoyment of youth sports (e.g., Wankel & Kreisel, 1985) and causal attributions of game outcomes (Iso-Ahola, 1977). A social psychological analysis of Little League sports has shown some major problems in these programs with concrete recommendations for improvement (Iso-Ahola, 1980c). The research literature is vast and suggests that adult intervention should be limited and coach effectiveness training be facilitated in youth sports (Iso-Ahola & Hatfield, 1986).

Play — Lost to Psychologists?

Traditionally, the question about why children play has been the dominant topic among leisure scholars. It is probably safe to say that in the late 1960s and early 1970s play research was the leading area of scholarship among leisure researchers, culminating with the publication of Ellis' (1973) optimal arousal theory of play. But since that time, play research has steadily lost ground to the point that it clearly plays second fiddle in today's leisure research. This is not to say that good play research is not done any more (for examples of good and interesting play experiments, see Barnett & Storm, 1981; Barnett, 1985; and for a recent review on developmental benefits of play for children, see Barnett, 1990). Concurrently with leisure researchers becoming less interested in play or more interested in other leisure phenomena, developmental psychologists have taken over play research. The number of books written (e.g., Hughes, 1991; Johnson et al., 1987) and articles published in developmental psychology journals during the last 15 years or so on various aspects of play is nothing short of amazing. Although much of this research has focused on the role of play in children's cognitive development, studies have also been reported on social aspects of play, a topic closer to the interests of leisure scholars. The importance of play was clearly shown by the conclusion Rice (1989) drew on the basis of her review of research on children's language acquisition: "Children's play is a primary source of language enrichment. Adult-directed teaching drills are not appropriate" (p. 155). While it is interesting to note developmental psychologists' discovery of the importance of play and their takeover of play research, this phenomenon raises some troubling questions, such as: Are leisure psychologists only to warm up certain research topics for mainstream psychologists/social psychologists who will eventually take over the research on these prehatched phenomena?

ABOUT THE FUTURE OF PSYCHOLOGICAL LEISURE RESEARCH

As the above review indicates, the volume of social psychological research on leisure is impressive. Our knowledge is quite advanced in some basic areas such as motivation and satisfaction, but it is also good in more applied areas like outdoor recreation and recreation resource management and therapeutic recreation. This, then, raises questions about the future research in the social psychology of leisure. Where do we go from here?

It seems that two major strategies of research should be followed. First, we should direct our energies to theory development and ask new questions in those areas where we have accumulated a good body of knowledge. We need to go beyond the factor analytic studies of leisure motivation and ask new research questions about leisure motivation: e.g., how are leisure motives acquired? How lasting are they? How do they change? What are the consequences of unfulfilled leisure needs and motives? Similarly, we know quite a bit about children's play, but we have not even answered one of the most basic questions about children's recreation: What experiences do parents expose their children to and what is the significance of such early exposures to various adult recreation experiences and subsequent psychological functioning? Mobily and his associates' work (1991, 1993) on adults' leisure repertoires needs to be extended to children's leisure repertoires as well.

Besides asking new research questions, we need to develop theories to guide our research. Although there are only two formal theories dealing with psychological aspects of leisure behavior, Iso-Ahola's (1986b) theory of substitutability of leisure behaviors and Tinsley and Tinsley's (1986) theory of attributes, benefits, and causes of leisure experiences, recent theoretical developments on ceasing leisure participation (Searle, 1991) and on leisure constraints (Crawford et al., 1991; Jackson et al., 1993) are very encouraging. Similarly encouraging is the theoretical work on recreation specialization (Ditton et al., 1992) and on social and psychological benefits of leisure (c.f., Wankel & Berger, 1990). Obviously, much more theoretical work is needed, because otherwise we end up with undirected accumulation of empirical facts and no ability to integrate such seemingly unrelated pieces of knowledge. One area that is in dire need of theory development is leisure satisfaction. A lot of empirical research has been done on leisure satisfaction, thereby providing a good basis for the development of a theory of leisure satisfaction (Mannell, 1989). The same applies to many other areas of existing research.

The second strategy of future research involves exploratory work. What is needed here is the opening of new areas of research or continuing those that have been started. One of these deals with the relationship between leisure and health. This relationship involves conceptually and empirically much more than computation of correlation coefficients between leisure participation and life satisfaction. It involves determination of the effect of various leisure lifestyles on physical and mental health (Iso-Ahola, 1994). It calls for research to determine the mediating role of leisure-related variables in the relationship between stressful life events and health (Caldwell et al., 1993; Caltabiano, 1988). A recent review of research suggests that leisure-related social interaction and self-determination buffer the effects of stress on health (Coleman & Iso-Ahola, 1993). Similarly, House's et al. (1988) review suggests that the social interaction that occurs in leisure may well be its most beneficial component. The field also begs for research on the relationship between leisure (e.g., leisure boredom) and unhealthy behaviors such as drug abuse (Iso-Ahola & Crowley, 1991). In short, the question about leisure and health is potentially one of the most important research topics on the horizon and promises to be an area where leisure psychologists and the entire profession can make headlines with their contributions.

There are many other important research topics for leisure psychologists. One of them has to do with marriage, decision-making, and leisure. Although it is the norm that both husbands and wives work in today's society, we know little about the role of leisure decisions in the lives of young couples. It is conceivable that how leisure decisions are made and how leisure is used between husbands and wives plays a critical role in contribution to or alleviation of marriage problems (Crawford & Huston, 1993; Hill, 1988; Holman & Jacquart, 1988). It is even possible that today's high divorce rate is rooted in couples' failure to use their leisure in personally and interpersonally rewarding ways.

Other research topics include the relationship between unemployment and leisure (see Haworth, 1986; Ingham, 1987) and the effects of leisure on work and productivity (Lounsbury & Hoopes, 1986). It is surprising that we have not studied the relationship between feelings of guilt and leisure either. Guilt feelings may not only be an important barrier to leisure participation, but may also account for differences in the quality of leisure experiences. In a similar vein, we have not studied the role and importance of sharing leisure experiences to the overall quality of leisure experiences. Is a leisure experience undermined by a failure or a lack of opportunity to "play the 19th hole?"

In addition to these kinds of relatively unexplored research topics, leisure psychologists are called on to explore the old phenomena or processes in new ways. For example, rather than studying personality correlates of leisure, new ways of looking at the issue include identity affirmation through leisure (Haggard & Williams, 1992) and self-awareness and leisure (Samdahl & Kleiber, 1989). Application of certain personality theories such as the self-schemata theory in the leisure context (e.g., Kendzierski, 1988) could be profitable. Leisure researchers are also called on to delve into basic features of leisure, such as leisure cycles and leisure rhythms that regulate our behaviors and well-being. The most obvious cycle is the 5-day work week and 2-day weekend. But, there are a lot of deviations from this norm, and it is conceivable that there are many smaller leisure cycles within a day. So, it is possible to have seasonal, weekly, and daily leisure rhythms. No research to date, however, has attempted to address what such cycles or rhythms are, what individual and group differences might exist in these cycles, and what the optimum leisure rhythms are from the psychological standpoint.

Research is also needed to investigate the relationship between work and leisure rhythms. It may well be that the highest level of productivity is not achieved by the fixed amount of hours worked, but by allowing people to balance their work and leisure rhythms in the course of each working day.

Related to the above is a question about exciting and routine leisure. Within a given leisure rhythm or cycle, what do people do to achieve the balance between sufficiently exciting and overly routine leisure? Are those whose leisure can be characterized as exciting psychologically and physically better off than those whose leisure appears routine to them? While we know quite a bit about the features of peak (flow) experiences, such experiences may be limited in time and space, thereby failing to capture most of one's leisure life. Research is needed to broaden our knowledge from peak experiences to the determination of antecedents and consequences of personally exciting leisure lifestyles.

CONCLUSION

The social psychology/psychology of leisure has an impressive body of knowledge. The research momentum begun in the early and mid-70s has been continued, leading to numerous and varied contributions today. As might be expected, knowledge is more advanced in some areas than others, and many important topics have not yet been addressed. There seems to be a good knowledge base on such basic concepts as motivation, satisfaction and attitudes. What is needed in these and other areas is theory development to guide our future research endeavors. The social psychological approach to research has also been utilized to create knowledge in applied areas like outdoor recreation and recreation resource management as well as therapeutic recreation and leisure counseling. Promising and potentially important research topics for the future include leisure and health; leisure, marriage and decision-making; leisure and unemployment; effects of leisure on work and productivity; leisure and guilt feelings; and the sharing of leisure experiences. In addition, some of the basic issues about leisure are still unresolved. These include a study of leisure cycles or rhythms and the relationship between exciting and routine leisure life.

Although leisure psychologists can be proud of their achievements, this is not time to rest on our laurels. To maintain the momentum, new textbooks need to be written and special journal issues edited. Leisure psychologists need to attract general social psychologists'/psychologists' attention, and this is best achieved by publishing some of their work in reputable psychology journals. They also have to continue to "recruit" general social psychologists to study leisure, because scholars such as Csikszentmihalyi will make lasting contributions to the field. But ultimately, the future of the field rests on the shoulders of young leisure psychologists, new Ph.D.s. Yet, annually the field produces a worrisomely small number of new leisure researchers who can be called leisure psychologists. This is probably the main obstacle the social psychology/psychology of leisure faces today, and unfortunately, there is no sign of improvement of the situation in the immediate future.

Finally, a methodological note is in order. It has become fashionable in recent years to criticize research methods employed for studying psychological phenomena. In particular, the experimental method has severely been criticized. Such a criticism, however, has been relatively nonexistent in the field of leisure studies, and with a good reason. Researchers have used a variety of methods to investigate psychological phenomena. A good example of this is research on perceived freedom and intrinsic motivation. Researchers have used quasi-experiments (Iso-Ahola, 1979a), laboratory experiments (Mannell & Bradley, 1986), personal interviews (Shaw, 1985a) and "experience sampling method" or beeper technology (Csikszentmihalyi & Graef, 1979) to investigate the same phenomenon. This kind of approach is unprecedented in psychological studies in general and demonstrates that leisure researchers are methodologically creative in their pursuit of new knowledge. Of course, the above example is still an exception rather than the rule but, nevertheless, is methodologically encouraging. As has been argued before (Iso-Ahola, 1980a, p. 77): "The balanced use of a variety of methods is the best guarantee of success in attempts to explain human social behavior in leisure environments." We need to be not only tolerant of different methodological approaches, but actively encourage the use of both quantitative and qualitative research methods in the social psychological study of leisure.

BIBLIOGRAPHY

Ajzen, I., and B. L. Driver (1991). Prediction of Leisure Participation from Behavioral, Normative, and Control Beliefs: An Application of the Theory of Planned Behavior. *Leisure Sciences, 13,* 185-204.

Andereck, K.L., and R. H. Becker (1993). Perceptions of Carry-Over Crowding in Recreation Environments. *Leisure Sciences, 15,* 25-35.

Argyle, M. (1992). *The Social Psychology of Everyday Life.* New York: Routledge.

Backman, S.J., and R. C. Mannell (1986). Removing Attitudinal Barriers to Leisure Behavior and Satisfaction: A Field Experiment Among the Institutionalized Elderly. *Therapeutic Recreation Journal, 20,* 46-53.

Barnett, L.A. (1985). Young Children's Free Play and Problem-Solving ability. *Leisure Sciences, 7,* 25-46.

Barnett, L.A., and B. Storm (1981). Play, Pleasure, and Pain: The Reduction of Anxiety Through Play. *Leisure Sciences, 4,* 161-176.

Barnett, L.A. (1990). Developmental Benefits of Play for Children. *Journal of Leisure Research, 22,* 138-153.

Becker, M.A., and D. Byrne (1984). Type A Behavior and Daily Activities of Young Married Couples. *Journal of Applied Social Psychology, 14,* 82-88.

Beard, J.G., and M. G. Ragheb (1980). Leisure Satisfaction: Concept, Theory, and Measurement. In S.E. Iso-Ahola (Ed.), *Social Psychological Perspectives on Leisure and Recreation* (pp. 329-353). Springfield, IL: Charles C. Thomas.

Beard, J.G., and M. G. Ragheb (1983). Measuring Leisure Motivation. *Journal of Leisure Research, 15,* 219-228.

Bird, C.E., and A. M. Fremont (1991). Gender, Time Use, and Health. *Journal of Health and Social Behavior, 32,* 114-129.

Bishop, D.W. (1973). *Psychological Adjustment and Leisure Time Activities.* Final Report for Grant MH 17913, Department of Recreation and Park Administration, University of Illinois.

Bishop, D.W., and C. A. Chace (1971). Parental Conceptual Systems, Home Play Environment, and Potential Creativity in Children. *Journal of Experimental Child Psychology, 12,* 318-338.

Bishop, D.W., and P. A. Witt (1970). Sources of Behavioral Variance During Leisure Time. *Journal of Personality and Social Psychology, 16,* 352-360.

Bradley, W., and R. C. Mannell (1984). Sensitivity of Intrinsic Motivation to Reward Procedure Instructions. *Personality and Social Psychology Bulletin, 10,* 426-431.

Brooks, J.B., and D. M. Elliott (1971). Prediction of Psychological Adjustment at Age Thirty from Leisure Time Activities and Satisfactions in Childhood. *Human Development, 14,* 51-61.

Brown, J.D. (1991). Staying Fit and Staying Well: Physical Fitness as a Moderator of Life Stress. *Journal of Personality and Social Psychology, 60,* 555-561.

Brown, P.J., and G. E. Haas (1980). Wilderness Recreation Experience: The Rawah Case. *Journal of Leisure Research, 12,* 229-241.

Caldwell, L.L., E. A. Smith, and E. Weissinger (1992). Development of a Leisure Experience Battery for Adolescents: Parsimony, Stability, and Validity. *Journal of Leisure Research, 24,* 361-376.

Caldwell, L.L., E. A. Smith, and E. Weissinger (1993). The Relationship of Leisure Activities and Perceived Health of College Students. *Society and Leisure, 15,* 545-556.

Caltabiano, M.L. (1988). *The Effect of Predisposing Variables and Leisure on the Relationship Between Stressful Life Events and Illness Symptomalogy.* Unpublished doctoral dissertation, James Cook University. Townsville, Australia.

Campbell, A., P. E. Converse, and W. L. Rodgers (1976). *The Quality of American Life: Perceptions, Evaluations, and Satisfactions.* New York: Russell Sage Foundation.

Cialdini, R., R. Borden, A. Thorne, M. Walker, S. Freeman, and L. Sloan, (1976). Basking in Reflected Glory: Three (football) Field Studies. *Journal of Personality and Social Psychology, 34,* 366-375.

Clough, P., J. Shepherd, and R. Maughan (1989). Motives for Participation in Recreational Running. *Journal of Leisure Research, 21,* 297-309.

Coleman, D., and S. E. Iso-Ahola, S.E. (1993). Leisure and Health: The Role of Social Support and Self-Determination. *Journal of Leisure Research, 25,* 111-128.

Copp, J.D. (1975, December). Why Hunters Like to Hunt. *Psychology Today, 9,* 60-62, 67.

Crawford, D.W., and T. L. Huston (1993). The Impact of the Transition to Parenthood on Marital Leisure. *Personality and Social Psychology Bulletin, 19,* 39-46.

Crawford, D.W., E. L. Jackson, and G. Godbey (1991). A Hierarchical Model of Leisure Constraints. *Leisure Sciences, 13,* 309-320.

Crouter, A. C., M. Perry-Jenkins, T. L. Huston and D. W. Crawford (1989). The Influence of Work-Induced Psychological States on Behavior at Home. *Basic and Applied Social Psychology, 10,* 273-292.

Csikszentmihalyi, M. (1975). *Beyond Boredom and Anxiety.* San Francisco: Jossey-Bass.

Csikszentmihalyi, M. (1982). Toward a Psychology of Optimal Experience. *Review of Personality and Social Psychology, 3,* 13-36.

Csikszentmihalyi, M. (1990). *Flow, the Psychology of Optimal Experience.* New York: Harper Perennial.

Csikszentmihalyi, M., and I. S. Csikszentmihalyi (1988). (Eds.). *Optimal Experience, Psychological Studies of Flow in Consciousness.* New York: Cambridge University Press.

Csikszentmihalyi, M., and R. Graef (1979, December). Feeling Free. *Psychology Today, 13*, 84-90, 98-99.

Csikzentmihalyi, M., and J. LeFevre (1989). Optimal Experience in Work and Leisure. *Journal of Personality and Social Psychology, 56*, 815-822.

Dattilo, J., and L. A. Barnett (1985). Therapeutic Recreation for Individuals with Severe Handicaps: An Analysis of the Relationship Between Choice and Pleasure. *Therapeutic Recreation Journal, 19*, 79-91.

DeCarlo, T.J. (1974). Recreation Participation Patterns and Successful Aging. *Journal of Gerontology, 29*, 416-422.

Deci, E.L. (1975). *Intrinsic Motivation*. New York: Plenum Press.

Dempsey, K. (1990). Women's Life and Leisure in an Australian Rural Community. *Leisure Studies, 9*, 35-44.

Ditton, R.B., A. J. Fedler, and A. R. Graefe (1983). Factors Contributing to Perceptions of Recreation Crowding. *Leisure Sciences, 5*, 273-286.

Ditton, R.B., D. K. Loomis, and S. Choi (1992). Recreation Specialization: Re-Conceptualization from a Social Worlds Perspective. *Journal of Leisure Research, 24*, 33-51.

Driver, B.L. (1972). Potential Contributions of Psychology to Recreation Resource Management. In J.F. Wohlwill, and D.H. Carson (Eds.), *Environment and Social Sciences: Perspectives and Applications* (pp. 223-244). Washington, D.C.: APA.

Driver, B.L., and R. C. Knopf (1977). Personality, Outdoor Recreation, and Expected Consequences. *Environment and Behavior, 9*, 169-193.

Driver, B.L., and S. R. Tocher (1970). Toward a Behavioral Interpretation of Recreation, with Implications for Planning. In B.L. Driver (Ed.), *Elements of Outdoor Recreation Planning* (pp. 9-31). Ann Arbor: The University of Michigan Press.

Driver, B.L. (1990). Focusing Research on the Benefits of Leisure: Special Issue Introduction. *Journal of Leisure Research, 22*, 93-98.

Dunn Ross, E., and S. E. Iso-Ahola (1991). Sightseeing Tourists' Motivation and Satisfaction. *Annals of Tourism Research, 18*, 226-237.

Ellis, G.D., and S. Niles (1985). Development, Reliability and Preliminary validation of a Brief Leisure Rating Scale. *Therapeutic Recreation Journal, 19*, 50-61.

Ellis, G.D., and P. A Witt (1986). The Leisure Diagnostic Battery: Past, Present, and Future. *Therapeutic Recreation Journal, 20*, 31-47.

Ellis, G.D., and J. T. Yessick (1989). Toward Person by Situation Research in Therapeutic Recreation. *Therapeutic Recreation Journal, 23*, 24-35.

Ellis, M.J. (1973). *Why People Play*. Englewood Cliffs, NJ: Prentice-Hall, Inc.

Ewert, A. (1985). Why People Climb: The Relationship of Participant Motives and Experience Level to Mountaineering. *Journal of Leisure Research, 17*, 241-250.

Eysenck, H.J. (1981). *A Model for Personality.* Berlin: Springer Verlag.

Forgas, J., and S. Moylan (1988). After the Movies: Transient Mood and Social Judgments. *Personality and Social Psychology Bulletin, 13,* 467-477.

Francken, D.A., and W. F. Van Raaij (1981). Satisfaction with Leisure Time Activities. *Journal of Leisure Research, 13,* 337-352.

Gilovich, T. (1983). Biased Evaluation and Persistence in Gambling. *Journal of Personality and Social Psychology, 44,* 1110-1126.

Graef, R., M. Csikszentmihalyi, and S. M. Gianinno (1983). Measuring Intrinsic Motivation in Everyday Life. *Leisure Studies, 2,* 155-168.

Graefe, A.R., J. J. Vaske, & F. R. Kuss (1984). Social Carrying Capacity: An Integration and Synthesis of Twenty Years of Research. *Leisure Sciences, 6,* 395-431.

Haggard, L.M., and D. R. Williams (1992). Identity Affirmation Through Leisure Activities: Leisure Symbols of the Self. *Journal of Leisure Research, 24,* 1-18.

Hammitt, W., L. Knauf, and F. Noe (1989). A Comparison of User vs. Researcher Determined Level of Past Experience on Recreation Preference. *Journal of Leisure Research, 21,* 202-213.

Hammitt, W.E., and M. E. Patterson (1991). Coping Behavior to Avoid Visitor Encounters: Its Relationship to Wildland Privacy. *Journal of Leisure Research, 23,* 225-237.

Harackiewicz, J.M., G. Manderlink, and C. Sansone (1984). Rewarding Pinball Wizardry: Effects of Evaluation and Cue Value on Intrinsic Interest. *Journal of Personality and Social Psychology, 47,* 287-300.

Harper, W. (1981). The Experience of Leisure. *Leisure Sciences, 4,* 113-126.

Harper, W. (1986). Freedom in the Experience of Leisure. *Leisure Sciences, 8,* 115-130.

Hautaluoma, J., and P. J. Brown (1978). Attributes of the Deer Hunting Experience: A Cluster-analytic Study. *Journal of Leisure Research, 10,* 271-287.

Hawes, D.K. (1978). Satisfactions Derived from Leisure-Time Pursuits: An Exploratory Nationwide Study. *Journal of Leisure Research, 10,* 247-264.

Haworth, J. (1983). Satisfaction Statements and the Study of Angling in the United Kingdom. *Leisure Sciences, 5,* 181-196.

Haworth, J. (1984). The Perceived Nature of Meaningful Pursuits and the Social Psychology of Commitment. *Society and Leisure, 7,* 197-216.

Haworth, J. (1986). Meaningful Activity and Psychological Models of Non-Employment. *Leisure Studies, 5,* 281-297.

Haworth, J., and Hill, S. (1992). Work, Leisure, and Psychological Well-being in a Sample of Young Adults. *Journal of Community and Applied Social Psychology, 2,* 147-160.

Henderson, K.A. (1990). The Meaning of Leisure for Women: An Integrative Review of the Research. *Journal of Leisure Research, 22,* 228-243.

Hill, M.S. (1988). Marital Stability and Spouses' Shared Time: A Multidisciplinary Hypothesis. *Journal of Family Issues, 9,* 427-451.

Hirschman, E.C. (1984). Leisure Motives and Sex Roles. *Journal of Leisure Research, 16,* 209-223.

Hoff, A.E., and G. D. Ellis (1992). Influence of Agents of Leisure Socialization on Leisure Self-Efficacy of University Students. *Journal of Leisure Research, 24,* 114-126.

Holman, T.B., and M. Jacquart (1988). Leisure-Activity Patterns and Marital Satisfaction: A Further Test. *Journal of Marriage and the Family, 50,* 69-77.

House, J.S., K. R. Landis, and D. Umberson (1988). Social Relationships and Health. *Science, 241,* 540-545.

Hughes, F.P. (1991). *Children, Play, and Development.* Boston: Allyn and Bacon.

Hull, R.B. IV, W. P. Stewart, and Y. K. Yi (1992). Experience Patterns: Capturing the Dynamic Nature of a Recreation Experience. *Journal of Leisure Research, 24,* 240-252.

Hultsman, W. Z. (1993). The Influence of Others as a Barrier to Recreation Participation Among Early Adolescents. *Journal of Leisure Research, 25,* 150-164.

Ibrahim, H., and R. Crandall (Eds.). (1980). *Leisure: A Psychological Approach.* Los Angeles, CA: Hwong Publishing.

Ingham, R. (1986). Psychological Contributions to the Study of Leisure - Part One. *Leisure Studies, 5,* 255-279.

Ingham, R. (1987). Psychological Contributions to the Study of Leisure - Part Two. *Leisure Studies, 6,* 1-14.

Iso-Ahola, S.E. (1977). Immediate Attributional Effects of Success and Failure in the Field: Testing Some Laboratory Hypotheses. *European Journal of Social Psychology, 7,* 275-296.

Iso-Ahola, S.E. (1979a). Basic Dimensions of Definitions of Leisure. *Journal of Leisure Research, 11,* 28-39.

Iso-Ahola, S.E. (1979b). Some Social Psychological Determinants of Perceptions of Leisure: Preliminary Evidence. *Leisure Sciences, 2,* 305-314.

Iso-Ahola, S.E. (1980a). *The Social Psychology of Leisure and Recreation.* Dubuque, IA: Wm. C. Brown Co.

Iso-Ahola, S.E. (Ed.). (1980b). *Social Psychological Perspectives on Leisure and Recreation.* Springfield, IL: Charles C. Thomas.

Iso-Ahola, S.E. (1980c). A Social Psychological Analysis of Little League Baseball. In S.E. Iso-Ahola (Ed.), *Social Psychological Perspectives on Leisure and Recreation* (pp. 171-218). Springfield, IL: Charles C. Thomas.

Iso-Ahola, S.E. (1983). Towards a Social Psychology of Recreational Travel. *Leisure Studies, 2,* 45-56.

Iso-Ahola, S.E. (1984). Social Psychological Foundations of Leisure and Resultant Implications for Leisure Counseling. In E.T. Dowd (Ed.). *Leisure Counseling, Concepts and Applications* (pp. 97-125). Springfield, IL: Charles C. Thomas.

Iso-Ahola, S.E. (1986). A Theory of Substitutability of Leisure Behaviors. *Leisure Sciences, 8,* 367-389.

Iso-Ahola, S.E. (1988). Research in Therapeutic Recreation. *Therapeutic Recreation Journal, 22,* 7-13.

Iso-Ahola, S.E. (1989). Motivation for Leisure. In E.L. Jackson & T.L. Burton (Eds.), *Understanding Leisure and Recreation: Mapping the Past, Charting the Future* (pp. 245-279). State College, PA: Venture Publishing Co.

Iso-Ahola, S.E. (1994). Leisure Lifestyle and Health. In D. Compton & S.E. Iso-Ahola (Eds.), *Leisure and Mental Health* (pp. 42-62). Park City, Utah: Family Development Resources.

Iso-Ahola, S.E., and J. Allen (1982). The Dynamics of Leisure Motivation: The Effects of Outcome on Leisure Needs. *Research Quarterly for Exercise and Sport, 53,* 141-149.

Iso-Ahola, S.E., J. Allen, and K. J. Buttimer (1982). Experience-Related Factors as Determinants of Leisure Satisfaction. *Scandinavian Journal of Psychology, 23,* 141-146.

Iso-Ahola, S.E., and K. J. Buttimer (1982). On the Measurement of Work and Leisure Ethics and Resultant Intercorrelations. *Educational and Psychological Measurement, 43,* 429-435.

Iso-Ahola, S.E., and E. D. Crowley (1991). Adolescent Substance Abuse and Leisure Boredom. *Journal of Leisure Research, 23,* 260-271.

Iso-Ahola, S.E. & B. Hatfield (1986). *The Psychology of Sports, a Social Psychological Approach.* Dubuque, IA: Wm. C. Brown Publishers.

Iso-Ahola, S.E., D. LaVerde, and A. Graefe (1989). Perceived Competence as a Mediator of the Relationship Between High Risk Sports Participation and Self-Esteem. *Journal of Leisure Research, 21,* 32-39.

Iso-Ahola, S.E., R. D. MacNeil, and D. J. Szymanski (1980). Social Psychological Foundations of Therapeutic Recreation: An Attributional Analysis. In S.E. Iso-Ahola (Ed.), *Social Psychological Perspectives on Leisure and Recreation* (pp. 390-413). Springfield, IL: Charles C. Thomas.

Iso-Ahola, S.E., and E. Weissinger (1985, October). *Relationship between Type A Coronary-Prone Behavior and Leisure Patterns.* Paper presented at the NRPA Leisure Research Symposium, Dallas, TX.

Iso-Ahola, S.E., and E. Weissinger (1987). Leisure and Boredom. *Journal of Social and Clinical Psychology, 5,* 356-364.

Iso-Ahola, S.E., and E. Weissinger (1990). Perceptions of Boredom in Leisure: Conceptualization, Reliability and Validity of the Leisure Boredom Scale. *Journal of Leisure Research, 22*, 1-17.

Ivancevich, J.M., and H. L. Lyon (1977). The Shortened Workweek: A Field Experiment. *Journal of Applied Psychology, 62*, 34-37.

Jackson, E.L. (1991). Leisure Constraints/Constrained Leisure: Special Issue Introduction. *Journal of Leisure Research, 23*, 279-285.

Jackson, E.L., D. W. Crawford, and G. Godbey (1993). Negotiation of Leisure Constraints. *Leisure Sciences, 15*, 1-11.

Johnson, J.E., J. F. Christie, & T. D. Yawkey (1987). *Play and Early Childhood Development*. New York: Harper Collins Publishers.

Kabanoff, B. (1980). Work and Nonwork: A Review of Models, Methods, and Findings. *Psychological Bulletin, 88*, 60-77.

Kendzierski, D. (1988). Self-Schemata and Exercise. *Basic and Applied Social Psychology, 9*, 45-59.

Kleiber, D. (1985). Motivational Re-Orientation in Adulthood and the Resource of Leisure. In D.A. Kleiber, & M. Maehr (Eds.), *Motivation and Adulthood* (pp. 217-250). Greenwich, CN: Jai Press Inc.

Kleiber, D., and R. Crandall (1981). Leisure and Work Ethics and Locus of Control. *Leisure Sciences, 4*, 477-485.

Kleiber, D., and M. J. Kane (1984). Sex Differences and the Use of Leisure as Adaptive Potentiation. *Society and Leisure, 7*, 165-173.

Kleiber, D., and R. Larson, & M. Csikszentmihalyi (1986). The Experience of Leisure in Adolescence. *Journal of Leisure Research, 18*, 169-176.

Knopf, R.C. (1983). Recreational Needs and Behavior in Natural Settings. In I. Altman & J.F. Wohlwill (Eds.), *Behavior and the Natural Environment* (pp. 205-240). New York: Plenum Publishing Corp.

Kobasa, S. (1979). Stressful Life Events, Personality, and Health: An Inquiry into Hardiness. *Journal of Personality and Social Psychology, 37*, 1-11.

Koocher, G.P. (1971). Swimming, Competence, and Personality Change. *Journal of Personality and Social Psychology, 18*, 275-278.

Kuentzel, W.F., and T. A. Heberlein (1992). Cognitive and Behavioral Adaptations to Perceived Crowding: A Panel Study of Coping and Displacement. *Journal of Leisure Research, 24*, 377-393.

Kuentzel, W.F., and G. D. McDonald (1992). Differential Effects of Past Experience, Commitment, and Lifestyle Dimensions on River Use Specialization. *Journal of Leisure Research, 24*, 269-287.

Langer, E., and J. Rodin (1976). The Effects of Choice and Enhanced Personal Responsibility for the Aged: A Field Experiment in an Institutional Setting. *Journal of Personality and Social Psychology, 34*, 191-198.

Larsen, R.J., and M. Kasimatis (1990). Individual Differences in Entrainment of Mood to the Weekly Calendar. *Journal of Personality and Social Psychology, 58*, 164-171.

Larson, R., J. Zuzanek, and R. C. Mannell (1985). Being Alone Versus Being with People: Disengagement in the Daily Experience of Older Adults. *Journal of Gerontology, 40,* 375-381.

Lepper, M.R., D. Greene, and R. E. Nisbett (1973). Undermining Children's Intrinsic Interest with Extrinsic Rewards: A Test of the "Overjustification" Hypothesis. *Journal of Personality and Social Psychology, 28,* 129-137.

London, M., R. Crandall, and G. W. Seals (1977a). The Contribution of Job and Leisure Satisfaction to Quality of Life. *Journal of Applied Psychology, 62,* 328-334.

London, M., R. Crandall, and D. Fitzgibbons (1977b). The Psychological Structure of Leisure: Activities, Needs, People. *Journal of Leisure Research, 9,* 252-263.

Lounsbury, J.W., and L. L. Hoopes (1985). Factors Associated with a Satisfying Vacation. *Journal of Leisure Research, 17,* 1-13.

Lounsbury, J.W., and L. L. Hoopes (1986). A Vacation from Work: Changes in Work and Nonwork Outcomes. *Journal of Applied Psychology, 71,* 392-401.

Madden, T.J., E. P. Scholder, and I. Ajzen (1992). A Comparison of the Theory of Planned Behavior and the Theory of Reasoned Action. *Personality and Social Psychology Bulletin, 18,* 3-9.

Manfredo, M.J. (1984). The Comparability of Onsite and Offsite Measures of Recreation Needs. *Journal of Leisure Research, 16,* 245-249.

Manfredo, M.J., S. M. Yan, and F. A. McGuire (1992). The Influence of Attitude Accessibility on Attitude-Behavior Relationships: Implications for Recreation Research. *Journal of Leisure Research, 24,* 157-170.

Mannell, R.C. (1978a, April). *Leisure Research in the Psychological Lab: Leisure a Permanent and/or Transient Cognitive Disposition?* Paper presented at the Second Canadian Congress on Leisure Research. Toronto, Canada.

Mannell, R.C. (1978b, October). *The Effects of Perceived Choice and Task Competitiveness on Time Perception, Situational Awareness and Affective States During Leisure Experiences.* Paper presented at the NRPA Research Symposium, National Recreation and Park Association, Miami, FL.

Mannell, R.C. (1980). Social Psychological Techniques and Strategies for Studying Leisure Experiences. In S.E. Iso-Ahola (Ed.), *Social Psychological Perspectives on Leisure and Recreation* (pp. 62-88). Springfield, IL: Charles C. Thomas.

Mannell, R.C. (1984). A Psychology for Leisure. *Society and Leisure, 7,* 13-21.

Mannell, R.C. (1989). Leisure Satisfaction. In E.L. Jackson & T.L. Burton (Eds.), *Understanding Leisure and Recreation: Mapping the Past, Charting the Future* (pp. 281-301). State College, PA: Venture Publishing Co.

Mannell, R.C. (1993). High Investment Activity and Life Satisfaction Among Older Adults: Overcoming Psychological Inertia through Committed, Serious Leisure and Flow Activities. In J. R. Kelly (Ed.), *Activity and Aging*. Beverly Hills, CA: Sage.

Mannell, R.C., and W. Bradley (1986). Does Greater Freedom Always Lead to Greater Leisure? Testing a Person X Environment Model of Freedom and Leisure. *Journal of Leisure Research, 18*, 215-230.

Mannell, R.C., and S. E. Iso-Ahola (1987). Psychological Nature of Leisure and Tourism Experiences. *Annals of Tourism Research, 14*, 314-331.

Mannell, R.C., J. Zuzanek, and R. Larson (1988). Leisure States and "Flow" Experiences: Testing Perceived Freedom and Intrinsic Motivation Hypotheses. *Journal of Leisure Research, 20*, 289-304.

Manning, R.E. (1985). Crowding Norms in Back Country Settings: A Review and Synthesis. *Journal of Leisure Research, 17*, 75-89.

Marsh, H.W., G. E. Richards, and J. Barnes (1986a). Multidimensional Self-Concepts: The Effect of Participation in an Outward Bound Program. *Journal of Personality and Social Psychology, 50*, 195-204.

Marsh, H.W., G. E. Richards, and J. Barnes (1986b). Multidimensional Self-Concepts: A Long-Term Follow-Up of the Effect of Participation in an Outward Bound Program. *Personality and Social Psychology Bulletin, 12*, 475-492.

McDonald, R., and C. Howe (1989). Challenge/Initiative Recreation Programs as a Treatment for Low Self-Concept Children. *Journal of Leisure Research, 21*, 242-253.

McIntyre, N. (1989). The Personal Meaning of Participation: Enduring Involvement. *Journal of Leisure Research, 21*, 167-179.

McIntyre, N., and J. J. Pigram (1992). Recreation Specialization Reexamined: The Case of Vehicle-Based Campers. *Leisure Sciences, 14*, 3-16.

Mills, A.S. (1985). Participation Motivations for Outdoor Recreation: A test of Maslow's Theory. *Journal of Leisure Research, 17*, 184-199.

Mobily, K.E., J. H. Lemke, and G. J. Gisin, (1991). The Idea of Leisure Repertoire. *Journal of Applied Gerontology, 10*, 208-223.

Mobily, K.E., J. H. Lemke, L. J. Ostiguy, R. J. Woodard, T. J. Griffee, and C. C. Pickens (1993). Leisure Repertoire in a Sample of Midwestern Elderly: The Case for Exercise. *Journal of Leisure Research, 25*, 84-99.

Neulinger, J. (1974). *The Psychology of Leisure*. Springfield, IL: Charles C. Thomas.

Neulinger, J., and M. Breit (1969). Attitude Dimensions of Leisure. *Journal of Leisure Research, 1*, 255-261.

Noe, F. (1987). Measurement Specifications and Leisure Satisfaction. *Leisure Sciences, 9*, 163-172.

O'Brien, G.E. (1981). Leisure Attributes and Retirement Satisfaction. *Journal of Applied Psychology, 66*, 371-384.

Orthner, D.K. (1975). Leisure Activity Patterns and Marital Satisfaction Over the Marital Career. *Journal of Marriage and the Family, 37*, 91-102.

Pierce, R.C. (1980). Dimensions of Leisure, I: Satisfactions. *Journal of Leisure Research, 12*, 5-19.

Quellet, G. (Ed). (1984). Psychological Studies of the Leisure Experience. *Society and Leisure, 7*, No. 1.

Ragheb, M.G. (1980). Interrelationships among Leisure Participation, Leisure Satisfaction and Leisure Attitudes. *Journal of Leisure Research, 12*, 138-149.

Reich, J.W., and A. Zautra (1981). Life Events and Personal Causation: Some Relationships with Satisfaction and Distress. *Journal of Personality and Social Psychology, 41*, 1002-1012.

Rice, M.L. (1989). Children's Language Acquisition. *American Psychologist, 44*, 149-156.

Riddick, C.C. (1986). Leisure Satisfaction Precursors. *Journal of Leisure Research, 18*, 259-265.

Riddick, C.C., and S. N. Daniel (1984). The Relative Contribution of Leisure Activities and Other Factors to the Mental Health of Older Women. *Journal of Leisure Research, 16*, 136-148.

Roadburg, A. (1983). Freedom and Enjoyment: Disentangling Perceived Leisure. *Journal of Leisure Research, 15*, 15-26.

Rohrbaugh, J.B. (1979, August). Femininity on the Line. *Psychology Today, 13*, 33-42.

Rosenhan, D.L. (1973). On Being Sane in Insane Places. *Science, 179*, 250-258.

Rubenstein, C. (1980, May). How Americans View Vacations. *Psychology Today, 13*, 62-76.

Russell, R.V. (1987). The Relative Contribution of Recreation Satisfaction and Activity Participation to the Life Satisfaction of Retirees. *Journal of Leisure Research, 19*, 273-283.

Samdahl, D.M. (1986). *The Self and Social Freedom: A Paradigm of Leisure.* Unpublished doctoral dissertation. University of Illinois.

Samdahl, D.M., and D. A. Kleiber (1989). Self-Awareness and Leisure Experience. *Leisure Sciences, 11*, 1-10.

Samdahl, D.M. (1992). Leisure in Our Lives: Exploring the Common Leisure Occasion. *Journal of Leisure Research, 24*, 19-32.

Savell, K. (1986). Leisure Efficacy: Theory and Therapy Implications for Therapeutic Recreation Programming. *Therapeutic Recreation Journal, 20*, 43-52.

Schleien, S.J., J. E. Rynders, T. Mustonen, and A. Fox (1990). Effects of Social Play Activities on the Play Behavior of Children with Autism. *Journal of Leisure Research, 22*, 317-328.

Schulz, R. (1976). Effects of Control and Predictability on the Physical and Psychological Well-Being of the Institutionalized Aged. *Journal of Personality and Social Psychology, 33*, 563-573.

Schutte, N., J. Malouff, J. Post-Gordon, and A. Rodasta (1988). Effects of Playing Video Games on Children's Aggressive and Other Behaviors. *Journal of Applied Social Psychology, 18,* 454-460.

Schreyer, R., D. Lime, and D. Williams (1984). Characterizing the Influence of Past Experience on Recreation Behavior. *Journal of Leisure Research, 16,* 34-50.

Schreyer, R., and J. W. Roggenbuck (1978). The Influence of Experience Expectations on Crowding Perceptions and Social-Psychological Carrying Capacities. *Leisure Sciences, 1,* 373-394.

Searle, M.S., (1991). Propositions for Testing Social Exchange Theory in the Context of Ceasing Leisure Participation. *Leisure Sciences, 13,* 279-294.

Searle, M.S., and M. J. Mahon (1993). The Effects of a Leisure Education Program on Selected Social-Psychological Variables: A Three Month Follow-up Investigation. *Therapeutic Recreation Journal, 27,* 9-21.

Sessoms, H.D. (1986). Of Time, Work, and Leisure Revisited. *Leisure Sciences, 8,* 107-113.

Shank, J.W. (1986). An Exploration of Leisure in the Lives of Dual Career Women. *Journal of Leisure Research, 18,* 300-319.

Shary, J.M., and S. E. Iso-Ahola (1989). Effects of a Control-Relevant Intervention on Nursing Home Residents' Perceived Competence and Self-Esteem. *Therapeutic Recreation Journal, 23,* 7-16.

Shaw, S. (1985a). The Meaning of Leisure in Everyday Life. *Leisure Sciences, 7,* 1-24.

Shaw, S. (1985b). Gender and Leisure: Inequality in the Distribution of Leisure Time. *Journal of Leisure Research, 17,* 266-282.

Shaw, S. (1986). Leisure, Recreation or Free Time? Measuring Time Usage. *Journal of Leisure Research, 18,* 177-189.

Shaw, S. (1992). Dereifying Family Leisure: An Examination of Women's and Men's Everyday Experiences and Perceptions of Family Time. *Leisure Sciences, 14,* 271-286.

Shelby, B., and T. A. Heberlein (1986). *Carrying Capacity in Recreation Settings.* Corvallis, OR: Oregon State University Press.

Shelby, B., T. A. Heberlein, J. J. Vaske, and G. Alfano (1983). Expectations, Preferences, and Feeling Crowded in Recreation Activities. *Leisure Sciences, 6,* 1-14.

Shelby, B., J. Vaske, and T. A. Heberlein (1989). Comparative Analysis of Crowding in Multiple Locations: Results from Fifteen Years of Research. *Leisure Sciences, 11,* 269-292.

Stebbins, R.A. (1992). *Amateurs, Professionals, and Serious Leisure.* Montreal: McGill-Queen's University Press.

Stewart, W.P. (1992). Influence of the Onsite Experience on Recreation Experience Preference Judgments. *Journal of Leisure Research, 24,* 185-198.

Stone, A. (1985). Prospective and Cross-Sectional Mood Reports Offer no Evidence of a "Blue Monday" Phenomenon. *Journal of Personality and Social Psychology, 49,* 129-134.

Stringer, P.F. (Ed.). (1984). The Social Psychology of Tourism. *Annals of Tourism Research, 11,* No. 1.

Tang, T.L.P. (1986). Effects of Type A Personality and Task Labels (work vs. leisure) on Task Preference. *Journal of Leisure Research, 18,* 1-11.

Tangney, J.P., and S. Feshbach (1988). Children's Television Viewing Frequency: Individual and Demographic Correlates. *Personality and Social Psychology Bulletin, 14,* 145-158.

Tinsley, H.E., T. C. Barrett, and R. A. Kass (1977). Leisure Activities and Need Satisfaction. *Journal of Leisure Research, 9,* 110-120.

Tinsley, H.E., and R. A. Kass (1978). Leisure Activities and Need Satisfaction: A Replication and Extension. *Journal of Leisure Research, 10,* 191-202.

Tinsley, H.E., and D. J. Tinsley (1986). A Theory of the Attributes, Benefits, and Causes of Leisure Experience. *Leisure Sciences, 8,* 1-45.

Vaske, J.J., M. P. Donnelly, T. A. Heberlein, and B. Shelby (1982). Differences in Reported Satisfaction Ratings by Consumptive and Nonconsumptive Recreationists. *Journal of Leisure Research, 14,* 195-206.

Vaske, J.J., B. Shelby, A. R. Graefe, and T. A. Heberlein (1986). Backcountry Encounter Norms: Theory, Method and Empirical Evidence. *Journal of Leisure Research, 18,* 137-153.

Vingerhoets, A., and B. Buunk (1987). Attitudes Towards Nudist and Public Beaches: Some Evidence of Dissonance Reduction and Gender Differences. *Journal of Leisure Research, 19,* 13-21.

Wade, M.G. (Ed.). (1985). *Constraints on Leisure.* Springfield, IL: Charles C. Thomas.

Wankel, L.M., and B. G. Berger (1990). The Psychological and Social Benefits of Sport and Physical Activity. *Journal of Leisure Research, 22,* 167-182.

Wankel, L.M., and P. S. Kreisel (1985). Factors Underlying Enjoyment of Youth Sports: Sport and Age Group Comparisons. *Journal of Sport Psychology, 7,* 51-64.

Wankel, L.M., and C. E. Thompson (1977). Motivating People to be Physically Active: Self-persuasion vs. Balanced Decision Making. *Journal of Applied Social Psychology, 7,* 332-340.

Watson, A., J. Roggenbuck, and D. Williams (1991). The Influence of Past Experience on Wilderness Choice. *Journal of Leisure Research, 23,* 21-36.

Weissinger, E. (1985). *Development and Validation of an Intrinsic Leisure Motivation Scale.* Unpublished doctoral dissertation, University of Maryland.

Weissinger, E., L. L. Caldwell, and B. L. Bandalos (1992). Relation Between Intrinsic Motivation and Boredom in Leisure Time. *Leisure Sciences, 14,* 317-326.

Weissinger, E., and S. E. Iso-Ahola (1984). Intrinsic Leisure Motivation, Personality and Physical Health. *Society and Leisure, 7,* 217-228.

Williams, D.R., J. W. Roggenbuck, and S. Bange (1991). The Effect of Norm-Encounter Compatibility on Crowding Perceptions, Experience and Behavior in River Recreation Settings. *Journal of Leisure Research, 23,* 154-172.

Williams, D.R., R. Schreyer, and R. C. Knopf (1990). The Effect of the Experience Use History on the Multidimensional Structure of Motivations to Participate in Leisure Activities. *Journal of Leisure Research, 22,* 36-54.

Witt, P.A., and D. W. Bishop (1970). Situational Antecedents to Leisure Behavior. *Journal of Leisure Research, 2,* 64-77.

Witt, P.A., and G. D. Ellis (1984). The Leisure Diagnostic Battery: Measuring Perceived Freedom in Leisure. *Society and Leisure, 7,* 109-124.

Wolfe, R.A., and C. C. Riddick (1984). Effects of Leisure Counseling on Adult Psychiatric Outpatients. *Therapeutic Recreation Journal, 18,* 30-37.

Yair, G. (1990). The Commitments to Long Distance Running and Levels of Activity: Personal or Structural? *Journal of Leisure Research, 22,* 213-227.

Young, R.A., and A. T. Kent (1985). Using the Theory of Reasoned Action to Improve the Understanding of Recreation Behavior. *Journal of Leisure Research, 17,* 90-106.

Zuckerman, M. (1979). *Sensation Seeking: Beyond the Optimal Level of Arousal.* Hillsdale, NJ: LEA.

Global Perspectives on the State of Leisure Research

Past, Present, and Future Research

Stanley Parker
University of Brighton
———————— **Eastbourne, England** ————————

INTRODUCTION

To attempt a review of leisure research on a global scale is a formidable task. I have been reading, talking about and taking part in leisure research for more than 25 years. During that time I have met many congenial people and visited many interesting places on the strength of various leisure conferences, seminars, etc. around the world as one of my favorite leisure activities. Nevertheless, not only do I find it difficult to keep up with all that is going on, but I am constantly coming across published research material that is new to me. Working with Alan Graefe on the non-North American sections of our recent handbook (Graefe and Parker, eds. 1987) has enabled me to lay some foundations for the present paper, but I have also drawn on other material. The handbook does, however, go into greater detail on some points and some of what I shall say here is not in the handbook.

There are two important limitations to what I shall attempt. First, I shall not refer to any leisure research that is confined to North America. A comprehensive review of such research, even in summary form, would require a paper much longer than this, written by someone better qualified to do so. I shall, however, refer to internationally comparative research that includes the U.S. or Canada and at least one other country. Second, my review will be confined almost entirely to publications in English or with a version or summary in English. Some research originally reported in a language other than English has been translated but many other relevant publications are available only in their original language.

Although I intend this paper to be broadly representative rather than selective (within the above limitations), inevitably I shall unintentionally omit some contributions to research that have an equal, if not greater, claim to be included. Please forgive the omissions and the degree of selectivity that has taken place.

I don't want to spend much time trying to define "leisure research." I shall take "leisure," "recreation" and "free time" to mean the same (although I don't believe they do). Leisure research includes, in my view, study of time use, activities or behavior, and experiences. "Research" (including "studies") takes many forms: surveys, interviews, observation, records, diaries, desk or library projects, etc.

Deciding how to organize this paper was a problem. I considered three possibilities. One was by discipline: what sociologists, psychologists, etc., around the world have found out or theorized about leisure—I rejected that because much leisure research cannot be classified by disciplines or cuts across more than one of them. I considered research by subject area: everything about sport brought together, then everything about the arts, and so on. This was tempting, but it would have required a large residual category of "leisure in general." So I settled for research by geographical area—of the people, activities, policies and so on researched, rather than of the location of the researcher. This, too, requires an important additional category: that of internationally comparative research.

UNITED KINGDOM

Outside of North America, the largest amount of leisure research has been carried out in the United Kingdom (England, Wales, Scotland and Northern Ireland—the Republic of Eire is considered separately below). The British Leisure Studies Association (LSA) was formed in 1975 and has held national and international conferences and regional seminars since that time. These conferences have been on a wide variety of leisure subjects, including (in rough chronological order); sport, public policy, futures community, tourism, urban society, culture, economics, the family, rural society, work, education, the media, youth, politics, the environment, health and well-being, and the welfare state. Proceedings of these conferences are now available from M. McFee LSA Publications, Chelsea School, University of Brighton, Eastbourne, BN20 7SP, England.

In 1982, the *Leisure Studies Journal* (LS) started publication. LS is an international journal, around 40 percent of the published material being by authors outside the UK. A bibliography of British publications on leisure from 1960-1977 (now out of print) contained over 1,000 items and noted that articles on leisure had been published in over 100 British journals.

I shall review leisure research in the UK in four broad sections: subject areas, populations, academic disciplines, and theory and methodology. These sections are somewhat arbitrary, because often a particular book, article, or research report deals with more than one of them. However, some method of organizing the material had to be chosen. From a much longer list of potential subject areas I have chosen 15. Some examples of exclusions are pornography, shopping, and warfare as leisure. The 15 are in alphabetical order, not in order of believed significance or my own preferences.

Arts and Culture

Generally speaking, research on the arts and cultural life in Britain has not been extensive—certainly less than that devoted to sport. There have been surveys of theater audiences (Mann, 1967) and the LSA conference in 1986 was devoted to various topics connected with the arts. The need to collect policy-oriented data from arts audience surveys is highlighted by Bruch (1981), while Pick (1981) analyzes the role of the arts administrator. The politics of the arts has received some attention in books by Hutchinson (1982) on the position of the Arts Council and O. Kelly (1984) on "storming the citadels" of state agencies on behalf of community arts. Tomlinson (1991) has written on cultural imperialism.

Countryside

It is a curious feature of British leisure research that country-side and rural recreation has received more attention than urban recreation. This is partly because of the controversial issue of conservation of resources versus recreation of people. The 1980 conference of the LSA was devoted to rural recreation (Ventris, 1980) and Mays (1982) has edited the proceedings of the Country-side Recreation Resources Advisory Group conference. The Countryside Commission published countryside research reviews for several years. Uzzell (1985) has written on management issues in the provision of countryside interpretation, and these issues figured prominently in the book by Glyptis (1991).

Education

Research on the relationship between education and leisure has encompassed a number of issues , notably the integration of education and leisure in community schools (Wimbush and Duffield, 1985), education experienced as leisure in adult evening classes (Jary, 1973) leisure and outdoor education (Gee, 1981), unemployment, leisure and education (Hargreaves, 1981) and education and leisure in post-industrial society (Carrol, 1981). The last three papers were among those published in the proceedings of an LSA conference on leisure and learning (Bacon, ed. 1981).

The Family

A number of British sociologists have shown interest in the subject of the family and leisure. The Rapoports (1975) seminal work was on leisure at different stages in the family life cycle, in which they investigated the "triple helix" of leisure, family and work. Young and Willmott (1973) and Bell and Healey (1973) looked at the implications for leisure of the "symmetrical" or democratic family of partners both having career and domestic responsibilities. A number of relevant papers were published in the proceedings of the LSA conference on leisure and family diversity (Strelitz, ed. 1979), including the topics of children's play, one-parent families, housewives, retirement, and family provision for arts and sport.

Futures

Veal (1987) has recently compiled a fascinating account of various writings about the potential role of leisure in future society. It seems that whenever there is a firmly held view about the way the future will develop there is a contrary view that can be argued just as convincingly. In some scenarios, the emphasis is on technology and the development of the advanced industrial economy, and leisure is not seen as being of much importance. But others, notably Gershuny (1978), forecast the growth of the self-service economy in which leisure could feature prominently. The third LSA conference had as its theme Forecasting Leisure Futures (Haworth and Parker, eds. 1976).

Home-based Leisure

Although over half of all leisure time is open within the home environment, this has been a neglected subject until recent years. Glyptis and Chambers (1982) studied the home as a leisure center and proposed an analysis of the structure and meaning of home-based leisure in relation to routine domestic tasks, to challenge concepts of leisure developed in the context of outdoor recreation. Cherry (1984) took a more historical perspective, noting how housing design and space, combined with increasing suburbanization, have resulted in the increased use of the home for leisure purposes.

Industrial Recreation

(See also Work). Research topics in this area have included the content of industrial recreation programs, the facilities available and used, club organization, and employee interest levels. Research on these and related topics by Bullen and others is summarized in the Yates Report on Recreation Management, (1984). Roberts (1983) carried out an investigation for the English Sports Council to see whether sports facilities adjacent to or near a place of work proved convenient and satisfying to employees.

Management

Although the management of people and resources is an important part of teaching in leisure studies programs in Britain, it was not until 1983 that the first book on the subject appeared (Torkildsen, 1991). He covers recreation provision in the public, commercial and voluntary sectors; management, programming and staffing of organization; marketing of facilities and services; and training for leisure and recreation management. The journal, *Leisure Management*, while commercial in orientation, occasionally reports research findings relevant to management problems and policies.

The Media

Considerable research has been done on the ways in which audiences consume popular cultural products (Bennett et al., 1981; Goodhart et al., 1975; Tunstall, 1983). LSA conference papers edited by Glyptis (1983) provide a range of different approaches to the relationship between media and audiences. Morley (1980) has researched the "decoding" process, examining how groups of different class, gender, ethnic and occupational composition make different readings of the same program. The record industry is the subject of a book by Frith (1983).

Parks

The Tourism and Recreation Research Unit of the University of Edinburgh (see, for example, 1980) has been responsible for a number of park surveys. Data on the attractions of parks for different age groups are reported—the younger tend to go for the facilities and the older for the peace and quiet. Cherry (1985) related the story of the national parks movement—a public sector response to vigorous advocacy by pressure groups both to protect the countryside and to open it up for the leisure of city dwellers. Donnelly (1986) describes the mass trespass of 1932: ". . . civil disobedience was employed in an attempt to regain access to land for the purpose of leisure."

Politics

This is an area of growing interest. One volume of the proceedings of the LSA international conference was devoted to the subject (Coalter, ed. 1984). Topics discussed included the social control of spare time, the politics of women's leisure, private enterprise or public interest, and political dimensions of leisure services. Bramham and Henry (1985) analyze the relationship between leisure policy and three political ideologies: liberalism, conservatism and socialism. Tomlinson and Whannel (1984) discuss politics at the Olympic games, and Sugden and Bairner (1986) look at the politics of leisure in the divided society of Northern Ireland. The book by Wilson (1988) has a chapter on politics and leisure in the UK and Houlihan (1991) deals with the government and politics of sport.

Reading

Perhaps not one of the more exciting aspects of leisure research, reading is nevertheless an important part of many people's leisure lives. For example, in Britain, about one-third of the total population are members of public libraries, mostly for escapist novels and other recreative reading. Average time spent reading a book per day has fallen from about 30 to 20 minutes over the last decade or so, while the quantities of sales and titles have risen steadily. Luckham (1984) suggests that reading may have held its own against TV and other leisure activities because of more space in the home and increased time spent alone.

Sports

This has received more research attention than any other leisure subject. Seventeen of the 106 articles published in the first five volumes of LS were on sport or games, higher than for any other subject (work and leisure came next with eight articles). The topics include football (three articles, two on violence), women in sport (three articles), athleticism, televised sport, and unusual sports such as karate-do and shinty. Sociologists have written books on sport (e.g., Dunning, 1971; Hargreaves, 1982; Jarvie and Walker, 1993) as have historians (e.g., Cunningham,

1980; Mangan, 1981; Taylor, 1992). Note that much research on "sport" is in one of the sports sciences (physiology, bio-mechanics and so on) and has little or nothing to do with leisure.

Tourism

British contributions to research on tourism have been relatively modest. Geographers rather than sociologists have been prominent in this work. Much statistical material is available from the official Tourist Boards (British, English, Scottish and Welsh). Although some attention has been paid to international tourism (e.g., Turner and Ash, 1975), most of the research has been on domestic tourism. The papers presented to the LSA conference on tourism (Duffield. ed. 1977) include tourism administration and policy, the economic costs and benefits of tourism, and implications for regional development.

Work

It is sometimes claimed that the study of leisure grew out of the study of work and that what is needed now is to recognize leisure as a field in its own right. Whether or not this is so, much work on leisure research continues to be devoted to the influence of work and leisure and (less often) vice versa. If "work" is extended to include unemployment, housework, voluntary work and retirement, then the amount of research is multiplied. Books on work that have something to say about leisure include Jenkins and Sherman (1979) and Robertson (1985). Parker (1983) discusses various aspects of the work-leisure relationship. Articles in LS deal with the professions (Haworth, 1984), the constraints of work (Chambers, 1986) and the meaning of work (Stokes, 1983). Three volumes of LSA conference proceedings (nos. 12, 15, and 23) deal centrally with work.

Populations

Turning now to look at British leisure research according to populations, most of the projects have been on six groups: women, youth, the elderly, the unemployed, disabled and ethnic minorities. I have space to comment only briefly on each:

1.   Women.   Research here is undoubtedly on the upgrade. A recent book with the telling title *All Work and No Play* is by Deem (1986). The first issue of LS contained what was in effect a debate on women's leisure between Deem and Gregory (1982), putting respectively a militant and moderate feminist view.

2.   Youth. Research on young people has been going on for some time, partly because of the "problem" nature of some of their free time activities. Early books included Leigh (1971) and Emmett (1971). Roberts (1983) has written a recent historical and contemporary account of working-class and middle-class youth cultures.

3.   The elderly.   While no book is devoted entirely to the leisure of the elderly, chapters in books by the Rapaports (1975), and Parker (1982) report relevant research. Bernard (ed., 1984) describes a number of community-based initiatives, while Long and Wimbush (1985) write on leisure around retirement.

4.   The unemployed.   Glyptis (1983) describes what local authority recreation departments are doing to help the unemployed. Hendry et al (1984) found that among the unemployed there was little continuation of school-based leisure activity into post-school life. Fryer and Payne (1984) show that "enforced leisure" has a positive outcome for some.

5.   The disabled. Most of the writing on the leisure of the disabled is about how to get them more involved in activities and to minimize the mobility and access problems.   The Sports Council (1982) and Countryside Commission (1977) have compiled bibliographies. The Committee of Inquiry into the Arts and Disabled People published a report (1985) and Pearson (1985) looks at access to arts venues.

6.   Ethnic minorities. Leaman and Carrington (1985) show how ethnic factors markedly affect attitudes to sport. Richardson (1984) has written on music, dance and West Indian youth subcultures. Papers by Kew and Michaelson (in Strelitz, ed. 1979) deal with family leisure in West Indian and Indian communities respectively.

Disciplines

I should now like to say a few words about academic disciplines and their contribution to leisure studies. Until recently in the UK, most leisure and recreation studies programs were offered only at postgraduate level. But now a small number of undergraduate degrees in leisure, recreation and sports studies have been instituted. "Leisure studies" is not a recognized discipline but rather is seen as an amalgam of more traditional disciplines and some material that does not fit into any of them. In terms of input to leisure studies the "big five" are probably sociology, (human) geography, (social) psychology, economics and history, roughly in that order. Other disciplines such as anthropology, geology, planning and social administration are involved more marginally.

The theory and methodology of leisure studies deserves special mention. Some pieces of empirical research are inspired by a particular theoretical standpoint, for example, a motivational approach to the use of free time or a Marxist analysis of sport in society. The research notes section in LS has featured some 15 items over the past six years, including time diary sampling (Haworth and Millar, 1986) self-reported participation rates (Boothby, 1987), and artists' fees in television (Granger and Galloway, 1982). Government statistical sources have been used to describe leisure activity rates (Veal, 1984) and employment in the leisure industries (Corley, 1982). Martin and Mason (1986, 1987) was mostly private sector data to describe patterns of leisure expenditure. Another type of research—personal leisure histories— has been pioneered by Hedges (1986).

OTHER WESTERN EUROPE

Leisure research in the Republic of Ireland (Eire) is not yet well developed. The guidance and Counseling Unit of the Department of Psychology, University College, Dublin, has been engaged in researching the leisure behavior of Irish adolescents since 1975. In 1980, it completed a study of the perceptions of work and leisure of Dublin school children (Chamberlain, 1983). The primary aims were to identify the extent to which leisure behavior exerts an influence on the acquisition of self-identity, and to estimate the importance that young people attach to concepts of work and leisure.

There are two other areas where research has been carried out and in which "leisure" is considered as an element in the overall content of the study:

1. Health: the principal agency is the Health Education Bureau. Their survey "Aspects of Work, Leisure, Health, and Fitness" (1983/84) speaks for itself in terms of the leisure component.

2. Education: there is a course in "Sociology of Sport and Leisure" taught at the Thomond College of Education, Limerick, as part of which students complete dissertations. Four theses relevant to leisure studies are known to have been completed in Irish universities since 1971. These are MA theses in education faculties, covering children's use of leisure, patterns of leisure viewing in 13- to 14-year-old children, and the leisure pursuits of university professors. Possibly there are other relevant theses in sociology and other departments.

In the Netherlands, much leisure research has been carried out, a high proportion of which has resulted in publications in English. The following is a summary of some of the main points made by Kamphorst in Graefe and Parker eds. (1987).

Up to 1975, between 2,500 and 3,000 research projects in the field of leisure, recreation tourism, sports and cultural activities had been carried out. Such a large number could easily give the impression that the Netherlands has a long history in leisure research. But this is only partly correct. Two main themes can be distinguished in dutch leisure research. The first is for space ordering and the second for the mental health of those with increased free time. Instead of "leisure research" projects, these might be called "applied studies in town and country planning" and "studies in public mental health."

Since 1975, one of the things that has contributed to the advance of leisure research is that improvements in internal organization have been made. First, in 1976, an Interuniversity Association for the Sociology of Leisure was founded, comparable to the British Leisure Studies Association. Second, since 1976, the Social and Cultural Planning Bureau (an advisory body for national policy) has published every two years a Social and Cultural Report, in which a chapter is devoted to developments in free time and leisure behavior.

To give some impression of the range of leisure projects carried out since 1975, the following titles are abstracted from the Selected Annotated Bibliography of Leisure, The Netherlands, Part II:

- Outdoor recreation: compensation or complement?
- The Bilts Dunes: a study of living circumstances in a summer camp
- Music and audience
- The social structure of the Dutch world of theater
- Visitors' centers and their patrons
- Cycling in the Netherlands
- Vacation behavior: a role-theoretical explanation
- Leisure in the 1950s: a description of free time spending
- Educational aspects of free time spending on outdoor recreation
- The perception and appreciation of Veluwe landscapes

A considerable amount of leisure research has been carried out in France, but relatively little of it has been translated into English. An outstanding contributor is Dumazedier, some of whose work *is* available in English (1967, 1974). The following summary of Dumazedier's work, together with that of a few other French scholars and institutes, is taken from the European Leisure and Recreation Association (1982).

Dumazedier's *Toward a Civilization of Leisure* (1967) stands as a declaration of independence for the sociology of leisure in France. The book emphasizes the sociological importance of leisure as "the very central element in the life-culture of millions upon millions of workers," and shows that it is misleading to define leisure by contrast merely to work. Several stages can be distinguished in the work Dumazedier has conducted with his group. In the 1960s, they focused on the relations between leisure and social stratification, giving special attention to leisure and level of education. With the coming of the '70s, topics of study were the relations between leisure and work life, family life, political activities and religion. A study was conducted on the problems of power that arose in the middle-sized French town (Annecy) between the leaders of voluntary associations and local government. Another direction of research was the study of cultural resistance coming from subcultures now in a situation of dependency on the dominant culture.

Interest developed in a theoretical perspective centered on the important question of values concerned with leisure, their strengthening as a consequence of the growth of free time, and their impact on other domains of life. This concern brought some members of the group to take up the study of leisure from the angle of "social times" (a concept much used by the French but difficult to translate into English).

In 1974, a research unit was set up dealing with the sociology of international tourism. Their major theoretical contributions deal with national and cultural identity, the socio-political system that develops around the exploitation of national cultures, and the economic and cultural impact of tourism on host societies.

Problems related to the increased leisure of old people have been studied, as have the possibilities of people with more free time spending part of it in the voluntary non-profit sector. A critical approach to the sociology of sport has been taken by Brohm, and the sociology of art has been researched by several authors, among whom Bourdieu is perhaps best known.

It may be concluded that the French sociology of leisure, after having been considered as merely a part of the sociology of work, has now established its autonomy, even though the concept of leisure is still a controversial topic. At any rate, leisure is no longer being defined as non-work. Neither is it synonymous with free time: leisure is *part* of free time, along with religious and political participation.

In West Germany (Federal Republic of Germany) there has been a reasonable amount of leisure research—less than in Britain and France, but more than in many other European countries. The following summary is of Tokarski's contribution in Graefe and Parker, eds (1987).

Today leisure in the FRG is gaining more importance and also becoming more problematic. A few studies point to the paradigm taking place: the decrease of the relative importance of work, in favor of leisure. The question is:Is leisure becoming the main meaning of life, as many people suggest? It is said that we are not prepared for more free time, which is often used as a means to secure work, not to improve living conditions or enrich people's lives. Politically leisure is understood as a means to solve problems other than those of leisure.

Empirical leisure research only began in the 1950s and '60s. It became quite an established field of research, yet did not really find a place in universities. Leisure research exists primarily outside the classical disciplines and is carried out in commercial research institutes, associations and ministries as a "socio-technical" field of work on short-term problems. We must doubt the chances of development of fundamental leisure research.

Leisure research in the universities is limited to two subjects; sociology and educational science. It has been pursued from narrow and subject-specific and educational science. It has been pursued from narrow and subject-specific viewpoints. While sociology has been mainly concerned with quantitative and descriptive studies, educational science has been especially interested in leisure problems and their solutions.

The area of sports is one of the relevant fields of research. Leisure centers are to a large extent centers for sports. The process of aging and leisure has been studied by Schmitz-Scherzer (1970), who suggests that leisure behavior is explained by three sets of determinants: ecological, social or socio-economic, and personal.

Leisure research in Italy has been reviewed by Koch-Weser Ammassari (See Graefe and Parker, eds. 1987 for the full account). In Italy, interest in the questions of leisure and free time dates back to the late '50s when the onset of automation suggested a reinterpretation of the meaning of work and non-work roles. Meetings and congresses were organized by cultural, professional and scientific associations on the interrelated topics of automation, industrial work , leisure, education and human development. Emphasis was given to the qualitative aspects of leisure and to the importance of personal rather than social dimensions of leisure behavior and experiences. This general outlook was challenged by Alberoni, who proposed that leisure and free time have different meanings according to social structure, and are a means of marginalizing the young, the old and women from full social participation. Italian social scientists have rarely been specifically interested in leisure, having tended to attribute to it only minor relevance among the phenomena of socio-cultural change. The pertinent empirical evidence is therefore scattered and fragmentary, to be found in the results of research studies primarily directed at attitudes and behavior of particular social groups (workers, women, adolescents, etc.) or undertaken to investigate social issues such as modernization, social mobility, education, religion, etc.

In 1980, Belloni carried out a time budget survey in Turin, investigating not only frequencies and durations of activities but also where these take place and in whose company. And in 1984,

Koch-Weser Ammassari studied differences in leisure styles among labor force men and women who were found to share configurations of typical and preferred leisure activities. Once interesting finding was a widespread "apathy"—a relative disenchantment with most leisure activities, which cuts across social strata. This contributes to the definition of a leisure style of its own, in contrast with technologically-oriented consumers, culturally aware individualists, and social traditionalists.

In Sweden, an international conference sponsored by the European Leisure and Research Association was held in 1983 at Vaxjo on the theme of "Leisure today and tomorrow," but unfortunately I do not have the papers presented there. In giving below a summary of the work of two Swedish scholars, I am therefore not representing the full range of leisure research in Sweden.

Swedner (1981, 1982) has written on leisure, culture and action research, based on his experience of working with under-privileged groups, particularly immigrants and slum-dwellers. He concluded that reasoning in the upper/middle class takes two forms: those who accept the culture barrier as inevitable and those who think the gap between "fine" culture and working-class culture can be bridged. These types of reasoning are paralleled in the working class, there being believers in class solidarity and "climbers." One reason for failing to bridge the cultural gap and alter the pattern of leisure life is the existence of an authorized national culture and leisure.

Olsen (1985) has researched the development of youth leisure policies. He presents the main themes in both the control and autonomy aspects of the early leisure policy debate in Sweden. He analyzes the parliamentary discussions on the leisure and moral development of children and young people. He shows that liberals and conservatives have been concerned with the threat to moral order caused by the "depravity of the young" and that they have supported measures aimed to instill in working-class children bourgeois values and norms.

Leisure research is known to have taken place in other West European countries such as Belgium, Denmark, and Spain, but the information I have is too sparse to justify even a cursory review. As time goes on and the communication network grows, this situation will no doubt be remedied.

EASTERN EUROPE

Leisure research in the former USSR has been traditionally dominated by time budget studies. However, there are signs that things are changing. The following extracts are taken from Olszewska and Pronovost (1982) and Riordan (1982).

Time budget studies were born in Russia—Strumilin's first inquiry was carried out in 1924. It still constitutes a favored methodology—a school of thought on the international level whose influence has been profound. But the question remains: What were they hoping to achieve with these studies? It seems that the prevailing approach was above all economic and quantitative, in that it consisted in measuring the achievements of the revolution in terms of work, culture and social well-being. The question of leisure was associated with a more global concept of culture. The classic dichotomy between working hours and free time was prevalent, being perceived as a long drawn-out battle by the working class, not only for access to a certain degree of well-being but also for the right to participate in cultural activities such as literature and the theater.

In the past, Soviet political manipulating of leisure resulted from centralized planning and administration designed to subordinate areas of social life such as leisure to the political and economic tasks of building a strong state. In recent years, however, certain internal forces within Soviet society have encouraged a dismantling of previously well-entrenched institutions and values in the field of leisure. Individuals have increasing free time and prosperity, a wider range of amenities and equipment to pursue leisure activities of their choice. How an individual spends his leisure time is becoming less ruled by the official utilitarian-instrumental approach. And this has implications that go far beyond the sphere of leisure.

The following account of leisure research in *Czechoslovakia* is taken from Filipcova in Romer, ed. (1982).

Four general stages can be identified in Czechoslovak leisure research:

1. The inter-war and immediate post-war period, influenced by the traditions of Czech bourgeois sociology.
2. The period 1948-1960 in which leisure research was primarily philosophical, historical, and pedagogical.
3. The period constituting the sociology of leisure proper (1960-1970).

4. The present period, characterized by a synthesis of the sociology of leisure, sociology of the way of life, and cultural sciences.

In the sixties, leisure was viewed in two ways. The first concerned the creation of conditions for an all-around development of personality. The second was economically oriented, being concerned with the expanded reproduction of labor as part of the development of the scientific and technological revolution.

At the present time, a series of empirical inquiries in different social environments is being carried out that aims at identifying different lifestyles and ways of using leisure. Such an approach to research should make it possible not only to describe the present situation but to explain it and discover the possibilities, mechanisms, and certain barriers to development.

Vitanyi and Fukasz in Romer, ed. (1982) are frequent participants in international conferences. They describe leisure research in *Hungary* as follows:

Hungarian sociologists started to study the problems of leisure more intensively in the mid-60s. The objectives have been to reveal as many aspects of social life as possible. Attention has been focused on free time activities, mainly because this yielded a useful approach to studying the way of life and, as a result of economic development, free time started to increase. We can distinguish four types of leisure research:
1. Classical time budget research (including international comparisons) (Szalai, 1972)
2. Demographic and statistical research
3. Longitudinal investigations, repeated at intervals for assessing changes in the use of free time and in the way of life
4. Sociological and socio-psychological research to establish and assess leisure models and way-of-life models. This has evolved primarily in the Research Institute for Culture and has led to a typology of leisure patterns and ways of life; a) unstable and deficient in stimuli (the "exodus" of the peasantry), b) search for stability and autonomy (urban, working-class background), c) open and in search of experiences (town dwellers, especially employed in services), d) emancipated and autonomous (chiefly professionals and white-collar workers).

For eight years until 1986, Anna Olszewska from *Poland* was president of the Leisure Research Committee of the International Sociological Association, in which capacity she helped to promote and disseminate such relevant research. Her compatriots Jung and Erdmann contributed papers to the Marly conference (Romer, ed. 1984).

In a thoughtful paper that is not easy to summarize, Jung examines the perception of free time in Polish economic thought and its consequences for leisure research. He makes three comments on the state of free time research in Poland: a) There is a lack of an integrated and coherent approach that would set out this *social* time as a separate topic for study and not a by-product of other research, b) There is a very instrumental and pragmatic perception of free time, and a desire to subject it to planning and rational decision, c) Polish economists still seem to feel that "free time" is an awkward concept and that those studying it require a serious "pretext." Jung (1990) has a later paper on the impact of the crisis on leisure patterns.

The paper by Erdmann was on the conditions and prospects for the development of neighborhood recreation. Investigations have been made into: 1) various forms of recreation and expected facilities among people with different demographic and socio-economic backgrounds, 2) the strategy of promoting participation in physical recreation, 3) the present system of recreation and methods for its improvement, 4) individual and social evaluation of recreational programs, 5) the efficacy of social initiatives.

The following notes on leisure research in the former *Yugoslavia* are taken from Mihovilovic (in Graefe and Parker, eds, 1987):

Investigations on the subject of leisure time in Yugoslavia in recent years fall into two groups: 1) those in various branches of the social sciences, directly or indirectly examining the problems of leisure activities, 2) those of leisure time as a separate field of activity, and a separate scientific discipline. Investigations have been concerned with the following questions:
- time budgets and the leisure time of contemporary men and women
- the life and work of people in urban and rural environments
- the influence of age, sex, education, profession, social status, income and environment on the use of leisure time
- where people with various characteristics spend their leisure time

- with whom they tend to spend their leisure time
- the effect of using leisure to homogenize social structures and reduce social inequalities
- how would people spend extra leisure time if they had the opportunity?

From the Marly conference (Romer, ed 1984) we learned something about leisure research in *Finland*. A paper by Sievanen was on outdoor recreation and the Finnish way of life. Data from a mailed questionnaire in two Finnish towns yielded eight different types of recreationists, based on the time of their participation (weekday, weekend or vacation), the number and types of recreational area visited, socio-economic category, and special interests in outdoor recreation such as hunting or fishing.

Another Marly paper by Eriksson looked at the impact of tourism on the economy and employment, with particular reference to Aland, an island in Finland. The author describes a model used to examine direct and indirect tourist expenditure, resulting employment and taxes. The method is intended to offer decision makers new and better information about the impact of tourism on the economy and employment in a region.

AUSTRALIA

Leisure research in Australia may be divided into that carried out at the federal (or national) level and that in the various states. I shall also briefly mention research in New Zealand as part of Australia. In each Australian state there is at least one College of Advanced Education (CAE) which offers leisure and recreation programs at the undergraduate and graduate levels, with associated research projects.

Australian journals that publish articles on leisure research include *Australian Parks and Recreation*, the *Journal of the Australian Council for Health, Physical Education and Recreation* (ACHPER), and *Recreation Australia*. Also there are articles in the (British) *Leisure Studies* by Australian authors: some examples are Van Moorst (1982) on leisure and social theory, Ternowetsky (1983) on holidays and socio-economic status, Dempsey (1990) on women's leisure, and Hamilton-Smith (1992) on leisure and optimal experience. Parker and Paddick (1990) have a book on *Leisure in Australia*.

Federal. The only ministry with direct responsibility for leisure and recreation matters is the Department of Sport, Recreation and Tourism. Its role is basically to initiate, coordinate, and fund research projects that enable the development and monitoring of sport and recreation programs. Other federal agencies that have an important influence on the socio-economic environment of leisure include the Australia Council (concerned with art and culture) and the various ministries having an impact on national economic policies, notably those responsible for the funding of education, social security and unemployment programs.

A good reference source is *Leisure and Recreation in Australia 1976-1983* (1984) available from the Leisure Information Center, Phillip Institute, Victoria. In this publication, leisure and recreation have been defined broadly as embracing the arts, holiday activities and tourism, indoor and outdoor activities, sport and other pursuits, including those not always recognized as recreational such as gambling, drinking and drug taking.

Australian Capital Territories (ACT). Leisure research has been limited there. In the sports studies field, areas of major interest are sport and the media, leisure history and sports psychology. Research in progress in the Recreation Planning group includes the place of sport in the (proposed) Museum of Australia, and the role of the voluntary sector in leisure provision. There is also some interest in education for leisure.

New South Wales. Research based at the Juring-gai CAE has resulted in two publications. Ponton, ed. (1982) presented the papers on a "user pays" seminar, and Brown, ed. (1983) did the same for a seminar on District Sports Councils.

Queensland. Tourism is a big industry there, and with it the development of entertainment and commercial recreation enterprises. The Queensland Recreation Council published a journal, Recreation Forum, on an ad hoc basis that deals with the recreation industry.

South Australia. Research projects being carried out by staff members at the Salisbury campus of the South Australian CAE include the relationship between public and private swimming pools, managerial styles among parks and recreation personnel, local applied studies for the layout of parks and trails, and the impact of recreation on sensitive ecological sites.

Tasmania. Tasmania's large tracts of rugged and undeveloped land are reflected in the research being carried out, much of which is related to improving the management of government-owned land for recreational purposes. Other areas of leisure research include motivational aspects such as why people do or do not participate in recreational activities.

Victoria. All leisure studies courses at the Phillip Institute of Technology are based in the social sciences, and there is a strong interest in research within the department, with some eight to ten major studies completed each year by staff and graduate students. The state Ministry of Youth, Sport and Recreation has several publications on sport and recreation policy.

Western Australia. The Western Australian Department for Youth, Sport, and Recreation has initiated and assisted with various projects. These have included recreational use of water catchments, preparing for retirement, sport and recreation for the disabled, and swimming for the over 50s.

New Zealand. The University of Otago (Dunedin) has people researching in outdoor recreation and urban geography. At Victoria University (Wellington) an MA in Recreation Administration is offered, requiring a thesis to be written.

SOUTH AMERICA

Leisure research in South America was given a considerable impetus by the formation in 1980 of the Latin American Leisure and Recreation Association (ALATIR). In a historical review of the development of ALATIR, Melendez (1987) notes that its antecedents were the Columbian Recreation Association, founded in 1956, and the Brazilian Recreation Association, founded in 1957. The charter members of ALATIR are Argentina, Bolivia, Brazil, Chile, Colombia, Costa Rica, Ecuador, Guatemala, Honduras, Mexico, Panama, Paraguay, Peru, and Uruguay. I am unable to give a balanced review of leisure research in all those countries, however, I shall indicate some of the research concerns in three of them.

In *Brazil*, the Center for Studies on Leisure —CELAZER— was created in 1978, supported by the Social Service of Commerce. On the occasion of the 10th World Congress of Sociology in Mexico City in August 1982, the Center published four monographs in both Spanish and English on various aspects of leisure research in Brazil. The first is on *Perspectives of Free Time in Brazil* and analyzes the prospects for free time and leisure up to the year

2000. Leisure values are shown to be those of culture, participation and of the body, illustrated by the popularity of going to the beach and carnival. *Intellectual Leisure and Cultural Development* distinguishes between imposed culture and chosen culture. The first is obligatory and regulated by institutions such as schools and business firms. By contrast, chosen culture refers to the activities done in one's free time. The third monograph, *Participative and Associative Leisure*, expands on the theme of social participation as an important use of free time. It is argued that associative leisure has been relatively neglected in leisure studies and that it is becoming less institutionalized, engaged in by all social classes, all age groups and both sexes. Finally, *Imposing and Proposing Cultural Handicraft Construction* reports a study in Sao Paulo that found a remarkably high proportion (87%) of the population practice manual activities in their spare time, notably cookery, gardening, and skilled work of various kinds.

De Moraes von Simson (1983) has analyzed the changing festive activities of central and southern Brazilian urban society during the past two centuries. She notes the rise of a dominant sector in society that impose cultural creations on the lower classes while at the same time adapting popular cultural traits to fit into a consumer-oriented capitalist system.

My reference to leisure research in Chile is confined to one area, recreation and the elderly (Chilean National Committee on Recreation, 1986). This research is very much part of a program of provision and education; an example of "action research," although it is not described as such. Until recently, the concept of recreation applied only to youngsters and sometimes to adults— never to the elderly. But in 1976, the YMCA extended its concern to work with the elderly. It set up organized camping activities for the elderly, helped to inaugurate recreational programs in residential homes, and promoted social participation in clubs for the elderly.

Again, the example of leisure research in Ecuador is taken from one area and says nothing about research probably carried out in other areas. And again it is very much action research. Caudillo (1983) describes the development and operation of Fundeporte, Quito's first organized public recreation program. Acting as consultant, Caudillo helped to program and deliver leisure activities to a public unaccustomed to these services. Fourteen workshops examined a variety of methods to assist management and operations personnel in understanding rules, regulations and policies governing Fundeporte. A workshop provided administrators with a program covering all aspects of efficient park and recreation maintenance, operation, programming, staffing, inventory, and evaluation.

MIDDLE EAST

Leisure research in this part of the world centers around two cultures: Jewish (Israel) and Muslim (principally Egypt).

My review of leisure research in Israel owes much to the work of Boas Shamir. Prior to the 1970s the study of leisure had not been on the academic agenda. In 1970, a major survey was carried out by Katz and his colleagues at the Communications Institute of the Hebrew University (Katz and Gurevitch, 1976). Based on a representative sample of 4,000 adults, the survey assessed by means of questionnaires and time budgets the degree of exposure to cultural activities and the level of participation in a large variety of leisure activities. In 1979, the Israeli Leisure and Recreation Association, formed shortly before, hosted an international conference to discuss the implications of the Katz study for the formulation of leisure policy in Israel.

Of particular interest is the study of leisure in the kibbutz. The interest stems from the collective community nature of the kibbutz, from the relative integration of various life spheres and from the major emphasis on work in the traditional kibbutz ideology (Rosner, 1979; Shamir and Ruskin, 1983).

For an account of leisure research in Egypt and other Muslim countries, we are indebted to Ibrahim (now in Whittier, California). His study of the leisure behavior of Cairo residents (1981) included the finding that they watched TV about one hour and fifteen minutes each weekday—not markedly different from the level ten or more years ago in other East and West capitals. In a further paper (1982) he examined the role of Islamic teaching in the development of a uniquely Muslim state of mind and leisure behavior. Traditional leisure activities include poetry, song, music, and dancing, but there are new activities: sport, TV and movie going. The urban centers of Islam are in dire need of open space and parks.

Ibrahim and Asker (1984) discuss the stature of sport in ancient and contemporary Egypt. Nasser's Egypt witnessed the spread of sport via rural and youth clubs where physical educators play important roles in increased sport participation today.

FAR EAST

Again, the picture I can paint is only sketchy, although that is probably a reflection of the undeveloped state of leisure research in this part of the world. But since the area contains three of the most populous countries, it would be wrong to exclude it.

The occasion of the 1986 meeting in Jaipur *India* of the Leisure Research Committee of the International Sociological Association gave a great boost to Indian leisure research. The papers presented there included Vaidya on the leisure time activities of railway coolies, Bhatty on the leisure of young people, Kawale on the leisure of divorcees, and Modi on leisurology. Modi (1985) has also written a book in which he presents empirical findings confirming the decline of many traditional leisure pursuits and the increasing popularity—particularly in urban areas—of films, radio, press and group-oriented games and sports. A conference of the World Leisure and Recreation Association was held in December 1993 in Japan.

In *Japan*, annual conferences are held by the Japanese Society of Leisure and Recreation Studies. In addition, the programs of the society include lectures, seminars, the publication of a research journal and exchange of information throughout the world. The Japanese Association for the Promotion of Leisure and Culture and the Japanese Institute for Advancement of Leisure also provide various lectures and seminars. The Japanese Association of Tourism organizes an annual tourism symposium.

Most research published during the 1970s was applied research, such as time budget studies, activity participation surveys and demand analysis. Basic research intended to test hypotheses and develop theories is not well developed. The recent appearance of the national fitness boom and the development of its programs in corporations and communities has started to attract the attention of researchers.

It is with some regret that I have to confess to having too little information to say anything about leisure research in *China*. Freysinger and Chen (1993) have written an article on leisure and family in China, and hopefully this will be followed by other research in the most populated country in the world.

AFRICA

Most leisure research in this continent has been done in South Africa, the most economically advanced country. I am indebted to Grobler (in Graefe and Parker, eds. 1987) for most of what follows.

The study of leisure time spending and recreational activities has only in recent years been done on a planned basis. Up to the 1970s, the few publications or unpublished papers on this subject were researched and written mostly with the aim of satisfying academic qualifications or as part of larger studies on, for example, urbanization, town planning or social anthropology. By the 1970s, the need for specialized knowledge on recreational activities and outdoor management became apparent. This led to the publication of a National Outdoor Recreation Plan by the Department of Planning and Environment in 1978 and the founding of the South African Association for Sport Science, Physical Education and Recreation. The members of this association, and especially of its Recreation Committee, took up the task of identifying and coordinating research on leisure and recreation.

Over the last two decades there has been considerable interest by overseas writers such as Jarvie (1985) in the patterns and policies of South African sport. The study of leisure and recreation patterns, and especially of the activities of the black population, is enormously complicated by two factors.

First, it is a developing country in which the way of life of each generation vastly differs from that of its predecessors. Second, the uniqueness of the South African situation is complicated by the policy of apartheid, which has been practiced by the white government since 1948. Various laws prohibit blacks and whites from spending their free time together.

So far as black Africa is concerned, a paper by June (in Romer, ed. 1984) raises the questions of whether free time could be a topic of study in such an area. He notes that surveys have shown an average work day in the non-industrial sector of something like four hours in a 25-day work year—far less than in industrial societies. Furthermore, the proportion of total expenditure categorized as "free time" is low in black Africa: two to six percent (excluding Zimbabwe) compared to eight to 12 percent in industrial countries. The use of free time is also different: in Burundi, an agricultural region, most of it is spent in resting, religious activities, feasting and walking. So the concept of free or unobligated time is more appropriate in such societies than leisure, which implies some use of products and services.

INTERNATIONAL COMPARATIVE RESEARCH

The best known project is the multinational time budget study carried out in the mid '60s and involving 12 countries (Szalai, 1972). A number of other leisure research projects have been carried out which involve gathering data in more than one country. Kelly (1986) has outlined the role of the World Leisure and Recreation Association (WLRA) Commission on Research in helping to promote international research. The first publication to result from this initiative is by Hantrais and Kamphorst, eds. (1987) on trends in the arts, reporting comparative findings in eight countries.

The Council of Europe has sponsored a considerable amount of internationally comparative sports research. A report by Rodgers (1977) analyzed patterns of participation in sport and problems of encouraging mass participation across eight countries. A further report by Claeys (1982) compared sports participation and motivation, with special reference to nonparticipants. A report has also been made by the Council of Europe (1985) on evaluation of the impact of Sport for All policies and programs across 15 countries.

A number of smaller internationally comparative projects have resulted in publications. Pine (1984) has compared community development and voluntary associations by means of case studies in Finland, England and Ireland. Two studies involve France and England: Hantrais (1984) on work, family and leisure, and Cross (1986) on the political economy of leisure, with special reference to the eight-hour day. Standeven and Thompson (1986) report on a project in England and Canada on education for leisure. Blumler (1992) has edited a comparative collection of papers on values at risk in West European broadcasting. Hummel (1994) has written on ecotourism development with examples from Nepal and Costa Rica.

In 1988, the LSA hosted a second international leisure conference at the University of Sussex, Brighton, and in 1993 there was
a third such conference at Loughborough University. A number
of papers by authors in different countries were offered to the
conferences, and no doubt, the stock of internationally comparative research projects will be increased.

CONCLUSIONS

I now come to the difficult task of trying to sum up what I
think can be learned from the foregoing review of leisure research around the world. I am going to make only a few points,
some of which I hope will be at least mildly provocative.

1. North American leisure research is extensive both in
topic coverage and in numbers of projects, but it is generally
more to an established pattern (and perhaps more bureaucratic?)
than is such research in most of the rest of the world.

2. The marriage of recreation and parks is found hardly
anywhere outside North America, one exception being Australia.

3. The contrast between research in Eastern Europe and the
West (including North America) is quite marked: in the West, the
emphasis is on leisure activities and recreation provision; in
Eastern Europe it is on time budgets and cultural participation.
However, there are signs in some East European countries that a
process of convergence with Western topics and methods is
starting to occur.

4. Leisure research in Britain is more international than in
North America, as reflected in the higher proportion of articles by
overseas writers in LS and in the traffic of overseas leisure
researchers coming to conferences in England.

5. WLRA and its regional offspring ELRA and ALATIR
have made a considerable contribution to internationalizing
leisure research, although it is clear that the potential for further
development is great.

6. In economically undeveloped areas such as black Africa
the concept of free or unoccupied time is more appropriate than
leisure, which implies some use of products and services.

7. In developing countries leisure research is at present
mainly for practical purposes such as providing people with
more opportunities and facilities for recreation. It is in only a

comparatively few countries (although surely the number will grow) that more basic leisure research is undertaken and contributions to cross-disciplinary research and theory building are made.

BIBLIOGRAPHY

Bacon, A.W. ed. (1981). *Leisure and Learning*. Eastbourne: Leisure Studies Association.

Bell, C., and P. Healey. (1973). The Family and Leisure. In M.A. Smith et al. eds. *Leisure and Society in Britain*. London: Allen Lane.

Bennett, T. et al. (1981). Popular Television and Film. London: British Film Institute /Open University.

Bernard, M. Ed. (1984). *Leisure in Later Life?* Beth Johnson Foundation.

Blumler, J. G. ed. (1992). *Television and the Public Interest*. London: Sage.

Boothby, J. (1987). Self-reported Participation Rates. *Leisure Studies*, (6) 1.

Bramham, P., and I. Henry. (1985). Political Ideology and Leisure Policy in the UK. *Leisure Studies (4)* 1.

Brown, P.R., ed. (1983). *District Sports Councils*. Lindfield: New South Wales Kuring-gai: CAE.

Caudillo, J. (1983). Fundeporte: A Noble Dream. *WLRA* Journal, March/April.

Chamberlain, J. (1983). Adolescent Perceptions of Work and Leisure. *Leisure Studies* (2) 2.

Chambers, D. (1986). The Constraints of Work and Domestic Schedules on Women's Leisure. *Leisure Studies* (5) 3.

Cherry, G. (1984). Leisure and the Home. *Leisure Studies* (3)1.

Cherry, G. (1985). Scenic Heritage and National Parks Lobbies and Legislation. *Leisure Studies* (4)2.

Chilean National Committee on Recreation. (1986). Recreation and the Elderly. *WLRA* Journal, April.

Claeys. U. (1982). *Rationalizing Sports Policies*, Council of Europe.

Coalter, F., ed. (1984). *Politics of Leisure*. Eastbourne: Leisure Studies Association.

Corley, J. (1982). Employment in the Leisure Industries in Britain, 1960-1980. *Leisure Studies* (1)1.

Council of Europe. (1985). *Evaluation of the Impact of Sport for All Policies*. Strasbourg: The Council.

Countryside Commission. (1977). *Provision for the Disabled in the Countryside*. Cheltenham: the Commission.

Cross. G. (1986). The Political Economy of Leisure in Retrospect. *Leisure Studies* (5)3.

Cunningham, H. (1980). *Leisure in the Industrial Revolution*. London: Croom Helm.

De Moraes von Simson. (1983). Cultural Changes, Popular Creativity and Mass Communication. *Leisure Studies* (2)3.

Deem, R. (1982). Women, Leisure, and Inequality. *Leisure Studies* (1)1.

Deem, R. (1986). *All Work and No Play*. London: Routledge.

Dempsey, K. (1990). Women's Life and Leisure in Australian Rural Communities. *Leisure Studies* (9)1.

Donnelly, P. (1986). The Paradox of Parks: Politics of Recreational Land Use. *Leisure Studies* (5)2.

Duffield, B., ed. (1977). *Tourism: A Tool for Regional Development*. Eastbourne: Leisure Studies Association.

Dumazedier, J. (1967). *Toward a Society of Leisure*. New York: Collier MacMillan.

Dumazedier, J. (1974). *Sociology of Leisure*. Amsterdam: Elsevier.

Dunning, E. (1971). *The Sociology of Sport*. London: Cass.

European Leisure and Recreation Association. (1982). *Trends in Leisure Research in Europe*. Budapest: The Association.

Emmett, D. (1971). *Youth and Leisure in an Urban Sprawl*. Manchester: University Press.

Freysinger, V. and Chen, T. (1993). Leisure and Family in China, *WLRA* Journal, Fall.

Frith, S. (1983). *Sound Effects*. London: Constable.

Fryer, D., and R. Payne. (1984). Proactive Behavior in Unemployment. *Leisure Studies* (3)3.

Gershuny, J. (1978). *After Industrial Society. The Emerging Self-Service Economy*. London: MacMillan.

Glyptis, S. (1983). Business as Usual? Leisure Provision for the Unemployed. *Leisure Studies* (2) 3.

Glyptis. S. (1991). *Countryside Recreation*. London:Longman.

Glyptis, S. and D. Chambers. (1982). No Place Like Home. *Leisure Studies* (1) 3.

Goodhart G., et al. (1975). *The Television Audience*. London: Saxon.

Graefe, A. and S. Parker, eds. (1987). *Recreation and Leisure: An Introductory Handbook*. State College, PA: Venture.

Granger, B., and L. Galloway. (1982). Comparing Artists Fees in Television. *Leisure Studies* (1)2.

Gregory, S. (1982). Women Among Others: Another View. *Leisure Studies* (1)1.

Hamilton-Smith, E. (1992). Work, Leisure and Optimal Experience. *Leisure Studies* (11)3.

Hantrais, L., P. Clark, and N. Samuel. (1984). Time-space Dimensions of Work, Family and Leisure. *Leisure Studies* (3)3.

Hantrais, L., & T. Kamphorst., eds. (1987). *Trends in the Arts: A Multinational Perspective*. Amersfoort: Bruno.

Hargreaves, J. (1982). *Sport, Culture and Ideology*. London: Routledge.

Haworth, J. (1984). Leisure, Work and Profession. *Leisure Studies* (3)3.

Haworth, J. (1986). Meaningful Activity and Psychological Models of Non-employment. *Leisure Studies* (5)3.

Hedges. B. (1986). *Personal Leisure Histories*. London: Sports Council/ ESRC.

Hendry, L., M. Raymond, and C. Stewart. (1984). Unemployment, School and Leisure. *Leisure Studies* (3)2.

Houlihan, B. (1991). *The Government and Politics of Sport*. London: Routledge.

Hummel, J. (1994). Ecotourism Development in Protected Areas of Developing Countries, *WLRA* Journal, Summer.

Hutchinson, R. (1982). *The Politics of the Arts Council*. London:Sinclair-Brown.

Ibrahim, H. (1982). Leisure Behavior Among Contemporary Egyptians. *Journal of Leisure Research* (13). p.87.

Ibrahim, H. (1982). Leisure and Islam. *Leisure Studies* (1)2.

Ibrahim, H., and M. Asker. (1984). Ideology, Politics and Sport in Egypt. *Leisure Studies* (3)1.

Jarvie, G. (1985). *Class, Race and Sport in South Africa's Political Economy*. London: Routledge.

Jarvie, G., and G. Walker. (1993). *Scottish Sport*. London: Leicester University Press.

Jary, D. (1973). Evenings at the Ivory Tower. In M.A. Smith et al., Eds, *Leisure and Society in Britain*. London: Allen Lane.

Jenkins, C., and B. Sherman. (1979). *The Collapse of Work*. London: Eyre Methuen.

Jung, B. (1990). The Impact of the Crisis on Leisure Patterns in Poland. *Leisure Studies* (9)2.

Katz, E., and M. Gurevitch. (1976). *The Secularization of Leisure*. London: Faber.

Kelly, J. (1987). The WLRA Commission on Research. *WLRA* Journal, special anniversary issue.

Kelly, O. (1984). *Community, Art, and the State*. London: Comedia.

Leaman, O., and B. Carrington. (1985). Athleticism and the Reproduction of Gender and Ethnic Marginality. *Leisure Studies* (4)2.

Leigh, J. (1971). *Young People and Leisure*. London: Routledge.

Long, J., and E. Wimbush. (1985). *Continuity and Change: Leisure Around Retirement*, London: Sports Council/ESRC.

Luckham, B. (1984). Book Reading. In J. White, Ed., *The Media and Cultural Forms*, Eastbourne: Leisure Studies Association.

Mangan, J. (1981). *Athleticism in the Victorian and Edwardian Public School*. Cambridge: University Press.

Mann, P. (1967). Surveying a Theatre Audience. *British Journal of Sociology* (18).

Martin, W., and S. Mason. (1986-7). *Current Trends in Leisure Studies*.

Melendez, N. (1987). The Historical Development of ALATIR. *WLRA* Journal, special anniversary issue.

Modi, I. (1985). *Leisure, Mass Media and Social Structure.* Jaipur:Rawat.

Morley, D. (1980). *The Nationwide Audience.* London: British Film Institute.

Olsen, H.D. (1985). The Development of Youth Leisure Policies in Sweden. *Leisure Studies* (4)1.

Olszewska, A., and G. Pronovost. (1982). Current Problems and Perspectives in the Sociology of Leisure. In T. Bottomore, Ed. *Sociology: The State of the Art.* International Sociological Association.

Parker, S. (1982). *Work and Retirement.* London: Allen and Unwin.

Parker, S. (1983). *Leisure and Work.* London: Allen and Unwin.

Parker, S., and R. Paddick. (1990). *Leisure in Australia.* Melbourne: Longman Cheshire.

Pearson, A. (1985). *Arts for Everyone: Guidance on Provisions for Disabled People.* London: Bedford Square Press.

Pick, J. (1980). *Arts Administrations.* London: Spon.

Pine, R. (1984). Community Development and Voluntary Associations. *Leisure Studies* (3)1.

Ponton, D., Ed. (1982). *The User Pays Seminar.* Lindfield, New South Wales: Kuring-gai CAE.

Rapoport, R. (1975). *Leisure in the Family Life Cycle.* London: Routledge.

Riordan, J. (1982). Leisure, the State and the Individual in the USST. *Leisure Studies* (1)1.

Roberts, K. (1983). *Youth and Leisure.* London:Allen and Unwin.

Robertson, J. (1985). *Future Work, Aldershot.* Hants: Gower.

Rodgers, H.B. (1977). *Rationalizing Sports Policies.* Strasbourg: Council of Europe.

Romer, M., Ed. (1984). LeTemps Libre et le Loisir. Paris: Association pour la Diffusion de la Recherbhe sur l'Action Culturelle.

Rosner, M. (1979). Changes in the Leisure Culture of the Kibbutz. *Leisure and Society* (2)2.

Shamir, B., and Ruskin, H. (1983). Type of Community as a Moderator of the Work-Leisure Relationship. *Journal of Occupational Behavior* (4).

Standeven, J. and G. Thompson. (1986). Northern Ireland: The Politics of Leisure in a Divided Society. *Leisure Studies* (5)3.

Stokes, G. (1983). Work, Unemployment and Leisure. *Leisure Studies* (2)3.

Strelitz, Z. Ed. (1979). *Leisure and Family Diversity.* Eastbourne: Leisure Studies Association.

Sugden, J., and A. Bairner. (1986). Northern Ireland: The Politics of Leisure in a Divided Society. *Leisure Studies* (5)3.

Swedner, J. (1981). The Swedish Experience: Life and Leisure in an Affluent Mixed Economy. In G.E. Cherry and A Travers, Eds. *Leisure in the 1980s.* Eastbourne: Leisure Studies Association.

Swedner, J. H. (1982). Leisure Culture and Action Research. *Leisure Studies* (1)2.

Szalai, A. (1972). The *Use of Time*. Mouton: The Hague.

Taylor, R. (1992). *Football and its Fans*. London: Leicester University Press.

Ternowetsky. (1983). Holiday Taking and Social Status in Australia. *Leisure Studies* (2)1.

Tomlinson, A., and G.Whannel. (1984). *Money Power and Politics at the Olympic Games*. New York: Longman.

Torkildsen, G. (1991). *Leisure and Recreation Management*. London: Spon.

Tourism and Recreation Research Unit. (1980). Pollok Park, 1979; a *Visitor Survey*. Edinburgh: University Dept. of Geography.

Tunstall, J. (1983). *The Media in Britain*. London: Constable.

Uzzell, D. 1985. Management Issues in Countryside Interpretation. *Leisure Studies* (4)2.

Van Moorst, H. (1982). Leisure and Social Theory. *Leisure Studies* (4)2.

Veal, A.J. (1984). Leisure in England and Wales. *Leisure Studies* (3)2.

Veal, A.J. (1987). *Leisure and the Future*. London: Allen and Unwin.

Ventris, N., Ed. (1980). *Leisure and Rural Society*. Eastbourne: Leisure Studies Association.

Wilson, J. (1988). *Politics and Leisure*. London: Constable.

Wimbush, E., and B. Duffield. (1985). Integrating Education and Leisure. *Leisure Studies* (4)1.

Young, M., and P. Willmott. (1973). *The Symmetrical Family*. London: Routledge.

Research on Women and Leisure

Past, Present, and Future Research

Karla A. Henderson
Curriculum in Leisure Studies and Recreation Administration
———— University of North Carolina at Chapel Hill ————

Susan M. Shaw
Department of Recreation and Leisure Studies
———————— University of Waterloo ————————

The year is 2005. Volume 35 of the *Journal of Leisure Research* has just arrived via electronic publishing. We have programmed the computer to highlight passages that discuss women, gender, and leisure. Although only one researcher has examined a topic pertaining specifically to women and leisure, the scan indicates that socialization and gender relations are discussed in virtually every article that addresses leisure behavior. Gender is clearly not the domain of women, but has important implications for how everyone lives their lives and experiences leisure. The computer review of the most recent issue of the *Journal of Park and Recreation Administration* also signals that two articles address programming for gay and lesbian families within the context of programming for families in general. The needs of a diversity of individuals whether male or female, gay or straight, black or white, employed or unemployed have become the focus of recreation and leisure research.

While society is still gendered, the variety of ways that gender is expressed has become evident in the early part of the twenty-first century. Further, the ways that research on women and gender can inform social change have become apparent over the past twenty years. Leisure researchers have internalized the idea that if research is to make a difference, it must make an impact on those being researched, leisure service providers, policy makers, and people in the society in general. The progress made from 1982-1993 in making the leisure (or lack of leisure) in women's lives visible, has given way in 1994-2005 to addressing the topics of gender as related to both male and female socialization and power relations. Along with leisure researchers' recognition of the needs and interests of women has come the concern about other disenfranchised groups (i.e., those individuals outside the dominant white, middle-class, able-bodied, male, heterosexual model) who largely were invisible in the leisure literature prior to the 1980s.

These first two paragraphs represent in a nutshell what the future holds for the study of women, gender, and leisure. Although major ideological changes are not likely in the next ten years, the study of women's leisure in the past and its potential application for positive social change have provided a firm basis for future research and for improvements in women's lives. Perhaps eventually the work of feminist researchers and those concerned with gender issues will no longer be needed because the tenets of feminism and the concern for women and other "invisible" groups will become common place in the leisure literature. Perhaps the next edition of this book on leisure research will not need a separate chapter on "women's leisure" because an acknowledgement and understanding of gender will be evident in all leisure research. As a prelude to the future, it may be useful to examine the past 30 years to see how the study of women and leisure has evolved and what the issues have been. The analyses herein are suggestive, not definitive, and should be considered as a "work in progress" in describing how current research on women and leisure might be further examined and interpreted.

A HISTORICAL PERSPECTIVE ON RESEARCH ON WOMEN'S LEISURE

The topics of women's leisure and gender issues have been discussed more frequently in the leisure research literature within the past 15 years than ever in the past. The importance of women's leisure experiences, especially those related to empowerment and the diversity of leisure meanings, has been acknowledged (e.g., Deem, 1986; Fox, 1992; Green, Hebron, & Woodward, 1987; Henderson, et al., 1989; Lenskyj, 1988; Shaw, 1985; Wearing & Wearing, 1988). The studies published about women's leisure, many from feminist perspectives, have given visibility to the analysis of gender issues. In addition, issues of gender are beginning to inform the leisure literature, not just as another demographic variable to add to the list to be studied, but as a focus of the impact of structured power relationships on social and economic everyday life (Deem, 1992).

As may be expected in the preliminary development of any line of research, the results have often been fragmented and sometimes contradictory. Although an integrated understanding of women's leisure seems desirable, it is not realistic since many perspectives exist and great diversity prevails in the situations of different women. Moreover, while few, if any, societies exist where men and women are treated equally (see the recent UN Report on the Status of Women), the specific nature of gender relations varies from culture to culture. With a broadened view of the world and a focus on various issues surrounding diversity, an expanding inclusive view of the meaning of gender as applied to an understanding of leisure behavior and the provision of leisure services is becoming essential. Studying women as a disadvantaged group may well sensitize us to understanding other deprived or oppressed groups.

Feminism has provided a world view for much of the research done on women and leisure, although not all research on women is feminist research, nor does it need to be. Feminism is a philosophical framework and practice that embodies equality, empowerment, and social change for women and men, and that seeks to eliminate the invisibility of women (Henderson et al., 1989). Although different approaches to feminism and feminist research exist, all have some commonalties. These similarities, according to Eichler (1980), are evident in the three broad functions which feminist research serves: to be critical of existent social structures; to serve as a corrective mechanism by providing an alternative viewpoint; and to lay the groundwork for a transformation of both social science and society.

Within this inclusive framework of feminist analysis and depending upon the perspective taken, feminism can mean equality or it can mean difference, liberal or radical, personal or political, and other apparent dichotomies (Henderson, 1990a; Henderson & Bialeschki, 1992). Thus, clear agreement does not occur over exactly how feminist theory can be used to understand gender and over how feminist goals can be reached.

Any examination of past research on women and leisure, therefore, needs to take into account how feminist analysis in a broad sense has evolved and changed over the years. While various scholars have attempted to devise frameworks to understand different approaches to the study of women (e.g., Dewar, 1987; Eichler, 1980; Evans, 1990; Lerner, 1975) Tetreault's (1985) feminist phase theory provides a useful historical perspective on the evolution of feminist research and writing. In a summary of historical changes in the study of gender, women, and leisure, Henderson (1994) adapted Tetreault's five phase model for a discussion of leisure research. To examine the leisure research, five conceptual phases were identified: invisible scholarship (i.e., "womanless"), compensatory scholarship (i.e., "add women and stir"), dichotomous differences scholarship (i.e., "sex differences"), feminist scholarship (i.e., "woman-centered"), and gender scholarship. Gender scholarship is the most recent stage and, as yet, has been least well defined and applied.

The value of this phase framework for analyzing the leisure literature of the past thirty years lies in how gender has become visible as a socially constructed, culturally transmitted organizer of our inner and outer worlds pertaining to leisure (Henderson, 1994). Further, it pushes researchers who have used theoretical structures developed primarily by, for, and about males to take account of different experiences, data, and methodologies (Rhode, 1990).

Invisible (Womanless) Scholarship

Little was written about women, let alone gender, in the leisure literature in North America from 1940 until the early 1980s (Henderson, 1993). Perhaps leisure researchers cannot be faulted for the omission since leisure research itself was not well organized until specialized research publications became available such as the *Journal of Leisure Research* in 1969 and *Leisure Sciences* in 1978. Between the inception of these journals and 1983, however, only 24 percent of the studies that used human subjects did any kind of analyses related to sex or gender and most of these studies reported statistical differences with little explanation of the meaning of the differences (Henderson, 1984). Just as in other disciplines (e.g., Tetreault, 1985), leisure scholars seemed to assume that the male experience was universal, representative of humanity, and constituted a basis for generalizing about all human beings. Little or no consciousness existed that women required additional or further study or that any variance existed in the predominant male view. Early theories of leisure such as theories of the relationship between work and leisure (Parker, 1972) did not incorporate or consider women's experiences, but remained androcentric. That is, work was conceptualized as paid work or labor market participation, while leisure was conceptualized as time away from paid work including family time and home-based activities. Thus, women's unpaid work in the home, as well as women's experiences of leisure, remained invisible. Not only women were left out of this scholarship but also people of color, people with disabilities, gay and lesbian people, low income, or any other group who did not fit societal norms.

Compensatory (Add Women and Stir) Scholarship

Related to the invisible scholarship was the emergence of compensatory scholarship in fields such as history and psychology. The "add women and stir" scholars were conscious that women might be missing from the analyses and that some examples or exceptions to the universal male experience might be needed. The leisure literature has a few cases of compensatory scholarship that appeared as the contemporary women's movement began to develop impetus.

Underlying the idea of compensatory research was a notion that women ought to be acknowledged, but such acknowledgement generally meant that women were judged in terms of their contributions based on typical male standards. That is, women were treated as if they represented a "minority" group, different in some ways from the "majority" white male standard. It is not uncommon in compensatory scholarship to find a single chapter or section of a text that described something about women's experiences (Andersen, 1993). These sections give the message that the book is really about men but women are different so they at least ought to be mentioned. Although corrected in subsequent editions, Godbey & Parker used three pages of their 1976 text to discuss "leisure activities of the sexes" (p. 85-87) but made little reference to women in other parts of the text except pertaining to "leisure and sexual behavior."

Dichotomous (Sex) Differences Scholarship

The realization that women existed and that they were in some way "different" than men resulted in leisure research in the 1970s and 1980s that addressed the dichotomous sex differences between males and females. A critique of the problems associated with studying differences between males and females suggested that although the study of differences can be helpful in understanding behavior, studying differences can also be problematic (Henderson, 1990a). Some say that identifying differences affirms women's value and special nature; others say it reinforces the status quo. Confirming that a situation exists does little to explain the motivations, satisfactions, and constraints to leisure behavior which may be due to the historical, cultural, and social context. Perhaps the main problem with dichotomous scholarship has occurred when differences are identified in the absence of any theoretical structure to explain those differences, or in the absence of any cultural or historical context in which to locate such differences.

One of the risks of atheoretical research is that if differences occur they can be seen to imply hierarchy; in other words, one group is seen to be superior or better than the other group. This risk is particularly an issue when differences are juxtaposed to white, male, middle class, European heterosexuality which provides the criteria for rationality, normality, and morality. Another risk is that such research can oversimplify and overclaim, and may also reinforce inequalities through the often unstated implication that if differences occur they must be inevitable or "natural." Yet a third risk is a tendency for researchers to create rather than discover difference, if that is their initial expectation.

Because differences may be a function of culture and can be seen to be socially constructed, explanations and interpretations of gender differences are often ideologically-based. Thus, well grounded and developed theoretical structures are needed to explain and guide differences research and to avoid intended or unintended biases. Research that has gone beyond making differences the conclusion of the research and has used theoretical assumptions for conducting the research has been conducted on patterns of participation (e.g., Searle & Jackson, 1985), on the distribution of leisure time (Shaw, 1985a), and on leisure meanings, definitions, and roles (Gloor, 1992; Samdahl, 1992; Shaw, 1985b).

Analysis of dichotomous differences research suggests that studying differences between males and females has helped to make females more visible in leisure research. Mere descriptions however, are not enough, and the research on differences that has been theoretically grounded, and thus placed in a broader context of gender relations as a whole, has contributed a greater understanding of women's leisure than a simple observing and recording that differences exist. Thus, the acknowledgment of differences can and has led into new directions especially when explanations for differences have been analyzed and when observed differences have been used as a stepping off point for further inquiry and further theoretical development.

Feminist (Women-Centered)Scholarship

Cultural feminists believe that it is women's qualities and experiences, not men's, that should be the measure of significance in society. Women-centered scholarship examines the experiences of women not in relation to men, necessarily, but in an attempt to understand the importance and meaning of women's lives. According to Tetreault (1985), in this scholarship what was formerly devalued in the content of women's everyday lives assumes new value as scholars investigate such areas as work, family and social relationships, and leisure.

A central problem that feminist researchers have addressed is how leisure itself should be conceptualized, and the inadequacy of traditional definitions for understanding women's leisure. Various scholars have commented on this definitional problem (e.g. Bella, 1989; Deem, 1986; Green, Hebron, & Woodward, 1987; Henderson, 1990b; Henderson & Bialeschki, 1991; Lenskyj, 1988; Wimbush & Talbot, 1988). As most leisure researchers have found, the construct of leisure has been highly subjective; leisure has been examined as time, activity, or experience. The notion of leisure as experience, however, is what is congruent with the way people think about their leisure in everyday life (Shaw, 1985b), and this approach is embodied in the literature about women's leisure today. Finding a definition of leisure more congruent with women's everyday experiences, and exploring gender differences in leisure experiences, has provided much of the motivation behind feminist empirical research on leisure meanings (e.g., Bialeschki & Henderson, 1986; Samdahl & Kleiber, 1989; Shaw, 1984). What has emerged from this research has been some agreement that leisure if freely chosen, is an enjoyable, self-enhancing, optimal experience that contributes to the quality of life. Additionally, and perhaps surprisingly, these characteristics seem to describe men's as well as women's experiences of leisure.

Understanding the experience of women has created a new world of meaning that has been hidden by androcentric thinking. Such women-centered research serves to counter the devaluation of women and, thus, to empower them. It has also challenged some of the traditional androcentric notions about leisure. For example, in conducting a study about constraints to leisure for women, Henderson, Stalnaker, & Taylor (1988) found that the assumption that constraints always mediated between desire for an activity and participation did not seem to fit. Instead, antecedent as well as intervening constraints were evidenced which have now been applied to other aspects of constraints research (e.g., Jackson, 1990). Feminist scholarship has helped to generate new ideas, patterns, and ways of examining the world. Thus, the focus on women has made leisure visible for women and has also opened the door for reinterpreting previous ideas about leisure behavior for both women and men.

Drawbacks also exist to this feminist women-centered scholarship. First, it can lead to female essentialism, the belief that the feminine nature is ideal and preferable to maleness. Another drawback is that the meaning of being female is a fluctuating, not a fixed state; being female has varied historically and contextually. Assuming that all females experience the world in the same way is risky. One's biological sex alone does not determine behavior, rather it is the way that an individual interprets his or her gender that is important. Women-centered scholarship needs to take into account historical, social, and/or economic factors that may create the situations to which women respond (Rhode, 1990). In other words, it is not possible to universalize the female experience or to suggest a "common" world exists for women except, perhaps, within a sense of common oppression. Race, age, education, cultural background, and other characteristics affect each female's experience in a way that cannot be generalized to all other females. Thus, for example, the research on leisure experiences has generally not included research on women of color, or women with diverse life experiences and life situations. The definitions developed so far, therefore, may not be inclusive of all women's experiences, but may be culturally specific. Research from a feminist women-centered perspective, however, is providing leisure scholars with new perspectives to consider in designing and interpreting research in a more inclusive manner.

Gender Scholarship

Gender or gender relations refers to cultural connections associated with one's biological sex. Thus, when biological sex is determined at birth as female or male, a huge number of cultural expectations are immediately associated with the child. Gender, then, refers to how women and men contribute to and are influenced by society. One's biological sex leads to a lifetime of relationships and expectations based on gender. Gender, therefore, may be defined as, ". . . a constitutive element of social relationship based on perceived differences between the sexes, and . . . a primary way of signifying relationships of power (Scott, 1986, p. 1067). Further, gender is an ongoing process rather than an inborn biological trait. The meaning of gender is constructed by society and each of us is socialized into that construction. Thus, gender is a set of socially constructed relations that are produced and reproduced through people's actions. At the societal level, gender relations can be seen as a set of structured power relations, while at the individual level they influence and are influenced by everyday activities and experiences.

The need to understand and analyze the meaning of gender for both females and males emerged as a dominant feminist model in other disciplines in the 1980s (Ferree, 1990). The analysis of gender relations appears to offer much potential in the 1990s for understanding leisure for women and men. Gender scholarship addresses the complexity of expectations, roles, and behavior associated with being male, as well as being female. Further, as Deem (1992) suggested, "gender is emphatically not 'a woman's problem!'" (p. 30). Researchers may apply a gender perspective to studying only women (e.g., Wearing, 1992), only men (e.g., Lynch, 1991), or may examine both sexes together (e.g., Samdahl, 1992; Whitson & Macintosh, 1989) from a perspective of interpreting how gender, as socially learned expectations, defines behavior. Gender interpretations can be applied to different facets of leisure such as constraints, definitions, benefits, participation, and satisfactions.

The earlier women-centered research tended to focus on meanings, definitions, and experiences of leisure, while the more recent gender scholarship has been more concerned with inequalities, integrity, and power relations. Shaw (in press) has argued that the dominant feminist approach to research on women's leisure has been seeking to understand how women's leisure is constrained as a result of gender relations and gendered life experiences. She also points out some new theoretical directions that are emerging, for example, like how leisure activities reinforce or reproduce structured gender relations and, alternatively, how leisure may sometimes be seen as a form of resistance to such power relations. These new research directions can be seen in the recent work of scholars such as Freysinger and Flannery (1992), Thompson (1992) and Wearing (1990; 1992). They represent the move toward broader and more inclusive theoretical frameworks and interpretations of the intersections between gender and leisure.

CONSIDERATIONS FOR FURTHER STUDY OF WOMEN, GENDER, AND LEISURE

If research on women, gender, and leisure is to evolve as was suggested in the short scenario at the beginning of this paper, then leisure researchers may want to consider how research on gender, women, and leisure ought to be conducted in the coming years. As leisure and feminist researchers incorporate a broader

understanding of gender issues, Henderson (1994) has suggested the following considerations be taken into account for
leisure research: the gendered context of leisure, the exploration
of difference and diversity, the use of multiple methods for
research, and the continuing evolution of feminist perspectives
as applied to gender.

Gendered Context of Leisure

A focus on gender and gender relations will allow researchers to move away from the dichotomous sex differences that have
been described previously in the literature into new understandings of female and male behavior. Gender theory analyses may
be related to roles, gender identities, socialization, and structured power relations as tied to leisure. Thus, as Henderson et al.
(1989) claimed, gender and leisure are acknowledged as mutually interactive. Recognition of this interactive relationship
serves to show the need for more research on both the effect of
gender on leisure (e.g., how gender identities, expectations about
femininity and motherhood, and economic and work inequalities affect leisure behavior) AND the effect of leisure on gender
relations (e.g., how stereotypical activities and/or ways in which
activities and time are socially structured function to reinforce or
challenge existing gender relations).

If the proposition is accepted that gender is a central axis
around which all social life revolves, then a gender analysis is one
way to analyze all research conducted concerning leisure behavior. The world of women is part of a world of men and vice versa.
In considering gender theory, our interpretations need to show
how some women's experiences and/or men's experiences lead
individuals to make choices contingent on contexts and relationships, not just because they are biologically female or male.
Leisure experiences also play an important role in the social
construction of masculinity as well as femininity. The growing
field of study concerning men and masculinity, particularly as it
relates to sport, attests to this role (e.g., Lynch, 1991; Kimmel &
Messner, 1989). To date, however, research on masculinity or the
gendered nature of men's leisure experiences is almost nonexistent in the leisure literature. This area needs more attention
from both male and female researchers.

As Shaw, Bonen and McCabe (1991) suggested in their analysis of constraints to leisure, "it is not being female ... per se which is the constraint, but rather the way in which this social location is experienced in society" (p. 299). The concept of gender is complicated, and thus, the explanations for how socialization and power influence behavior will not be simple explications. Gender scholarship requires that researchers move beyond observations to analysis and interpretation. The use of gender as an analytic framework for leisure studies will have to take into account the situation and context in which it is uncovered and described. Thus, attention to theoretical development as well as empirical data collection will become more important. Acknowledged or not, gender is continually being constructed and negotiated in our individual worlds and in our society. The role of leisure in this process and the effect of leisure on this process need much further exploration.

Differences and Diversity in Leisure Behavior

The issues of differences and diversity are becoming more recognized in research practice and in understanding leisure behavior. The acknowledgement of gender differences can lead leisure research into new directions if differences become the starting point for further inquiry and not the conclusion of the research or the explanation of results.

The construction of differences is central to classism, ethnocentrism, and homophobia, as well as sexism (Rothenberg, 1990). Differences can divide people, but the diversity created by differences can also enrich life. The key is in determining, and thus potentially reducing, inequalities without abolishing all differences or seeking to make everyone the same. In other words, it is important to recognize that differences exist among women and among men, as well as between women and men. In the absence of oppression, discrimination, and inequalities, these differences may be cause for celebration rather than change.

As feminists have espoused in recent years, being female or male is not only an individual experience, but also a cultural experience. Talking about women globally is impossible without falling into the trap that renders some women invisible, particularly women who are not European-American, heterosexual, able-bodied, and middle class (Fox, 1992). Further, acknowledgement does not compensate for exclusion. If feminists are to make gender theory inclusive, women and men who represent a diversity of race, class, and other positions in society must be studied. Radford-Hill (1986) suggested that the political viability of feminism as an agency of change depends on the ability to build a movement that is inclusive rather than exclusive, one that can mobilize from a broad base of support.

Using Multiple Methods in Research

To understand the situational context of gender and leisure behavior, multiple methods in research will need to be employed. The research on women over the past 10 years, in particular, has used a variety of methods, but with more propensity toward qualitative research than has been seen in other areas of leisure research. The value of qualitative methods is being recognized by the field; the qualitative approach has opened the door for discovering the qualitative meanings of leisure experiences for both females and males. Large scale studies have been useful, although sometimes such studies have failed to recognize the different experiences of women and others. Survey methods can often benefit from, and build upon, understandings gained from more exploratory and experiential qualitative studies. The need, then, is not only to use multiple methods, but to use triangulated methods that inform and allow researchers to build upon each other's insights. Although multiple methods per se are not a gender issue, the use of methods allows for a broader understanding of how people interact in their lives.

As observers (i.e., leisure researchers) of gender behavior and relations, we also become its creators (Hare-Mustin & Marecek, 1988). Once leisure researchers seek to define and construct gender within an area like leisure, a process of creating meanings occurs. These meanings require self-examination to assure that the world of meaning that we create and construct is the world in which we want to live. Researchers who study women or men from a gendered perspective must be careful not to make the mistakes that have been made in the past in studying any one group and assuming the human experience is represented. Inclusive theorizing requires leisure scholars to question who creates knowledge, the universality of theory, the problems with generalizing to all women (or all men), and the impact of diversity on leisure research and leisure behavior. The future of leisure behavior research will depend upon an ability to build theories that are inclusive and that examine leisure from a broad base of cultural perspectives that address the diverse life experiences of females and males in a variety of situations.

Inclusion of Feminist Perspectives

Feminist perspectives that recognize the significance of gender and the need to move toward greater integrity for all people ought to continue to guide the research that is conducted related to women's leisure and gender issues. The negative connotations sometimes associated with feminism as a political agenda will need to be recognized, but the perspectives that feminism can offer as a philosophical framework will be essential in helping to construct and deconstruct our understanding of gender and leisure. Feminism will be most useful if researchers are able to apply all the possible approaches to feminism in addressing issues in leisure research and practice (Henderson et al., 1989; Henderson & Bialeschki, 1992). Feminism can also help to assure that females are kept in the picture and do not become invisible again. The importance of gender, however, cannot be the singular domain of feminists if it is to be understood. Although the goal of most feminist researchers has been to use critical feminist analyses to ground research in feminist social theory and to challenge androcentric notions, gender analysis offers a framework for all leisure researchers. As long as gender impacts behavior, feminists will need to remind us continually of the value of women's experiences (Jaggar, 1991).

Perhaps a day will come when feminist perspectives will no longer be needed and gender socialization, relations, and inequities will not be an issue in our society. Perhaps someday leisure behavior will be completely a matter of choice and not a result of constraints or lack of opportunities due to cultural expectations. We are not, however, close to that utopia. Leisure researchers will need to be cognizant of the changing meanings surrounding the construction of gender and the influence of differences.

This examination of women, gender, and leisure over the past 30 years has taken us from a point where women were invisible to a point where we are beginning to understand women, men, and their relationships to each other through leisure. Leisure and feminist researchers have suggested that leisure, as a common expression of human behavior, often can be further understood by analyzing and interpreting it within the context of gender relations. Broadening our perspectives and examining leisure within the context of gender may give insight into understanding other aspects of the human condition such as race, class, sexual orientation, physical ability, and aging. The process has been and will continue to be one of discovery, recognizing, and creating patterns—patterns where leisure experiences grounded in a gender context can now make a new kind of sense, or make sense for the first time.

TRANSFORMING THE GENDERED MEANINGS OF LEISURE IN WOMEN'S LIVES

The research about women and leisure in the past and the focus on the gendered meanings of leisure for males and females in the future will only be useful when social change is addressed in the present. If research on, for, and about women and men does not lead to empowerment regardless of life circumstances, then its usefulness can be questioned. A number of researchers have tried to address what research on women and gender means for leisure providers, policy-makers, women themselves, and the society at large (e.g., Deem, 1986; Duquin, 1991; Fasting, 1987; Fox, 1992; Freysinger & Flannery, 1992; Green, Hebron, & Woodward, 1987; Henderson, 1992; Hunter & Whitson, 1992). Analyses of the gendered meanings of leisure for women or men, however, are of little consequence unless they can be translated into practice and improving our quality of life.

As individuals interested in research and practice surrounding women's leisure, the first step to transforming women's leisure may be to describe some of the aspirations that women may have for their leisure. The incorporation of research on men from a gendered perspective, and on diversity among women and among men implies expanding this notion of social change to incorporate people in a variety of life situations. It also implies research directed towards societal change and/or social structural change. This issue of research for social change raises a number of questions. For example, in an ideal world, would we expect women's leisure to be like men's leisure? Are there more valuable and less valuable forms of leisure? To what extent is it the role or purpose of research to bring about social change either on the macro or micro level?

These questions are not easy to answer, but hopefully this difficulty does not mean that future researchers will shy away from such questions. Advances in our understanding of women's lives and of gender issues in society have come about because of people who have been willing to take a stand on difficult issues. Future progress will also depend on people willing to question and critique existing ideas, theories, and practices. The challenge for researchers, and perhaps particularly for researchers in the controversial area of gender relations, is ongoing.

REFERENCES

Andersen, M. L. (1993). *Thinking about Women: Sociological Perspectives on Sex and Gender* (third edition). New York: Macmillan Publishing Company.

Bella, L. (1989). Women and Leisure: Beyond Androcentrism. In E. Jackson & T. Burton (Eds.), *Understanding Leisure and Recreation: Mapping The Past, Charting the Future*, (p. 151-180). State College, PA: Venture Publishing Co.

Bialeschki, M.D., and K. A. Henderson (1986). Leisure in the Common World of Women. *Leisure Studies, 5*, 299-308.

Deem, R. (1986). *All Work and no Play? The Sociology of Women and Leisure*. Milton Keynes, England: Open University Press.

Deem, R. (1992). The Sociology of Gender and Leisure in Great Britain. *Loisir & Societe/Society & Leisure, 15*(1), 21-38.

Dewar, A.M. (1987). The Social Construction of Gender in Physical Education. *Women's Studies International Forum, 10*(4), 453-465.

Duquin, M.E. (1991). Sport, Women, and the Ethic of Care. *Journal of Applied Recreation Research, 16*(4), 262-280.

Eichler, M. (1980). *The Double Standard*. New York: St. Martin's.

Evans, M. (1990). The Problem of Gender for Women's Studies. *Women's Studies International Forum, 13*(5) 457-462.

Fasting, K. (1987). Sports and Women's Culture. *Women's Studies International Forum, 10*(4), 361-368.

Ferree, M.M. (1990). Beyond Separate Spheres: Feminism and Family Research. *Journal of Marriage and the Family, 52*, 866-884.

Fox, K. (1992). Choreographing Differences in the Dance of Leisure: The Potential of Feminist Thought. *Journal of Leisure Research, 24*(4), 333-347.

Freysinger, V.J., and D. Flannery (1992). Women's Leisure: Affiliation, Self-determination, Empowerment and Resistance? *Loisir & Societe/Society and Leisure, 15*(1), 303-322.

Gloor, D. (1992). Women Verses Men? The Hidden Differences in Leisure Activities. *Loisir & Societe/Society and Leisure, 15*(1), 39-62.

Godbey, G., and S. Parker (1976). *Leisure Studies and Services: An Overview.* Philadelphia: W.B. Saunders Company.

Green, E., S. Hebron, and D. Woodward (1987). *Leisure and Gender: A Study of Sheffield Women's Leisure Experience.* London: The Sports Council and Economic and Social Research Council.

Hare-Mustin, R.T., and J. Marecek (1988). The Meaning of Difference: Gender Theory, Postmodernism, and Psychology. *American Psychologist, 43*(6), 455-464.

Henderson, K.A. (1984, October). *An Analysis of Sexism in Leisure Research.* Paper presented to the NRPA Leisure Research Symposium, Orlando, FL.

Henderson, K.A. (1990a). Anatomy is not Destiny: A Feminist Analysis of the Scholarship on Women's Leisure. *Leisure Sciences, 12,* 229-239.

Henderson, K.A. (1990b). An Oral History Perspective on the Containers in Which American Farm Women Experienced Leisure. *Leisure Studies, 9,* 121-133.

Henderson, K.A. (1992). Women and Leisure in the Future: Planning for a Vision. *Journal of Applied Recreation Research, 17*(2), 115-129.

Henderson, K.A. (1993). A Feminist Analysis of Selected Professional Recreation Literature about Girls/Women from 1907-1990. *Journal of Leisure Research, 25*(2), 165-181.

Henderson, K.A. (1994). Perspectives on Analyzing Gender, Women, and Leisure. *Journal of Leisure Research, 26* (2), 119-137.

Henderson, K.A., and M. D. Bialeschki (1991). A Sense of Entitlement to Leisure as Constraint and Empowerment for Women. *Leisure Sciences, 13,* 51-65.

Henderson, K.A., and M. D. Bialeschki (1992). Leisure Research and the Social Structure of Feminism. *Loisir & Societe/Society & Leisure, 15*(1), 63-77.

Henderson, K.A., M. D. Bialeschki, S. M. Shaw, and V. J. Freysinger (1989). *A Leisure of One's Own: A Feminist Perspective on Women's Leisure.* State College, PA: Venture Publishing, Inc.

Henderson, K.A., D. Stalnaker, and G. Taylor (1988). The Relationship Between Barriers to Recreation and Gender-Role Personality Traits for Women. *Journal of Leisure Research, 20,* 69-80.

Hunter, P.L., and D. J. Whitson (1992). Women's Leisure in a Resource Industry Town: Problems and Issues. *Loisir & Societe/Society and Leisure, 15*(1), 223-244.

Jackson, E.L. (1990). Variations in Desire to Begin a Leisure Activity: Evidence of Antecedent Constraints. *Journal of Leisure Research, 22,* 55-70.

Jaggar, A.M. (1991). Feminist Ethics: Projects, Problems, Prospects. In C. Card (Ed.), *Feminist Ethics,* (pp. 78-104). Lawrence: University Press of Kansas.

Kimmel, M.S., and M. A. Messner (Eds.). (1989). *Men's Lives.* New York: Macmillan.

Lenskyj, H. (1988). Measured Time: Women, Sport, and Leisure. *Leisure Studies, 7,* 233-240.

Lerner, G. (1975). Placing Women in History: Definitions and Challenges. *Feminist Studies, 3,* 5-14.

Lynch, R. (1991, July). *The Cultural Repositioning of Rugby League Football in Australia.* Paper presented to the World Leisure and Recreation Association Congress, Sydney, Australia.

Parker, S. (1972). *The Future of Work and Leisure.* London: Granada.

Radford-Hill, S. (1986). Considering Feminism as a Model for Social Change. In T. DeLauretis (Ed.). *Feminist Studies/Critical Studies* (pp. 157-172). Bloomington, IN: Indiana University Press.

Rhode, D.L. (Ed.) (1990). *Theoretical Perspectives on Sexual Difference.* New Haven: Yale University Press.

Rothenberg, P. (1990). The Construction, Deconstruction, and Reconstruction of Difference. *Hypatia, 5*(1), 42-57.

Samdahl, D. M. (1992, October). *The Effect of Gender Socialization on Labeling Experience as "Leisure."* Paper presented to the NRPA Leisure Research Symposium, Cincinnati, OH.

Samdahl, D. M., and D. A. Kleiber (1989). Self-Awareness and Leisure Experience. *Leisure Sciences, 11*(1), 1-10.

Scott, J. W. (1986). Gender: A Useful Category of Historical Analysis. *American Historical Review, 91,* 1053-1075.

Searle, M. S., and E. L. Jackson (1985). Socioeconomic Variations in Perceived Barriers to Recreation Participation Among Would-Be Participants. *Leisure Sciences, 7,* 227-249.

Shaw, S.M. (1984). The Measurement of Leisure: A Quality of Life Issue. *Loisir et Societe/Society & Leisure, 7,* 91-107.

Shaw, S.M. (1985a). Gender and Leisure: Inequality in the Distribution of Leisure Time. *Journal of Leisure Research, 17*(4), 266-292.

Shaw, S. M. (1985b). The Meaning of Leisure in Everyday Life. *Leisure Sciences, 7*(1), 1-24.

Shaw, S.M. (in press). Gender, Leisure, and Constraints: Towards a Framework for the Analysis of Women's Leisure. *Journal of Leisure Research, 26*(2)

Shaw, S.M., A. Bonen, and J. F. McCabe (1991). Do More Constraints Mean Less Leisure? Examining the Relationship Between Constraints and Participation. *Journal of Leisure Research, 23*(4), 286-300.

Tetreault, M.K. (1985). Feminist Phase Theory: An Experience-Derived Evaluation Model. *Journal of Higher Education, 56* (4), 364-384.

Thompson, S. (1992). "Mum's Tennis Day": The Gendered Definition of Older Women's Leisure. *Loisir & Societe/Society and Leisure, 15*(1), 271-290.

Wearing, B. (1990). Beyond the Ideology of Motherhood: Leisure and Resistance. *Australian and New Zealand Journal of Sociology, 26,* 36-58.

Wearing, B. (1992). Leisure and Women's Identity in Late Adolescence: Constraints and Opportunities. *Loisir & Societe/Society & Leisure, 15*(1), 323-342.

Wearing, B. M., and S. L. Wearing (1988). All in a Day's Leisure: Gender and the Concept of Leisure. *Leisure Studies, 7,* 111-123.

Wimbush, E., & M. Talbot (Eds). (1988). *Relative Freedoms.* Milton Keynes: Open University Press.

Whitson, D., and D. Macintosh (1989). Gender and Power: Explanations of Gender Inequalities in Canadian National Sport Organizations. *International Review of Sociology of Sport, 24*(2) 137-150.

Leisure Programs and Services for Older Adults

Past, Present, and Future Research

Richard D. MacNeil
Department of Sport, Health, Leisure and Physical Studies
————————— University of Iowa —————————

INTRODUCTION

In what has become almost a cliche around college campuses, a story is often told about a philosophy professor whose final examination required students to respond in one page or less to the following question: "Take a position for or against Truth. Prove the validity of your position." While not quite analogous to this story, the invitation to produce a meaningful treatise on a topic as broad as the history and future of research regarding leisure programs and services for older adults within strict editorial limits is indeed a challenge.

While the total volume of such research is not necessarily overwhelming, it is the scope and breadth of the research which makes its synthesis difficult. The leisure phenomena as experienced by older adults is multidimensional. Consequently, literature entries have been made in such diverse disciplines as sociology, psychology, economics, and political science to name a few. Moreover, the rapidly expanding field of gerontology has produced a growing body of leisure-related articles in a wide variety of publications.

Given this situation, the need for parameters to guide the development of this paper is obvious. First, to the degree to which it is possible, priority will be given to the review of articles/studies which have been printed in journals and books which have a specific leisure/recreation focus (e.g., Journal of Leisure Research (JLR), Therapeutic Recreation Journal (TRJ), Activities, Adaptation and Aging (AAA). Second, the term "research" will be broadly interpreted and publications which are deemed important but which may be philosophical or atheoretical in nature, will also be included in this review. Finally, the author will exercise personal discretion with respect to chronological time and divide the paper into the following three frames: (1) the Past, the 1930s through the mid-1970s; (2) the Present, mid-1970s through the early-1990s; and (3) the Future, the 1990s and projections into the next decade.

THE PAST: 1930s TO THE MID-1970s

The Social Security Act and Its Impact

The historical roots of leisure with respect to older adults has been ascribed to the passage of the Social Security Act in 1935 (Bell, 1976). In the first few decades following its initial passage, an increasing number of writers (e.g., Caplow, 1954; Morse & Weiss, 1955) responded to questions/problems related to the newly acquired leisure status of older people. According to Bell, a critical question addressed by researchers during this period was whether or not leisure, in the form of retirement, would "impose a new and negatively valued burden upon the elderly" (1976, p. 51).

The emergence of research directed toward leisure and older adults began in earnest during the 1950s. While the issue of retirement and the concomitant expansion in unobligated time remained the preeminent topic of concern for investigators, several new questions began to receive attention. These questions included: (1) How might leisure experiences contribute to successful retirement?; (2) What are the leisure interests and participation patterns of older adults and what factors may influence these interests and patterns?; (3) How might these patterns be affected by different environmental settings?

Research Themes: Leisure and Successful Retirement

According to Bell (1976), by the late 1950s the concept of retirement had changed from a life event to a social process. As a process, retirement assumed the character of a social role. It is in this context that the two most prominent and widely publicized theories related to successful adjustment to later life were developed. The first of these, the Disengagement Theory, hypothesized that high levels of life satisfaction in old age are associated with older persons reducing the number and importance of societal roles (Cumming & Henry, 1961). When viewed from the perspective of leisure involvement, the Disengagement Theory suggests that successful aging involves the gradual withdrawal from the activities and interactions that marked middle adulthood.

In direct contrast, the Activity Theory was formulated by Burgess (1960), as an application of symbolic interaction theory to social gerontology. As explained by Ward, Activity Theory suggests that "personal satisfaction depends on a positive self-image which is validated through continued active participation in middle-aged roles" (1979, p. 104). With respect to leisure, the implication of the Activity Theory is that the greater the level of activity involvement, the greater the life satisfaction, and that the more roles that are lost and not replaced, the greater the drop in life satisfaction (Havighurst, Neugarten, & Tobin, 1968).

Debate regarding the validity of the two theories became a persistent theme in gerontological literature during the 1960s and 1970s. Numerous researchers (e.g., Maddox & Eisdorfer, 1962; Maddox, 1963; Lemon, Bengston & Peterson, 1972; DeCarlo, 1974; Graney, 1975; Peppers, 1977) addressed this issue in their work, most often with inconsistent and conflicting results. It should be noted that attempts to compare findings between these studies have proved futile owing to wide variations in methodology and analytical approaches. Interestingly, the two theories which produced this sudden surge of research were both primarily based on data derived from the Kansas City studies of the 1950s.

A third explanation of the relationship between leisure and successful adjustment to retirement was proposed by Atchley in 1971. Atchley's Identity Continuity Theory was offered as a direct response to an earlier work by Miller (1965) who suggested that retirement produced an identity crisis for most people because leisure roles cannot replace job roles as a source of self-respect. It is Atchley's contention, however, that retirement does not produce a dramatic change in sources of self-identity and that "leisure can be one of the greatest sources of continuity across the lifespan" (1977, p. 177). Leisure, therefore, can be a major contributor to successful retirement.

Research Themes: Leisure Interests and Patterns

In a pioneering work published in 1960, Max Kaplan explored trends in American leisure patterns and their implications to older persons. His call for increased research dealing with the leisure patterns of older adults was heeded by a number of authors. Some of these works were aimed at uncovering the range of leisure choices available to seniors (Stafford, 1957). Other works (e.g., Cordroy, 1965; Gross, 1963) addressed the benefits derived from leisure activity participation by older citizens. Still others were concerned with the identification of factors which influenced or restricted the choice of activities of seniors (e.g., Horton, 1959; Hoar, 1961; James, 1958).

In one of the first studies which utilized an interview format to explore the specific activities of older adults, Cowgill and Baulch (1962) found that the leisure patterns of their subjects were dominated by home-centered and family-oriented activities. This finding proved to be consistent with the research completed by Ford (1962) in her analysis of the activities and interests of older residents in eight cities in Indiana and also with the data obtained in a study by the U.S. Department of Health, Education, and Welfare (1963). Among the most popular pastimes identified in these studies were television viewing, visiting for pleasure, reading, hobbies, and church-related activities.

One of the major changes in this era of research endeavors was a decline in the negative associations of leisure. According to Bell (1976, p. 153), by the 1960s "leisure came to be viewed not as a unique experience in the life of the retired, but rather as an extension or continuation of a previously-developed pattern of behavior." Evidence supporting this view was produced in the studies of Zborowski (1962), and Desroches and Kaiman (1964).

Research Themes: Leisure Patterns and Programs, the Environment as a Variable

The influence of various environmental settings upon the leisure patterns of seniors began to capture the attention of investigators during the late 1960s. Bultena and Wood (1970) for example, studied 322 retired men in the four planned retirement communities in Arizona and found that continuity existed in the pre- and post-retirement activity levels of subjects and that their retirement itself was more often prompted by a desire for increased leisure than was that of persons remaining in their home communities. Cross-sectional participation surveys of outdoor activities were conducted by the Outdoor Resources Review Commission in 1960, 1965, and 1972. In addition, there was a rapid increase in the number of publications dealing with leisure programs in the nursing home setting. Most of the early papers dealing with recreation in nursing homes tended to be philosophically oriented with a strong emphasis upon establishing the need for such services (e.g., Routh, 1967, 1970; Hardie, 1970) or, examinations of the current status of such services (e.g., Tague, 1968, 1970; Peters & Verhoven, 1970). A few investigations, however, reported positive effects resulting from the implementation of leisure programs with nursing home residents (e.g., Jewell, 1967; Reichenfeld, et al., 1973; deLerma-Salter, 1975).

Summary: "The Past"

The years between 1930 and 1975 witnessed an ever-expanding literature base in terms of the study of aging with leisure as a variable. This expansion was marked by increases in the total quantity of published papers, in the areas of investigation, and in the development of more sophisticated research designs. These advances enabled researchers to begin to formulate viable theories that were more analytical in nature. However, despite this growth, in the mid-1970s our empirical knowledge of leisure and its implications to older adults remained limited at best, and most of the information we had garnered grew from the work of individuals associated with non-leisure disciplines and published in non-leisure-oriented publications.

THE PRESENT: MID-1970s- EARLY 1990s

Growth and Expansion

The decision to select the decade of the mid-1970s to early-1990s as representing "The Present" in this paper is based upon a number of important demographic trends and professional developments which came together during this period. Although demographers had long suggested that America "was graying," it was not until the 1970s that the implications of this trend finally began to impact social policy. With the number of people over age 65 exceeding 20 million and the growth of advocacy groups (e.g., American Association of Retired Persons, The Grey Panthers, Senior Citizens Coalition) dedicated to representing the collective interests of the elderly, the American public continually pressured policy makers to expand services and programs for the aged. In response, federal funding for service and research on aging increased dramatically during the 1970s (Poon & Welford, 1980).

Paralleling this movement, the field of recreation and leisure became established as a legitimate human service profession during the 1970s. University programs dedicated to educating leisure professionals grew rapidly. After several formative decades, a generation of researchers with a distinct leisure orientation began to emerge. Fueled by the nation-wide interest in older adults, the growing commitment of the federal government to the provision of services to the elderly, and the emergence of leisure scientists and service providers, a profound transition in the nature of research on aging and leisure occurred. This transition is nowhere more evident than in the expansion of the publication marketplace.

Prior to 1975 recreation researchers were limited to publishing their studies in only a few leisure journals (e.g., JLR, TRJ). Between the mid-1970s and the mid-1980s, however, there was a dramatic proliferation in this market. Since 1979, for instance, all of the following leisure and aging books have been published: Kaplan (1979); Shivers and Fait (1980); Teague, MacNeil and Hitzhusen (1982); Osgood (1982); National Recreation and Park Association (1983); Teaff (1985); Leitner and Leitner (1985); Carruthers, et al. (1986); Foster (1986); MacNeil and Teague (1987 and 1992); Keller (1990); Elliott and Sorg-Elliott (1991); and Arrigo, Lewis, and Mattimore (1992).

In terms of journals, the *JLR*, which had published only one leisure and aging study prior to 1976, printed eight between 1976 and 1985, and seven additional works between 1986 and 1992. The *TRJ* published 25 articles on this topic between 1976 and 1985 and featured a special issue dedicated to this topic in 1980. Since 1986, another 22 manuscripts focused upon older adults have been published by the *TRJ*. *Parks and Recreation* produced two special issues on aging in 1981 and 1986 and published over two dozen papers on the subject during the 1980s, and Activities, Adaptation and Aging, established in 1980 is oriented specifically toward the production of empirical, theoretical, and programmatic articles on leisure and aging.

Subjects of Investigation: Retirement

As the outlets for publication expanded, so too did the volume of research being completed. Interestingly, however, the topics being investigated had not changed noticeably from previous times. Retirement, the cornerstone of most early studies, continued to be explored by researchers, although the focus of their work was somewhat different. Noting that the hypothesized social and psychological traumas associated with retirement had not materialized in research findings, Atchley (1976) theorized that those problems that do come with retirement are not so much a product of the inability of individuals to cope psychologically and/or physically with retirement, but instead are flaws in the retirement preparation system.

The theme that society should better prepare individuals for the retirement process was prevalent in the 1980s. In one theoretical paper, Kleiber and Thompson (1980) presented a thoughtful literature review of factors that influence adjustment to retirement and discussed implications for the development of pre-retirement education programs. Weiner provided an overview of a pre-retirement education program that focused on the role of leisure planning in two separate publications (1980, 1981). Tedrick discussed leisure competency in a 1983 work. In addition, Kaminski-da Roza discussed the process known as "phased retirement" as an alternative strategy for preparing the worker for the role of retiree (1985).

More recently, Singleton and Keddy (1991a, 1991b) authored a pair of articles based upon an investigation of the perceptions of employees of a Canadian university regarding retirement. There was a general agreement among subjects that the topic of leisure, including the use of free time and the selection of leisure activities, should be included in a pre-retirement preparation program. This suggestion was supported by Ginsberg (1988) who proposed a three-step approach to developing a personal-ized leisure program for retirees. In another recent paper, Blanding (1992) developed a thoughtful rationale for the inclusion of the leisure service profession in pre-retirement planning.

An important empirical study concerned with the impact of retirement on leisure participation was reported by Glamser and Hayslip (1985). The researchers, who conducted this six-year longitudinal study utilizing 110 male retirees, found evidence which suggested that leisure involvement prior to retirement was an important factor in retirement activity and adjustment. This finding is consistent with results obtained by Peppers (1976) and Bosse and Ekerdt (1981).

Subjects of Investigation: Life Satisfaction

As our knowledge of the adjustment process associated with retirement grew, leisure researchers increasingly began to focus on the broader dimension of life satisfaction in later life. A primary concern of these investigations was upon the potential relationship of leisure and the subjective well-being of seniors. In a comprehensive review of literature published on this subject, Baack (1985) found considerable support for activity and social interaction as major factors related to life satisfaction in seniors. Baack's conclusion, which was drawn primarily from non-recre-ation sources, is generally supported by leisure-oriented re-search as well.

Ragheb and Griffith, for instance, focused on the contribu-tion of leisure activity participation and leisure satisfaction to life satisfaction of older individuals. In essence, the researchers concluded that for their subjects, the higher the frequency of participation in leisure activities, the higher the life satisfaction; the more the leisure participation, the higher the leisure satisfaction and the greater the leisure satisfaction, the greater the life satisfaction (1982). They further produced data that suggested that leisure satisfaction (the meaning, attitude or quality of leisure) contributed much more to the life satisfaction of seniors than did simple leisure participation. This finding is consistent with the conclusion reached by Russell (1987) whose results indicated that frequency of participation in recreation activities has no significant relationship to life satisfaction in retirement, but satisfaction with recreation activities does have a significant and positive relationship even when compared to the variables of gender, age, marital status, income and mobility. Studies conducted by Mancini and Orthner (1980); TerBurgh and Teaff (1986); Agostino, Gash and Martinsen (1981); and Mishra (1992) produced additional evidence which suggests that personally satisfying recreational activities can have a positive effect upon the perceived life satisfaction of retirement-aged individuals.

Using a sample consisting entirely of older women, Riddick and Daniel also found the existence of a significant relationship between increases in leisure participation and increases in life satisfaction (1984). A similar conclusion was offered by Romsa, Bondy and Blenman (1985). However, in contrast, Salamon (1985) found evidence that indicated that affiliation, not active involvement, was more positively related to life satisfaction. This finding suggests that life satisfaction is far too complex of a concept to be simply defined by a single variable or theory.

With most research supporting a relationship between the two concepts, one might ask why leisure may be a vital contributor to the life satisfaction of retirees? Studies conducted using older adult subjects have consistently produced findings that indicate that through the provision of choice, perceptions of control can be positively affected (Mannell, Zuzanek, & Larson, 1988; Shary & Iso-Ahola, 1989; Purcell & Keller, 1989). More significantly, four studies, one conducted by Peppers (1976), another by Ray (1979), a third by MacTavish and Searle (1991) and a fourth by Savell (1991) have shown that perceived control over activity choices can have a positive influence on the life satisfaction and well-being of older adults.

Iso-Ahola and Weissinger have summarized the evidence as follows:

Empirical research leaves little doubt about the fact that intrinsically motivated leisure is positively and significantly related to psychological or mental health. Those who are in control of their leisure lives and experiences and feel engaged in and committed to leisure activities and experiences are psychologically healthier than those who are not in control over their leisure lives and feel detached and uncommitted (1984, p. 41).

Subjects of Investigation: Leisure Participation Patterns

Studies conducted to explore the leisure participation patterns of the elderly became more prevalent during the 1970s and 80s. As Howe has observed, these studies tended to be descriptive, enumerating either the amount of time spent engaging in leisure activities, the variety or types of activities pursued, or the frequency in which people engaged in leisure (1985, p. 9). Representative of these investigations were the works of Gordon, Gaitz and Scott (1976), Scott and Zoerink (1977), McAvoy (1979), Singleton (1984) and Thornton and Collins (1986). Although methodological differences make comparisions between these studies somewhat tentative, it can be generally stated that older adults report participating in activities that are more sedentary, home-centered, and informal than do adults of younger ages (MacNeil, et al., 1987).

While the studies identified above generally used a broad cross-section of the elderly population, other investigators began to focus on more specific segments of this group. Morgan and Godbey (1978), for instance, found that while the number of activities participated in dropped slightly, the frequency of participation in activities actually increased among subjects who had entered an age-segregated environment. Also using a population who resided in an age-segregated environment, Russell (1987) found that the most frequently participated in forms of recreation included those involving the mass media (i.e., watching TV, reading newspapers), social activities (visiting friends, attending parties), and cultural activities (i.e., dancing, theater attendance).

Blazey (1984) reported on the use of two theme parks by elders, and Keller (1984) focused on the activities of centenarians. Both Kivett and Orthner (1980) and Heinemann, et al. (1988) found that the leisure preferences of rural elderly with visual impairments showed considerable similarity to the general population of rural elderly.

Strain and Chappell's work (1982) on outdoor recreation patterns of rural elderly found that the subjects favored outdoor pursuits that were sedentary in nature and required little physical exertion. In perhaps the most comprehensive study of rural aged, Mobily, et al. found evidence that suggested: (1) higher level of leisure activity involvement among elderly than had been implied in past studies (1984); (2) generally positive attitudes toward leisure among rural aged (1984); and (3) that age, self-perceived health, leisure attitude, life satisfaction and sex were the most influential factors associated with the leisure repertoires of their subjects (1986).

A number of researchers have also addressed the topic of barriers to leisure participation. Such investigations have been primarily descriptive in nature and oriented toward a pragmatic concern about what prohibits older individuals from participating in desired leisure activities (Howe, 1985). Among the works completed on this topic are McGuire (1981, 1982, 1984), Scott and Zoerink (1977), Godbey and Blazey (1983), Strain and Chappell (1982), Mobily, et al. (1984), and Buchanan and Allen (1985). The data reported in these studies generally suggest that lack of time, money, transportation, and companions, fear of crime, and poor health present the major barriers to the leisure participation of the elderly. Similarly, Mobily, et al. (1993) found that participation in physical activity by elderly subjects was significantly affected by weather conditions.

Subjects of Investigation: Recreation Programming

An extensive volume of literature addressing the development and delivery of recreation programs was produced during this period. The overwhelming majority of these publications were intended for a non-scientific audience and thus, they typically highlighted specific activities or participant characteristics. A large percentage of the aging papers printed in the *Journal of Leisureability, Activities, Adaptation and Aging,* and *Therapeutic Recreation Journal* are of this nature.

Much of this work has been completed utilizing an institutionalized population and long-term care setting. For example, Mobily (1981) explored the attitudes of institutionalized aged towards physical activity and developed a series of objectives for such programs in this setting. Backman and Mannell (1986) utilized a leisure counseling program to produce a positive change in attitudes toward leisure in a total care facility. Other researchers have studied approaches to increasing attendance at recreational activities (Gillespie, et al., 1984), while McGuire investigated the preferences of aged subjects toward recreational leaders and co-participants (1985), and the effects of the use of video games on the quality of life of residents (1984). Card (1989) studied the effect of an organized recreation program on the perceived leisure functioning of six mentally ill elderly living in a nursing home. Forsythe (1989) examined a variety of therapeutic activities that could be utilized for isolated residents in long-term care settings.

The use of recreational activities and programs with disoriented older individuals has also received increasing attention. Portnoy (1992), for example, has outlined a host of reminiscence activities that are applicable to a residential care environment. In their text on recreation programming for older adults (1991), Elliott and Sorg-Elliott provide a helpful chapter on working with confused clients. Perhaps the most substantive work in this area has been produced by Caroline Weiss who in a series of articles (1987, 1989, 1990) has offered a variety of creative and effective ideas for recreation programming for disoriented seniors.

Finally, perceived satisfaction with recreation programs was studied by Riddick and DeSchriver (1984) and Hupp (1986). In the first work, the researchers found that an outdoor day camp experience was satisfying to nursing home residents despite the fact that the activity professionals offering the program assessed the experience as not being satisfying to the residents. The 294 non-institutionalized female subjects of the second study associated leisure program satisfaction with qualities such as Achievement, Relaxation, and Environment.

Subjects of Investigation: Implications of Societal Aging and the Leisure Service Profession

Recognition of the fact that we are rapidly becoming a "grey society" has led to the publication of a growing number of papers dedicated to exploring the possible implications of this trend for the leisure service profession. As representative of this, during the past three years, *Parks and Recreation* has published three papers that explore the theoretical linkage between aging and the profession (i.e., McCormick, 1991; Kelley, 1992; & Penalta & Uysal, 1993). Similarly, two recent papers have examined various sociodemographic variables associated with the "baby boom generation" and discussed these in reference to possible implications for leisure programming in the future (MacNeil, 1991a; Tedrick & MacNeil, 1991). In addition, the status of gerontological content in professional preparation programs in recreation and leisure studies curriculum (MacNeil, 1991b) and hospitality management curriculum (MacNeil, Ego, & Mobily, 1993) has been studied. The last two investigations found a veritable dearth of academic preparation with respect to the aging process and older adults. Possible explanations for this finding are varied, but one relevant fact is the noted reluctance of future leisure service professionals to work with older adults (MacNeil, et al., 1990; Barber & Magafas, 1992).

Summary: The Present

In comparison to the previous period, there were several significant developments between the mid-1970s and early 1990s. Among the most profound was the emergence of leisure-oriented writers/researchers interested in the phenomena of aging and older adults, and the development of a marketplace for the dissemination of their works. Although the topic of retirement remained of interest, the debate over its impact upon an individual's self-identity gave way to other leisure-related themes. Investigations dealing with leisure and life satisfaction and leisure patterns and preferences of the aged added much to our body of knowledge. But while the total volume of literature on leisure and aging grew during this time, the actual percentage of these published works that are based upon scientific examination remain minimal. Moreover, of the printed research, most was descriptive in nature and geared toward pragmatic concerns (e.g., improving program attendance, describing participation rates), which have little explanatory or predictive value. Further, a trend of having research follow theory seemed to develop during this period.

THE FUTURE

The final segment of this paper offers projections about the aging and leisure research agenda for the remainder of the century. This section will be divided into two topic areas. First, projections based upon emerging demographic trends will be discussed. Next, trends identified in a review of recent publications will be used to project directions for future work. Suggestions with respect to potential research topics and methodologies will be offered.

Projections Based on Demography

The most obvious of demographic trends is the expected growth in the size of the elderly population. While there were only three million Americans 65 or older in 1900, this age group surpassed the 25 million mark in the early 1980s and is projected to rise to close to 65 million by the year 2050. On the surface alone, these figures suggest that the leisure service profession must prepare itself to meet burgeoning numbers of older consumers. In order to do this, continued efforts to understand and predict the leisure needs and behaviors of seniors must be undertaken. However, rather than using the traditional cross-sectional, descriptive techniques that used age as a variable to determine leisure patterns, researchers might consider examining this problem from the life cycle or life stage approach. Such an approach will likely prove to be a more reliable predictor of leisure patterns than chronological age (e.g., Kelly, 1978; Witt & Goodale, 1981; Buchanan & Allen, 1985; Mobily, 1987; Butcher, 1993; Witt & Jackson, 1993).

In addition, it is significant to note that the most rapid of late life growth is occurring in the age 80 and over subgroup. As the susceptibility to disabling conditions increases with age, we can predict that the number of aged persons who have severe functional deficits will continue to increase in forthcoming years. Consequently, investigations designed to explore the impact of functional impairments on the leisure patterns of older adults are needed. In addition, research designed to increase the effectiveness of leisure services to "at-risk" populations in the community (e.g., Leitner & Merenbloom, 1979; Wilhite, 1987) as well as in long-term care settings must be undertaken (Byrd, 1983; Savell, 1991). For this latter group, the "efficacy approach," originally proposed in leisure literature by Iso-Ahola (1980a, b), seems to be a particularly appropriate theoretical model for consideration.

Another trend that merits attention concerns the changing sociocultural status of older persons. Evidence clearly indicates that present retirement-age adults are healthier, better educated and more financially stable than were their peers of previous generations (Dychwald, 1990). In practical terms this means that our existing knowledge base about seniors may need continual updating. Godbey suggested that these changes are likely to mean that seniors in the future "will participate in a broader range of leisure behavior than did previous generations. . ." (1983, pp. 82-83). Although some projections have been made about the types of leisure services which may grow in demand as "baby boomers" age (i.e., MacNeil, 1991a; Tedrick & MacNeil, 1991), the basis for the predictions are intuitive rather than empirical. Quantitative research must be conducted to help determine which variables have the highest predictive value in regard to the leisure behavior of future generations of seniors.

Finally, the landmark decision by the federal government to repeal mandatory retirement presents a new challenge to leisure researchers. The new reality is that for most individuals the decision to retire can now be based upon personal choice rather than company policy. What will be the impact of leisure attitudes and behaviors upon the decision to retire? Will the reported relationship between leisure satisfaction and life satisfaction (e.g., Ragheb & Griffith, 1982; Riddick & Daniel, 1984; Romsa, et al., 1985; Russell, 1987) remain as significant among persons over 65 who continue to work? Will leisure-oriented preretirement programs (e.g., McGhee, 1987; Weiner, 1980, 1981) continue to proliferate? Each of these questions needs further inquiry.

Projections Based on Literature Review

Recent years have witnessed a persistent call for increased sophistication in leisure-oriented research (e.g., Ragheb, 1984; Kelly, 1986). As was mentioned repeatedly, the volume of scientifically-based research in aging and leisure is small and what exists is primarily atheoretical in nature and descriptive by design. In a discipline as grounded in a service mission as is ours, there will always be a place for applied research. Nonetheless, there is a need for more basic research to help establish theoretical underpinnings for the field which can then guide further scientific inquiries. This author would agree with Godbey's (1983) assessment that increased emphasis should be placed on longitudinal research. In addition, single-subject methodology (i.e., Dattilo, 1986) is especially well-suited to clinical research in the long-term care setting. The need for replication of existing studies is also evident.

Paralleling the national emphasis placed upon preventative health, there has been a recent proliferation of leisure literature addressing this topic with older populations (e.g., Emery & Blumenthal, 1990; Teague, 1987; Keller, 1986; DiGilio & Howze, 1984; Riddick & Freitag, 1984). The philosophical context upon which most of these works are based is that individuals can influence their state of health through lifestyle management. While the assumptions behind this approach are scientifically well established in disciplines like exercise physiology, research directed toward evaluating the leisure profession's contribution to this process is limited. It is easy to speculate about the positive relationship between leisure, health and aging, but without scientific testing, we are limited to conjecture!

As the number of aged confined to long-term care continues to rise, increased interest in the application of leisure services to confused and disoriented elderly has been evident in the literature (e.g., Mobily & Hoeft, 1985; Weiss & Kronbert, 1986; Weiss & Thurn, 1987; Weiss, 1989; Weiss, et al., 1990). Given demographic data about projected increases in the over 80 population, the need for more information about leisure's role in the prevention management and treatment of cognitively impaired persons is evident.

Considerable attention has been given to the need for improvement in the professional preparation (and certification) of those who work with older adults (e.g., MacLean, 1983; Binkley, 1983; MacNeil, 1984; MacNeil & Barber, 1986; MacNeil, et al., 1990). There is a need for researchers to identify competencies required by those who work with the aged, and to test methods that might best be utilized to develop these competencies in the future. In addition, the need for more opportunities to integrate gerontological content into leisure and recreation coursework is evident (MacNeil, 1991b; MacNeil, et al., 1993).

There is also an obvious void in the literature with respect to various ethnic and racial minorities. This is particularly true in light of the fact that the number of racial/ethnic minority elderly, including black/African Americans and Hispanics, are projected to grow at a rate faster than the general elderly population in the U.S. Most of our knowledge regarding the leisure behavior of older adults has been drawn from descriptive, cross-sectional studies. In almost all cases, chronological age was used as a variable in this stratification approach. Since minority elderly are not distributed randomly throughout the country or in metropolitan areas, it is likely that they have been under-represented in research conducted thus far. Few references could be found in leisure and recreation literature dealing with minority elderly (e.g., Ego, 1983; Creecy, Wright & Berg, 1982; Brooks-Lambing, 1972; Holmes, et al., 1979; Allison & Smith, 1990). Consequently, research efforts devoted to studying the leisure needs, patterns and preferences of older minority individuals is warranted.

Finally, another population that has been largely ignored in terms of aging-related needs and habits are individuals with developmental disabilities. The publication of the text, Activities with Developmentally Disabled Elderly and Older Adults (Keller, 1990), provided a general conceptual overview of this subject to leisure service audiences. Empirical investigations remain rare, although the pioneering work of Hawkins (1991; 1993) has added much to our knowledge base in this field. The expansion and replication of such work certainly merits attention in future years.

CLOSING COMMENTARY

As stated in the introduction, the charge given this paper required the writer to synthesize the evolution and projected future of research on the topic of leisure and aging. A strict editorial policy on page limit immeasurably affected the direction of the project. As such, the final product is marked by a shotgun analysis of past and future trends. Generalizations abound! Oftentimes, the desire to provide a critical commentary on a study had to be sacrificed for the sake of brevity.

Upon completion, however, two overwhelming impressions emerge. The first is that our knowledge of the leisure phenomenon and its relationship to aging individuals has experienced rapid advancement in a relatively short period of time. This growth in knowledge is highlighted by the proliferation of printed papers, of leisure-oriented writers and researchers, and markets for publication. The second impression is that so much of our new-found knowledge must be described as speculative at best. The simple truth is that most of what we accept as fact has not been obtained by, or subjected to, rigorous scientific inquiry.

As a consequence, it would seem relatively easy to be critical of the state of the art in aging and leisure research. However, such an assessment ignores a fundamental principle; the acquisition of knowledge is a painstakingly slow process. It is not surprising that most of the existing theories about aging which are addressed by leisure writers are products of systematic inquiry in such disciplines as sociology, psychology, or biology; disciplines whose roots run far deeper than our own. In comparison, the leisure discipline remains in its infancy. While this is not to excuse our profession's noticeable slowness in advancing knowledge through scientific investigation, this writer, for one, is optimistic about the future of leisure-oriented research in relation to aging and older adults.

BIBLIOGRAPHY

Agostino, J., Gash, T., and J. Martinsen (1981). The Relationship Between Recreational Activity Programs and Life Satisfaction of Residents of Thunder Bay Homes for the Aged. *Activities, Adaptation and Aging, 1,* 4, 5-16.

Allison, M., and S. Smith (1990). Leisure and the Quality of Life Issues Facing Racial and Minority Elderly. *Therapeutic Recreation Journal, 25,* (4), 9-28.

Arrigo, S., A. Lewis, and H. Mattimore (1992). *Beyond Bingo: Innovative Programs for the New Senior.* State College, PA: Venture Publishing, Inc.

Atchley, R. (1971). Retirement and Leisure Participation: Continuity or Crisis? *The Gerontologist, 11,* 11-17.

Atchley, R. (1976). *The Sociology of Retirement.* New York: Schenkman.

Atchley, R. (1977). *The Social Forces in Later Life (2nd ed.),* Belmont, CA: Wadsworth Publishing Company.

Baack, S. (1985). Life Satisfaction among Older Persons: A Review of the Literature. *Leisure Commentary and Practice, 3,* 1 and 2.

Backman, S., and R. Mannell (1986). Removing Attitudinal Barriers to Leisure Behavior and Satisfaction: A Field Experiment among the Institutionalized Elderly. *Therapeutic Recreation Journal, 20,* 3, 46-53.

Barber, E., and A. Magafas (1992). Therapeutic Recreation Majors' Work Preference. *Therapeutic Recreation Journal, 26* (4), 53-54.

Bell, B.D. (Ed.). (1976). *Contemporary Social Gerontology: Significant Developments in the Field of Gerontology.* Springfield, IL: Charles C. Thomas.

Binkley, A. (1983). Continuing Education for Personnel Serving the Aged. *Aging and Leisure* (pp. 115-119). Alexandria, VA: National Recreation and Parks Association.

Blanding, C. (1992). Planning for Retirement: Can We Help? *Parks and Recreation, 27,* (3), 36-40.

Blazey, M.A. (1984). Theme Park Use by Older Persons: An Exploratory Investigation. *Abstracts from the 1984 Symposium on Leisure Research, 97.*

Bosse, R., and D. Ekerdt (1981). Change in Self-Perception of Leisure Activities with Retirement. *The Gerontologist, 21,* 650-654.

Brooks-Lambing, M. (1972). Leisure Time Pursuits Among Retired Blacks by Social Status. *The Gerontologist, 12,* 63-69.

Buchanan, T., and L. Allen (1985). Barriers to Recreation Participation in Later Life Cycle Stages. *Therapeutic Recreation Journal, 14,* 3, 39-50.

Bultena, G., and V. Wood (1970, Winter). Leisure Orientation and Recreational Activities of Retirement Community Residents. *Journal of Leisure Research, 2,* 3-14.

Burgess, E.W. (1960). *Aging in Western Societies.* Chicago: University of Chicago Press.

Butcher, J. (1993). Physical Leisure Through the Lifespan: The Case of the Master's Swimmer. *Proceedings of the 7th Canadian Congress in Leisure Research, 155-158.*

Byrd, M. (1983). Letting the Inmates Run the Asylum: The Effects of Control and Choice on the Institutional Lives of Older Adults. *Activities, Adaptation and Aging, 3,* 3, 3-11.

Caplow, T. (1954). *Sociology of Work.* Minneapolis: University of Minnesota Press.

Card, J. (1989). Perceived Leisure Functioning of Nursing Home Patients: Does Recreation Make a Difference? *Activities, Adaptation and Aging, 13,* 1/2), 29-40.

Carruthers, C., I. Sneegas and C. Ashton-Shaeffer (1986). *Therapeutic Recreation: Guidelines for Activity Services in Long-Term Care.* Urbana, IL: University of Illinois at Urbana-Champaign.

Cordroy, E. (1965). *The Need for Health Activities and Social Services Through Recreation for Senior Citizens in Azusa*. Master's thesis. California State College of Los Angeles.

Cowgill, D., and N. Baulch (1962). The Use of Leisure Time by Older People. *The Gerontologist, 2*, 47-50.

Creecy, R., R. Wright, and W. Berg (1982). Correlates of Loneliness Among Black Elderly. *Activities, Adaptation and Aging, 3*, 2, 9-16.

Cumming, E., and W. Henry (1961). *Growing Old: The Process of Disengagement*. New York: Basic Books.

Dattilo, J. (1986). Single-Subject Research in Therapeutic Recreation: Applications to Individuals with Disabilities. *Therapeutic Recreation Journal, 29*, 1, 76-87.

DeCarlo, T. (1974). Recreation Participation Patterns and Successful Aging. *Journal of Gerontology, 20*, 416-422.

deLerma-Salter, C., and C. Salter (1975). Effects of an Individualized Activity Program on Elderly Patients. *The Gerontologist, 15*, 404-408.

Desroches, H., and B. Kalman (1964, April). Stability of Activity Participation in an Aged Population. *Journal of Gerontology, 19*, 211-214.

DiGilio, D., and E. Howze (1984). Fitness and Full Living for Older Adults. *Parks and Recreation, 19*, 12, 32-37.

Dychtwald, K. (1990). *Age wave*. New York: Bantam Books.

Ego, M. (1983). Triple Jeopardy: The Urgent Need for Humanistic Delivery of Leisure Services to the Minority Elderly. *Leisure and Aging* (pp. 128-134). Alexandria, VA: National Recreation and Park Association.

Elliott, J.E., and J. Sorg-Elliott (1991). *Recreation Programming and Activities for Older Adults*. State College, PA: Venture Publishing Co.

Emery, C., and J. Blumenthal (1990). Perceived Change Among Participants in an Exercise Program for Older Adults. *Gerontologist, 30* (4), 516-521.

Ford, P. (1962). *An Analysis of Leisure Time Activities and Interests of Aged Residents of Indiana*. Doctoral dissertation. Bloomington, IN: Indiana University.

Forsythe, E. (1984). One-to-One Therapeutic Recreation Activities for the best and/or room bound. *Activities, Adaptation and Aging, 13* (1/2), 63-76.

Foster, P.M. (1986). *Therapeutic Activities with the Impaired Elderly*. New York: Haworth Press.

Gillespie, K., R. McLellan, and F. McGuire (1984). The Effects of Refreshment on Attendance at Recreational Activities for Nursing Home Residents. *Therapeutic Recreation Journal, 18*, 3, 25-29.

Ginsberg, B. R. (1988). Structuring Your Retirement Leisure Time. *Parks and Recreation, 23* (5), 46-49.

Glanser, F., and B. Hayslip (1985). The Impact of Retirement on Participation in Leisure Activities. *Therapeutic Recreation Journal, 14, 3,* 28-38.

Godbey, G. (1983). *Research on Aging and Leisure: Some Reflections. In Aging and Leisure* (pp. 78-86). Alexandria, VA: National Recreation and Park Association.

Godbey, G., and M. Blazey (1983). Old People in Urban Parks: An Exploratory Investigation. *Journal of Leisure Research, 15,* 228-244.

Gordon, D., M. Gaitz, and J. Scott (1976). Leisure and Lives: Personal Expressivity Across the Lifespan. In R.H. Binstock & E. Shanas (Eds.), *Handbook of Aging and the Social Sciences* (pp. 310-341). New York: Van Nostrand Reinhold.

Graney, M.L. (1975). Happiness and Social Participation in Aging. *Journal of Gerontology, 30,* 701-706.

Gross, S.W. (1963). *Opening the Door to Creative Experience for the Aging Through an Art Program.* Master's thesis. Maryland Institute of Art.

Hardie, E. (1970). Therapeutic Recreation for the Institutionalized Ill Aged: A Rationale. *Therapeutic Recreation Journal, 4, 3,* 9-11.

Havighurst, R., B. Neugarten, and S. Tobin (1968). Disengagement and Patterns of Aging. In B. Neugarten (Ed.), *Middle Age and Aging.* Chicago: University of Chicago Press.

Hawkins, B. A. (1991). An Exploration of Adaptive Skills and Leisure Activity of Older Adults with Mental Retardation. *Therapeutic Recreation Journal, 25,* (4), 9-28.

Hawkins, B. A. (1993). An Exploratory Analysis of Leisure and Life Satisfaction of Aging Adults with Mental Retardation. *Therapeutic Recreation Journal, 27,* (2), 98-109.

Heinemann, A. W., J. Colorez, and R. Larson (1988). Leisure States and "Flow" Experiences: Testing Perceived Freeeom and Intrinsic Motivation Hypotheses. *Journal of Leisure Research Gerontologist, 28* (2) 181-184.

Hoar, J. (1961). A Study of Free-Time Activities of 200 Aged Persons. *Sociology and Social Research, 45,* 157-162.

Holmes, D., M. Holmes, L. Steinbach, and T. Hausner (1979). The Use of Community-Based Services in Long-Term Care by Older Minority Persons. *The Gerontologist, 19,* 389-396.

Horton, D.A. (1959). *An Analysis of Selected Factors Influencing the Choice of Leisure-Time Activities of Senior Citizens in Conway, Arkansas.* Master's thesis. Iowa City, IA: University of Iowa.

Howe, C. (1985, November). *An Overview of Older Adult Leisure Engagement: Leisure Use and Activity Theory.* Paper presented at the Gerontological Society of America.

Hupp, S. (1986). Satisfaction of Older Women in Leisure Programs. *Abstracts from the 1986 Symposium on Leisure Research, 47.*

Iso-Ahola, S. (1980a). Perceived Control and Responsibility as Mediators of the Effects of Therapeutic Recreation on the Institutionalized Aged. *Therapeutic Recreation Journal, 14,* 1, 36-43.

Iso-Ahola, S. (1980b). *Social Psychological Perspectives on Leisure and Recreation.* Springfield, IL: Charles C. Thomas Publishers.

Iso-Ahola, S., and E. Weissinger (1984, June). Leisure and Well-Being: Is There a Connection? *Parks and Recreation, XVIII,* 40-44.

James, E. (1958). *Factors that Affect Participation of Members in the Program of Gold Age Club of Williamsport, Pennsylvania.* Master's thesis. The Pennsylvania State University.

Jewell, D. (1967). *An Activity Program for the Social Rehabilitation of the Institutionalized Geriatric Mental Patient.* Master's thesis. Carbondale, IL: Southern Illinois University.

Kaminski-deRoza, V. (1985, Summer). Phased Retirement: An Experiential View. *Activities, Adaptation and Aging, 6,* 4, 9-30.

Kaplan, M. (1979). *Leisure: Lifestyle and Lifespan.* Philadelphia: W. B. Saunders.

Kaplan, M. (1960). The Uses of Leisure. In C. Tibbits (Ed.), *Handbook of Social Gerontology* (pp. 407-443). Chicago, IL: University of Chicago Press.

Keller, M. J. (1984). Leisure Patterns and Adjustment of Centenarians. *Abstracts from the 1984 Symposium on Leisure Research, 96.*

Keller, M. J. (Editor). (1990). *Activities with Developmentally Disabled Elderly and Older Adults.* Binghamton, NY: Haworth Press.

Keller, M. J., and N. Turner (1986). Creating Wellness Programs with Older People: A Process for Therapeutic Recreators. *Therapeutic Recreation Journal 20,* 4, 6-14.

Kelley, J. (1992). Aging: It is Our Business. *Parks and Recreation, 28* (3), 36-42.

Kelly, J. (1978). Recreation Prediction by Age and Family Life Cycle. *The Third Nationwide Outdoor Recreation Plan, Appendix II, Survey Technical Report 4.* (pp. 151-159). Washington, D.C.: U.S. Department of Interior.

Kelly, J. (1986). Theories, Models and Metaphors: Agendas for Leisure Research. Keynote address presented to the Psychological/Social Psychological Aspects of Leisure Behavior Topic Area. 1986 Symposium on Leisure Research.

Kivett, V., and D. Orthner (1980). Activity Patterns and Leisure Preferences of Rural Elderly with Visual Impairments. *Therapeutic Recreation Journal, 14,* 2, 43, 48.

Kleiber, D., and S. Thompson (1980). Leisure Behavior and Adjustment to Retirement: Implications for Pre-Retirement Education. *Therapeutic Recreation Journal, 14,* 2, 5-17.

Leitner, M., and S. Leitner (1985). *Leisure in Later Life: A Sourcebook for the Provision of Recreational Services for Elderly.* New York: Haworth Press.

Leitner, M., and S. Merenbloom (1979). Senior Day Care Centers Ensure Fun for the Impaired Aged. *Parks and Recreation, 14,* 58-64.

Lemon, B.W., V. L. Bengston, and J. A. Peterson (1972). An Exploration of the Activity Theory of Aging: Activity Types and Life Satisfaction Among In-Movers to a Retirement Community. *Journal of Gerontology, 27,* 511-523.

MacLean, J. (1983). Too Hot in the Kitchen: Sociological Environments for Older Americans. *Aging and Leisure* (pp. 15-29). Alexandria, VA: National Recreation and Parks Association.

MacNeil, R. (1984). Gerontology and Leisure in Post-Secondary Curriculum. *Parks and Recreation, 19,* 6, 48-52.

MacNeil, R. D. (1991b). Gerontology and Recreation/Leisure Studies Curriculum: A Status Report. *Schole: A Journal of Leisure Studies and Recreation Education, 6,* 68-79.

MacNeil, R. D. (1991a, September/October). The Recreation Profession and the Age Revolution: Times They Are a 'Changing'. *Illinois Park and Recreation, 22* (5), 22-25.

MacNeil, R., and E. Barber (1986). Aging and the Compression of Infirmity: Implications for the Recreation Profession. *Journal of Expanding Horizons in Therapeutic Recreation, 1,* 43-48.

MacNeil, R., M. Ego, and K. Mobily (1993). Gerontology and Hospitality Management in Post-Secondary Curriculum. *Proceedings of the 7th Canadian Congress on Leisure Research,* 102-105.

MacNeil, R., D. Hawkins, E. Barber, and R. Winslow (1990). The Effect of a Client's Age Upon the Employment Preferences of Therapeutic Recreation Majors. *Journal of Leisure Research, 22,* (4), 329-340.

MacNeil, R., and M. Teague (1987). *Aging and Leisure: Vitality in Later Life.* Englewood Cliffs, NJ: Prentice-Hall.

MacNeil, R., M. Teague, F. McGuire, and J. O'Leary (1987). Older Americans and Outdoor Recreation: A Literature Synthesis. *Therapeutic Recreation Journal, 21,* 1, 18-25.

MacTavish, J., and M. Searle (1991). Older Individuals with Mental Retardation and the Effect of a Physical Activity Intervention on Selected, Social Psychological Variables. *Therapeutic Recreation Journal, XXV* (2), 55-71.

Maddox, G. (1963, December). Activity and Morale: A Longitudinal Study of Selected Elderly Subjects. *Social Forces, 42,* 195-204.

Maddox, G., and C. Eisdorfer (1962, March). Some Correlates of Activity and Morale Among the Elderly. *Social Forces, 40,* 254-260.

Mancini, J., and D. Orthner (1980). Situational Influences on Leisure Satisfaction and Morale in Old Age. *Journal of the American Geriatrics Society, 28,* 466-471.

Mannell, R., J. Zuzanek, and R. Larson (1988). Leisure States and "Flow" Experiences: Testing Perceived Freedom and Intrinsic Motivation Hypotheses. *Journal of Leisure Research, 20,* 289-304.

McAvoy, L. (1979). The Leisure Preferences, Problems and Needs of the Elderly. *Journal of Leisure Research, 11*, 40-47.

McCormick, S. (1991). The Greying of Parks and Recreation. *Parks and Recreation, 26* (3), 60-64.

McGhee, V. (1987). Preretirement Education: Challenge or Crisis? In R. MacNeil and M. Teague (Eds.), *Aging and Leisure: Vitality in Later Life* (pp. 322-348). Englewood Cliffs, NJ: Prentice-Hall.

McGuire, F. (1981). Freedom to Choose: The Total Environmental Approach. *Parks and Recreation, 16*, 12, 51-55.

McGuire, F. (1982). Constraints on Leisure Involvement in the Later Years. *Activity, Adaptation and Aging, 3*, 2, 47-54.

McGuire, F. (1984). A Factor Analytic Study of Leisure Constraints in Advanced Adulthood. *Leisure Studies, 6*, 313-326.

McGuire, F. (1984). Improving the Quality of Life for Residents of Long-Term Care Facilities Through Video Games. *Activities, Adaptation and Aging, 6*, 1, 1-18.

McGuire, F. (1985). Recreation Leader and Co-Participant Preferences of the Institutionalized Aged. *Therapeutic Recreation Journal, 19*, 2, 47-54.

Miller, S. (1965). The Social Dilemma of the Aging Leisure Participant. In A. Rose W. Peterson (Eds.), *Older People and Their Social World* (pp. 77-92). Philadelphia: F. A. Davis.

Mishra, S. (1992). Leisure Activities and Life Satisfaction in Old Age: A Case Study of Retired Governmental Employees Living in Urban Areas. *Activities, Adaptation and Aging, 16* (4), 7-26.

Mobily, K. (1981). Attitudes of Institutionalized Elderly Iowans Toward Physical Activity. *Therapeutic Recreation Journal, 15*, 3, 30-40.

Mobily, K. (1987). Leisure, Lifestyle and Lifespan. In R. MacNeil & M. Teague (Eds.), *Aging and Leisure: Vitality in Later Life* (pp. 155-180). Englewood Cliffs, NJ: Prentice-Hall.

Mobily, K., and T. Hoeft (1985). The Family Dilemma, Alzheimer's Disease. *Activities, Adaptation and Aging, 6*, 4, 63-71.

Mobily, K., D. Leslie, J. Lemke, R. Wallace, and F. Kohout (1986). Leisure Patterns and Attitudes of the Rural Elderly. *Journal of Applied Gerontology, 5*, 4, 201-214.

Mobily, K., R. Nilson, L. Ostiguy, and R. MacNeil (1993). Seasonal Variation in Physical Activity in Elderly Adults. *Proceedings of the 7th Canadian Congress on Leisure Research*, 175-180.

Mobily, K., R. Wallace, F. Kohout, D. Leslie, J. Lemke, and M. Morris (1984). Factors Associated with the Aging Leisure Repertoire: The Iowa 65+ Rural Health Study. *Journal of Leisure Research, 16*, 4, 338-343.

Morgan, A., and G. Godbey (1978). The Effect of Entering an Age-Segregated Environment Upon the Leisure Activity Patterns of Older Adults. *Journal of Leisure Research, 10,* 177-190.

Morse, N.C., and R. S. Weiss (1955). The Function and Meaning of Work and the Job. *American Sociological Review, 20,* 693-700.

Osgood, N. (Ed.). (1982). *Life after Work: Retirement Leisure Recreation and the Elderly.* New York: Praeger.

Penalta, L., and M. Uysal (1993). Aging and the Future of the Travel Market. *Parks and Recreation, 27* (9), 96-99.

Peppers, L.G. (1976). Patterns of Leisure Adjustment to Retirement. *Gerontologist, 16,* 441-446.

Peters, M., and P. Verhoven (1970). A Study of Therapeutic Recreation Services in Kentucky Nursing Homes. *Therapeutic Recreation Journal, 4,* 4, 19-22.

Poon, L., and A. Welford (1980). Prologue: A Historical Perspective. In L. W. Poon (Ed.), *Aging in the 1980s.* Washington, D.C.: American Psychological Association.

Portnoy, E. (1992). Creative Programming and Reminiscence Activities for Older Persons in Residential Care. *Activities, Adaptation and Aging, 16* (4), 27-37.

Purcell, R., and M. J. Keller (1989). Characteristics of Leisure Activities Which May Lead to Leisure Satisfaction Among Older Adults. *Activities, Adaptation and Aging, 13* (4), 17-29.

Ragheb, M. (1984). Leisure Measurements. *Abstracts from the 1984 Symposium on Leisure Research,* p. 58.

Ragheb, M., C. Griffith (1982). The Contribution of Leisure Participation and Leisure Satisfaction to Life Satisfaction of Older Persons. *Journal of Leisure Research, 14,* 4, 295-306.

Ray, R. O. (1979). Life Satisfaction and Activity Involvement: Implications for Leisure Service. *Journal of Leisure Research, 11,* 112-119.

Reichenfeld, H., K. Csapo, L. Carriere, & R. Gardner (1973). Evaluating the Effect of Activity Programs on a Geriatric Ward. *The Gerontologist, 13,* 305-309.

Riddick, C., and S. Daniel (1984). The Relative Contribution of Leisure Activities and Other Factors in the Mental Health of Older Women. *Journal of Leisure Research, 16,* 136-148.

Riddick, C., and M. DeSchriver (1984). Derived Satisfaction From an Outdoor Day Camp Program: The Perspectives of Nursing Home Residents Versus Activity Professionals. *Abstracts from the 1984 Symposium on Leisure Research,* p. 98.

Riddick, C., and R. Freitag (1984). The Impact of an Aerobic Fitness Program on the Body Image of Older Women. *Activities, Adaptation and Aging, 6,* 1, 59-70.

Romsa, G., P. Bondy, and M. Blenman (1985). Modeling Retirees' Life Satisfaction: The Role of Recreational Life Cycle, and Socio-Environmental Elements. *Journal of Leisure Research, 17,* 1, 29-39.

Routh, T. (1970). Realistic Recreation in Nursing Homes. *Therapeutic Recreation Journal, 4,* 4, 23-25.

Routh, T. (1967). Recreation in Nursing Homes. *Therapeutic Recreation Journal, 1,* 1, 3-5.

Russell, R. (1987). The Importance of Recreation Satisfaction and Activity Participation to the Life Satisfaction of Age-Segregated Retirees. *Journal of Leisure Research, 19* (4), 273-283.

Salamon, M. (1985). Sociocultural Role Theories in the Elderly: A Replication and Extension. *Activities, Adaptation and Aging, 7,* 2, 111-122.

Savell, K. (1991). Leisure, Perceptions of Control and Well-Being: Implications for the Institutionalized Elderly. *Therapeutic Recreation Journal, 25* (3), 44-59.

Scott, E., and D. Zoerink (1977). Exploring Leisure Needs of the Aged. *The Journal of Leisurability, 4,* 4, 25-31.

Shary, J., and S. E. Iso-Ahola (1989). Effects of a Control-Relevant Intervention on Nursing Home Residents' Perceived Competence and Self-Esteem. *Therapeutic Recreation Journal, 23,* 7-15.

Shivers, J., and H. Fait (1980). *Recreational Service for the Aging.* Philadelphia: Lea & Febiger.

Singleton, J. (1984, Fall). Outdoor Recreation Participation Patterns Among the Elderly. *Activities, Adaptation and Aging, 6,* 1, 81-89.

Singleton, J., and B. Keddy (1991a). Planning for Retirement. *Activities, Adaptation and Aging, 16,* (2), 49-55.

Singleton, J., and B. Keddy (1991b). Women's Perceptions of Life After Retirement. *Activities, Adaptation and Aging, 16* (2), 57-65.

Stafford, V. (1957). Recreation Planning for Older People: Adding Life to Years. *Bulletin of the Institute of Gerontology,* Iowa, Vol. 4, No. 4.

Strain, L., and N. Chappell (1982). Outdoor Recreation and the Rural Elderly: Participation, Problems and Needs. *Therapeutic Recreation Journal, 16,* 4, 42-48.

Streib, G., and C. Schneider (1971). *Retirement in American Society.* New York: Cornell University Press.

Tague, J. (1968). *Leisure Time Activities in Selected Nursing Homes.* Doctoral dissertation. University of Southern California.

Tague, J. (1970). The Status of Therapeutic Recreation in Extended Care Facilities: A Challenge and an Opportunity. *Therapeutic Recreation Journal, 4,* 3, 12-17.

Teaff, J. (1985). *Leisure Services with the Elderly.* St. Louis: C. V. Mosby.

Teague, M.L. (1980). Aging and Leisure: A Social Psychological Perspective. In S. Iso-Ahola, (ed.) *Social Psychological Perspectives on Leisure and Recreation* (pp. 219-257). Springfield, IL: Charles C. Thomas.

Teague, M.L. (1987). *Health Promotion: Achieving High-Level Wellness in the Later Years.* Indianapolis: Benchmark Press.

Teague, M., R. MacNeil, and G. Hitzhusen (1982). *Perspectives on Leisure and Aging in a Changing Society.* Columbia, MO: University of Missouri.

Tedrick, T. (1983). Leisure Competency: A Goal for Aging Americans in the Eighties. In *Aging and Leisure* (pp. 87-91). Alexandria, VA: National Recreation and Park Association.

Tedrick, T., and R. MacNeil (1991). Sociodemographics of Older Adults: Implications for Leisure Programming. *Activities, Adaptation and Aging, 15,* (3).

TerBurgh, C., and J. Teaff (1986). Relationship Between Leisure and Life Satisfaction of Older Catholic Women. (p. 48). *Abstracts from the 1986 Symposium on Leisure Research.*

Thornton, J., and J. Collins, J. (1986, March). Patterns of Leisure and Physical Activities Among Older Adults. *Activities, Adaptation and Aging, 8,* 2, 5-27.

Ward, R.A. (1979). *The Aging Experience: An Introduction to Social Gerontology.* New York: J. B. Lippincott Company.

Weiner, A. (1980). Pre-Retirement Education: Accent on Leisure. *Therapeutic Recreation Journal, 14,* 2, 18-31.

Weiner, A. (1981). Pre-Retirement Education: Assisting in the Transition from a Work to a Leisure Role. In M. Teague, R. MacNeil, & G. Hitzhusen, *Perspectives in Leisure and Aging in a Changing Society* (pp. 352-383). Columbia, MO: University of Missouri.

Weiss, C. (1989). TR and Reminiscing: The Pursuit of Elusive Memory and the Art of Remembering. *Therapeutic Recreation Journal, 23*(3), 7-18.

Weiss, C., and J. Kronberg (1986). Upgrading TR Service to Severely Disoriented Elderly. *Therapeutic Recreation Journal, 20,* 1, 32-42.

Weiss, C., M. Markue-Patch, and J. Thurn (1990). Meals, Memories, and Memoirs: A Culinary Odyssey. *Therapeutic Recreation Journal, 24* (4), 10-22.

Weiss, C., and J. Thurn (1987). A Mapping Project to Facilitate Reminiscence in a Long-Term Care Facility. *Therapeutic Recreation Journal, 21,* 2, 46-53.

Wilhite, B. (1987). REACH Out Through Home Delivered Recreation Services. *Therapeutic Recreation Journal, 21,* 2, 29-38.

Witt, P., and E. Jackson (1993). Constraints to Leisure Across the Family Lifecycle: Extension and Re-Examination. *Proceedings of the 7th Canadian Congress on Leisure Research*, 162-166.

Witt, P., and T. Goodale (1981). The Relationships Between Barriers to Leisure Enjoyment and Family Stages. *Leisure Sciences, 4*, 29-49.

U.S. Department of Health, Education and Welfare. (1963). *Human Aging: A Biological and Behavioral Study*. Bethesda, MD: Public Health Service.

Zborowski, M. (1962, July). Aging and Recreation. *Journal of Gerontology, 17*, 302-309.

Tourism and Commercial Recreation

Past, Present, and Future Research

Richard R. Perdue
College of Business
——————— University of Colorado ———————

Laura Valerius
Department of Leisure Studies
——————— University of Illinois ———————

ABSTRACT

The purpose of this paper is to examine how tourism and commercial recreation research has changed over the past ten years and to provide our perspective of how it might change over the next ten years. The basis of this paper is our subjective experiences both in conducting tourism research and as members of the Travel and Tourism Research Association and a content and citation analysis of selected tourism publications.

INTRODUCTION

Because of its diversified nature, travel and tourism is receiving increasing recognition as a vehicle for regional and community economic development. Consequently, state and local governments have become, over the past ten years, increasingly involved in tourism and commercial recreation (Pritchard, 1982). State government budgets for travel and tourism have grown from 53.2 million dollars in 1977 to 234 million dollars in 1987, a growth of 440 percent (Stacey, 1987). As a result of this growth, a recognized need and, perhaps more importantly, budget for quality research in tourism and commercial recreation has also evolved over the last ten years (Rovelstad & Blazer, 1983).

During these same ten years, there has been a substantive growth in the number of university recreation and parks degree programs with a tourism and/or commercial recreation option or concentration. Over 50 percent of the curriculums listed in the 1985-1986 SPRE Curriculum Catalog list a tourism and/or commercial recreation option. Further, a substantial share of recently advertised academic positions focus on tourism and commercial recreation.

As a result of these two forces, the research and academic opportunities, the number of researchers in the affiliated areas of parks, recreation, and leisure who focus their efforts on tourism and commercial recreation has grown very rapidly in the last ten years. The purpose of this paper will be to examine how tourism and commercial recreation research has changed over the same ten years and to provide our perspective of how it might change over the next ten years.

Two bases for this paper exist. First, a content and citation analysis was conducted of trends in selected tourism publications over the last ten years. Second, and much more subjective, are our experiences both in conducting and publishing tourism research and as members of both the National Recreation and Park Association and the Travel and Tourism Research Association. The paper is structured to, first, provide the methodology and results of the content and citation analyses. Next, two underlying characteristics of tourism and commercial recreation research are discussed. Finally, what we consider to be the important current and future trends in tourism and commercial recreation are presented.

THE CONTENT AND CITATION ANALYSIS

Introduction

Sociologists of science have argued that scholarly publications can be used to identify the structure and trends in an area of inquiry (Wells & Picou, 1981). Four recent publications have examined the trends and developments in recreation research. Three of those publications reported content analyses of the titles and institutional affiliations of authors (Lewko & Crandall, 1980; Szymanski, 1980; McLellan, 1980). The fourth publication reported a citation analysis of selected recreation research literature (Van Doren, Holland & Crompton, 1984). For this paper, both a content and a citation analysis of selected tourism publications over the past ten years was conducted.

Specifically, four volumes of the *Journal of Travel Research* (*JTR*) and the *Annals of Tourism Research* (*ANNALS*) were studied: 1977, 1980, 1983, and 1986. Of the different tourism research journals, these two were selected for two reasons. First, they represent the primary publication outlets for recreation researchers, defined as individuals affiliated with parks, recreation and leisure academic units. Second, they represent the range of tourism and commercial recreation research. *JTR* has grown from an applied marketing tradition. Conversely, the *ANNALS* has evolved from a more basic social science tradition, particularly sociology, anthropology, and geography.

Methodology

All of the articles published in *JTR* during the four study years were examined. However, only those articles published in non-thematic issues of the *ANNALS* were included in the study; it was felt that including the thematic issues would bias any identification of research trends. Since the first and third issues of each *ANNALS* volume were thematic, the data from the *ANNALS* were, consequently, weighted by a factor of two to avoid over-representation of *JTR*.

The content analysis examined trends in the institutional affiliation of tourism research authors, the topics of tourism research, and tourism research methodologies. The unit of analysis for the content analysis was the research article, research note, or theory note. The total number of articles examined was 121 (Table 1). By year, the articles were distributed as follows: 35 articles in 1977, 24 in 1980, 29 in 1983, and 33 in 1986.

The citation analysis was modeled after an analysis of the recreation research literature by Van Doren, Holland and Crompton (1984). Each citation from the selected articles was examined to determine its date, type (e.g., research journal, book, proceedings, etc.), field of study (e.g., marketing, sociology, geography, etc.), and, for journal publications, the name of the journal. The unit of analysis for the citation analysis was the individual citation. Each citation constituted one unit of analysis, regardless of the number of times it was cited in the article. The

Table 1
Study Sample

Year	Journal of Travel Research		Annals of Tourism Research	
	Articles	Citations	Articles	Citations
1977	26	163	9	109
1980	17	206	7	194
1983	21	282	8	210
1986	21	312	12	358
Total	85	963	36	871

total number of citations included in the study was 1,834. By year, the number of citations was 272 in 1977, 400 in 1980, 492 in 1983, and 670 in 1986 (Table 1).

For both the content analysis and the citation analysis, the coding was performed by the authors. Following the initial analysis, all coding was reviewed for consistency. As with all open-ended coding formats, a certain amount of judgment was required to code the articles and citations. In particularly judgmental situations, a general "other" category was available on each study variable.

Content Analysis Results

The contribution to tourism research of recreation researchers has grown substantively over the past ten years (Table 2). In 1977, only 2.7 percent of the articles were published by recreation researchers. In 1986, that percentage had grown to 26.7 percent. Importantly, this growth of recreation researcher contributions has not affected the general topics of tourism research. Rather, it has resulted from recreation researchers adopting or focusing on the traditional research problems of tourism. The research topics in the study journals have been very consistent (Table 3). Tourism planning was the major research topic in each of the four study years. Although the trends are relatively erratic, studies focusing on tourism impacts and tourism statistics have generally declined. Similarly, articles describing tourism research methodologies have grown. Articles focusing on tourism marketing and tourist behavior have been a relatively constant and important area of tourism research. Substantial differences exist between the two study journals. *JTR* has continued to focus on tourist behavior and applied tourism marketing. In contrast, the *ANNALS* has consistently focused on tourism planning and impacts. These differences reflect the fact that the editors and institutional homes of both journals have not changed over the study period.

Survey research has consistently represented 45 to 50 percent of the published tourism research (Table 4). Other particularly important methodologies include the analysis of existing statis-

Table 2
Academic Affiliation of Tourism Authors
(Percentage Distributions)

Academic Affiliation	1977	1980	1983	1986	Overall
Recreation, Parks and Leisure	2.7	6.9	35.5	26.7	18.3
Geography	18.9	27.6	12.9	8.9	16.2
Marketing	18.9	13.8	9.7	17.8	15.5
Economics	8.1	13.8	9.7	15.6	12.0
Sociology	13.5	10.3	3.2	4.4	7.7
All others	37.9	27.6	29.0	26.6	30.3

Table 3
Percentage Distribution of Tourism Research Articles
by Research Topic

Research Topic	1977	1980	1983	1986	Overall
Tourism planning and development	45.5	35.5	21.6	44.4	37.6
Tourism behavior	29.5	16.1	37.8	11.1	23.6
Tourism impacts	27.3	22.6	21.6	8.9	19.7
Tourism marketing	15.9	16.1	10.8	24.4	17.2
Tourism research methods	4.5	9.7	18.9	13.3	11.5
Tourism statistics	11.4	6.5	5.4	8.9	8.3

*column totals exceed 100.0 due to some articles being assigned to multiple topics.

Table 4
Percentage Distribution of Tourism Research Articles
by Research Methodology

Research Methodology	1977	1980	1983	1986	Overall
Survey research	46.5	48.4	48.6	46.5	47.4
Analysis of existing statistics	11.6	12.9	24.3	30.2	20.1
Observation	18.6	19.4	10.8	9.3	14.3
All other methods	23.3	19.4	16.2	14.0	18.2

tics, many of which were actually collected by survey methods, and observation. As with research reported in the *Journal of Leisure Research* and *Leisure Sciences*, very little experimental research is published in tourism and commercial recreation.

Citation Analysis Results

The results of the citation analysis reflect both consistency and change. Of the publications cited, there has been a substantive growth in the number of citations from research and professional journals (Table 5). The number of citations drawn from both federal government and consultant reports has, during the same time period, declined substantively. However, the field of study represented by the citations has been relatively consistent; publications from the tourism literature have consistently represented between 38 and 41 percent of the citations in the study journal (Table 6). Of particular importance to this paper, the percentage of the citations being drawn from the recreation and parks literature has changed less than one percent over the last ten years, ranging between 5.8 and 6.7 percent.

As would be expected, *JTR* and the *ANNALS* were consistently the dominant journals cited (Table 7). The *Journal of Leisure Research* was represented by between 2.6 and 5.4 percent of the citations, but there was no consistent pattern of growth or decline. Similarly, the percentage of citations drawn from the *Journal of Marketing* and *Journal of Marketing Research* has fluctuated over the study period, but collectively represents approximately 7 percent of the citations.

Following the analysis by Van Doren, Holland and Crompton (1984), the median age of the citations was examined both for all citations and for only those citations drawn specifically from

Table 5
Percentage Distribution of Citations by Type of Publication

Type of Publication	1977	1980	1983	1986	Overall
Journal (research or professional)	24.4	38.2	38.0	41.1	37.3
Book (not an edited volume)	27.0	17.2	26.8	19.9	22.1
Magazine/newspaper (public media)	11.0	4.9	3.0	9.7	7.1
Edited book	2.6	5.2	7.8	6.4	6.0
Federal government report	11.5	6.4	3.7	4.5	5.7
Consultant report (inc. USTDC)	7.3	8.1	3.7	4.0	5.3
State government report	3.7	6.7	3.0	3.9	4.3
University report	3.7	6.7	3.0	3.9	4.3
Conference proceedings	2.9	3.5	5.8	2.5	3.7
Thesis/Dissertations	2.6	1.5	2.6	1.8	2.1
Local government report	0.3	0.0	0.6	0.7	0.4
Other	4.2	5.4	0.6	0.8	2.2

Table 6
Percentage Distribution of Citations by Field of Citation

Field of Citation	1977	1980	1983	1986	Overall
Tourism	37.8	39.6	46.6	40.5	41.5
Sociology/Anthropology	9.4	5.2	8.7	8.3	7.9
Social Sciences (general)	11.5	9.3	4.6	6.6	7.4
Recreation, Parks & Leisure	5.8	6.4	6.7	5.8	6.2
Economics	6.0	8.8	6.1	4.6	6.1
Marketing	5.8	5.9	2.0	6.5	5.1
Geography	2.6	4.4	7.5	2.5	4.3
Others	24.1	28.5	23.8	31.2	28.6

tourism and commercial recreation literature. In both cases, the median age of the citations has grown substantively (Table 8). The median age of the tourism citations has grown from 3.26 to 6.30 years. For comparison, Van Doren, Holland and Crompton (1984) reported a median age between nine and ten years for the recreation citations in the *Journal of Leisure Research* and *Leisure Sciences*.

Table 7
Percentage Distribution of Journal Citations by Journal Cited

Journal Cited	1977	1980	1983	1986	Overall
Journal of Travel Research	11.8	11.9	12.4	18.7	14.9
Annals of Tourism Research	6.5	6.6	14.6	14.7	12.1
Journal of Marketing Research	4.3	8.8	1.1	4.7	4.7
Journal of Leisure Research	5.4	2.6	4.9	4.0	4.1
Journal of Marketing	7.5	1.8	0.0	4.3	2.9
Cornell Hotel & Restaurant Administration Quarterly	0.0	1.8	4.9	0.9	2.1
Tourism Management	NA	NA	0.4	3.1	1.4

Table 8
Median Age of Citations by Journal

	All Citations			Tourism Citations Only		
Year	Journal of Travel Research	Annals of Tourism Research	Both	Journal of Travel Research	Annals of Tourism Research	Both
1977	4.26	5.26	4.74	2.61	3.93	3.26
1980	7.16	6.18	6.51	5.57	5.70	5.67
1981	7.08	8.47	8.04	5.53	7.31	6.45
1986	6.97	7.23	7.15	5.25	6.82	6.30

CHARACTERISTICS OF TOURISM AND COMMERCIAL RECREATION RESEARCH

The Publication of Tourism and Commercial Recreation Research

Perhaps the first difficulty in describing tourism and commercial recreation research is to identify the differences between the two areas and to understand the nature of the research being conducted and published. In this paper, commercial recreation is defined as privately-owned business involved in the supply and distribution of recreation commodities with the primary purpose of long-term economic profit (Perdue & Thomason). Tourism is more broadly defined as the "sum of the phenomena and relationships arising from the interaction of tourists, business suppliers, host governments, and host communities in the process of attracting and hosting tourists and other visitors" (McIntosh & Goeldner, 1986). While these definitions may appear academic, they are very important to understanding the published research. Commercial recreation is dominated by small businesses. As such, the available dollars for commercial recreation research are very limited. Further, with the exception of a few camping studies funded by either the U.S.D.A. Forest Service or National Park Service and a few marina and charter boat fishing studies funded by either the National Marine Fisheries Service or Sea Grant, almost none of the existing commercial recreation research has been published. For the most part, commercial recreation research is proprietary research conducted by consultants for a specific business client with the purpose of gaining market advantage.

Tourism research can be divided into three general groups. First, a large amount of research is conducted by private corporations in the lodging, transportation, finance, and publishing industries. As with the commercial recreation research, very little of this tourism research is published. However, some of it, particularly the operations research in the transportation and lodging industries, is highly sophisticated. The fact that it is not published does not imply poorer quality. Rather, the purpose of the research is to gain market advantage. Publishing the results would, in effect give up that market advantage.

A second body of tourism research is that conducted for local and state governments, focusing on marketing and economic development. This area of research can be further subdivided into that conducted by academic institutions and that conducted by consultants. As with the two areas of research previously discussed, very little of the consultant research is published. For the most part, there is very little reward to consultants for publishing in refereed journals. Again, this does not imply that their research is of poorer quality; it simply is not available to review as part of the body of literature in tourism and commercial recreation. The research conducted by academic institutions can also be further subdivided into that by the extension services at land grant universities and that by research faculty members. Again, much of the extension research is not published in the refereed journals. Numerous extension service publications exist, but are generally difficult to obtain after a few years.

The third body of tourism research is that conducted primarily by sociologists and anthropologists examining the social impacts of tourism development, particularly in rural and developing areas. This research has been widely published not only in the tourism literature, but also in the sociological, anthropological and geographical literature.

In conclusion, this section makes four points. First, virtually none of the commercial recreation research is published. Second, very little of the tourism research is published. Third, of the published tourism research, two distinct bodies of work can be identified, that which views tourism as a positive element of economic development and that which views tourism as a negative social impact on indigenous cultures. Fourth, and perhaps most importantly, a substantial share of tourism research is conducted by consultants who exist within a very different reward system than academic researchers. At least in our view, there is very little evidence to suggest that the consultant research is better or worse than the academic research. However, the consultant's reward system is such that it is in their best interest to not report their methodologies or specific results. Further, it is also in their best interest to be outstanding salespersons. Attending a Travel and Tourism Research Association conference is an interesting experience for an individual accustomed to academic research meetings. Many of the presentations are by consultants who, in effect, indicate they can solve the problems of the world, provide very little detail about how that might be accomplished, and "here's my business card." Importantly, however, the calligraphy of their presentations is outstanding. When compared to the academic presentations, the quality of the consultant presentations is generally much, much higher.

Tourism is a Rodney Dangerfield Area

A second critical underpinning of tourism and commercial recreation research is the personality of most tourism organizations. The lay professional organizations and government offices of tourism are obsessed with proving the economic importance of travel and tourism to the local and/or state government. By and large, tourism professionals feel they don't get the respect they deserve. Since the available research dollars are heavily centered in the state tourism offices, assessing economic impact is, consequently, a crucial component of most tourism research. Further, showing a high impact is politically very important. While we're not suggesting unethical behavior by tourism researchers, it's important to understand the underlying motive of most organizations that fund tourism research. Their interest is not necessarily science.

CURRENT AND FUTURE TRENDS IN TOURISM AND COMMERCIAL RECREATION RESEARCH

The results of the content and citation analyses of the *Journal of Travel Research* and the *Annals of Tourism Research* in combination with our subjective experiences provide numerous insights into the past and present of tourism and commercial recreation research. Five points are, in our opinion, particularly relevant and have important implications for the future of tourism and commercial recreation research. First, tourism and commercial recreation research has been and continues to be remarkably stable in terms of the research topics and methodologies. Certainly, new theories, hypotheses, and procedures have evolved, but the general concerns and methods of research have been relatively consistent. So long as the editors of the two primary tourism and commercial recreation journals do not change, there is no reason to believe that the general research concerns and procedures, at least in the published research, will change. As a function of the available resources, however, it is our opinion that greater research opportunity and effort will be conducted on issues of tourism marketing and economic impact as opposed to the negative social and environmental impacts of tourism development. In many ways, the available funding drives the research being conducted in tourism and commercial recreation.

Second, recreation researchers have become much more active in publishing in the tourism literature. This documents the general perception that a greater and greater percentage of the researchers in the affiliated areas of parks, recreation, and leisure are focusing their efforts on tourism and commercial recreation. Importantly, however, the percentage of citations from the recreation literature and journals has not grown. The implication of these conflicting trends is that recreation researchers necessarily must learn and adopt the tourism research literature in order to be effective in that environment. The shifting of recreation re-searchers to tourism and commercial recreation is not simply the application of recreation concepts and theories of tourists. Rather, it involves and will continue to involve learning the literature and methodology of tourism.

Third, tourism and commercial recreation research is becom-ing more scientific. Both the percentage of citations drawn from research journals and the number of citations per article is growing. In our judgment, this indicates that the research is becoming more dependent upon previous technical and scien-tific publications. Given this trend and two additional findings, first, that the number of refereed publication outlets is not growing or, for that matter, changing in any substantive way and, second, that there is a growing number of researchers, the scientific quality of the published research will necessarily con-tinue to improve in the future.

Fourth, contrary to the opinions of most futurists, our find-ings do not indicate a decline in the useful age of the tourism research literature. In fact, the median age of tourism citations is growing significantly. Again, the implication of this finding is of increasing maturity and quality of the tourism research.

Fifth, a substantial growth is occurring in the amount of money being allocated within universities for tourism research. Numerous universities are establishing Centers of Tourism Re-search. The purposes of these centers are two-fold. First, they can serve as a clearinghouse to coordinate research by individuals from a variety of academic homes. Second, they may enhance the ability of universities to attract tourism research dollars. Regard-less of their success in attracting outside dollars, these centers represent an important commitment to tourism that has not previously existed. Additionally, the agricultural experiment stations at many land grant universities are committing substan-tial monies to tourism research, particularly as related to rural communities and alternative revenues to agricultural land own-ers. In coastal areas, some university Sea Grant programs have also funded tourism research in recent years. Finally, numerous state universities are establishing Centers for Rural Economic Revitalization, which in many cases are funding rural tourism development research.

There is, however, a negative potential underlying the cur-rent popularity of tourism. Historically, tourism support has been inversely related to the economic climate. During periods when the general economy has declined, the support for tourism and tourism development has increased. Conversely, during periods when the general economy has grown, the support for tourism has declined. Much of the support for tourism research that exists today, particularly in the universities, is a result of the general decline of traditional industries, most frequently agriculture. One of the interesting questions of the future is whether that support will continue if and when these traditional industries recover.

REVISITING OUR PROJECTIONS

It is not often that we have the opportunity to re-visit a past writing, particularly one that made an effort to project future trends in research content and methodology. In 1988, we made five projections about the future of tourism and commercial recreation research. Now, in 1994, we can claim accuracy on two of those projections. While batting .400 would be great in major league baseball, we're not sure what it represents about our ability to project future research in tourism and commercial recreation.

First, our successes. Research topics focusing on marketing and impacts continue to be the primary focus in the tourism and commercial recreation area. Market segmentation, accountability assessment, and consumer persuasion continue to be key marketing topics. Similarly, the economic and social impacts of tourism continue to be a key concern.

Similarly, we were accurate in projecting the continued involvement of recreation, park, and leisure study (RPLS) faculty in conducting and publishing tourism and commercial recreation research. Perhaps this is best represented by the number of RPLS researchers that are now members of the editorial boards and key research committees in the tourism area. Importantly, however, some of the key RPLS researchers have moved into other types of academic positions. For example, Muzaffer Uysal, Wes Roehl, and Mark Bonn, among others, have moved into Hotel and Restaurant Administration Schools. Similarly, Dave Sneppenger, Mark Pritchard, one of us, and others have moved into Business Schools. Consequently, it's not easy to effectively track the contributions of RPLS researchers in the tourism area.

Now, for our failures. We projected that the available monies for tourism and commercial recreation would continue to grow. It is extraordinarily difficult to measure our accuracy on this projection. However, continued cutbacks in academic budgets have seriously affected the available resource pool. Similarly, state tourism offices have also experienced increasing budget stress which translates, in many cases, into lower research expenditures.

Two of our projections focused on the level and quality of science conducted in the tourism and commercial recreation area. We were optimistic in projecting that the quality of science would continue to evolve and improve. Based only on our subjective review, we are not convinced that this has happened. In many ways, it seems that the quality of our research has plateaued over the last two years. Optimistically, we believe this is nothing more than a natural lull in the evolution of our work. However, it appears that we need to more aggressively stretch the boundaries of our theoretical and methodological knowledge in tourism and commercial recreation.

Further, it is time that we establish the unique identity, if one exists, of tourism and commercial recreation. Rather than continuing to simply borrow concepts and methodologies from other areas, particularly marketing and sociology/psychology, it is time that we establish the ways in which tourism and commercial recreation behavior is different from other types of behavior and the implications of those differences for tourism development, marketing, and policy. Instead of continuing to study tourists alone, it is time that we begin studying tourists as compared to other types of people and tourism as compared to other types of development. Perhaps that is the next stage in our theoretical and methodological evolution.

Request for reprints: Richard R. Perdue, College of Business, University of Colorado, Boulder, CO 80309-0419.

BIBLIOGRAPHY

Lewko, J. and R. Crandall. (1980). Research Trends in Leisure and Special Populations. *Journal of Leisure Research, 12*(1): 69-79.

McIntosh, R. and C. Goeldner. (1986). *Tourism: Principles, Practices, Philosophies, 5th edition.* New York: John Wiley & Sons, Inc.

McLellan, R. (1980). The State of the Art . . . Research. *Parks and Recreation, 15*(7): 62-67, 90.

Perdue, R. and P. Thomason. 1987. Commercial Recreation. In Parker, S. & A. Graefe (ed). *Recreation and Leisure: An Introductory Handbook.* University Park, PA: Venture Publishing.

Pritchard, G. (1982). Tourism Promotion: Big Business for the States. *The Cornell Hotel and Restaurant Administration Quarterly, 23*(2): 48-57.

Rovelstad, J. and S. Blazer. (1983. Research and Strategic Marketing in Tourism: A Status Report. *Journal of Travel Research 11*(2): 2-7.

Stacey, J. (1987). States Bankroll Tourism. *USA Today.* March 4.

Szymanski, D. (1980). An Index for Determining Trends in Selected Leisure Journals and Publications. *Therapeutic Research Journal, 14*(3): 42-51.

Van Doren, C.S., S. M. Holland, and J. L. Crompton. (1984). Publishing in the Primary Leisure Journals: Insights into the Structure and Boundaries of our Research. *Leisure Sciences, 6*(2): 239-256.

Wells, R. and J. Picou. (1981). *American Sociology: Theoretical and Methodological Structure.* Washington, D.C.: University Press of America.

Outdoor Recreation: Resource Planning and Management

Past, Present, and Future Research

H. Ken Cordell
USDA Forest Service
Athens, GA

ABSTRACT

Improvement of planning and management technology and better information will continue as needs never quite fulfilled. Research must continue to try to fill these needs. Decisions in the future will tolerate less intuition and emotion and will require more fact and solid evaluation. Over the past 30 years, great strides have been made to advance outdoor recreation planning and management. Some of the issues of the past, when ORRRC was active, seem less ominous today, in part because of the wealth of research accomplished since then. Research was stimulated by ORRRC, and there is reason for pride when we review the importance and obvious influence of that research. The issues of today are not totally different from those of 1960. The distinguishing characteristic is the rising intensity with which those issues are viewed. Contemporary concerns center on presenting the importance of recreation, protection of environments and resources, providing quality and appropriate opportunities, access, and assuring credible and meaningful information. Research addressing resource, user, and manager interactions and describing the determinants of change are the areas with least accomplishment. These areas having the least accomplishment present perhaps the greatest need. In future research, stronger ties to theory will be needed, especially the theories of relevant social and biological sciences. Understanding the full implications of research findings requires a firm grounding in theory and a tie back to preceding research. Follow up with preceding research and greater care with interpreting the findings will vastly improve the relevance and standing of outdoor recreation/resource planning and management. This abstract describes an invited paper presented as a feature paper for the Outdoor Recreation/Resource Planning and Management Session of the National Leisure Research Symposium, New Orleans, Louisiana, September 18-22, 1987.

INTRODUCTION

The natural resources in this country are vast and complex. "Proper" management of these resources becomes ever more critical as our population grows, our values change, and the bidding accelerates for rights to a slice of the resource pie. The end is not in sight, nor will it ever be. Improvement of management and better information will continue as needs never quite fulfilled because the target is a moving one.

Planning is one of the more critical phases of management. Planning implies a look to the future in an attempt to anticipate change and to target appropriate management responses. Planning and management are "hand in glove" perspectives. They address the same issues; only their scope and time frames differ. Planning is a process that provides systematic examination of the many potential changes, targets, alternatives and issues of management and, in doing so, brings better focus to future management.

As challenges to the way resources are or might be used and managed escalate, there is less room for intuitively and emotionally based decisions. To better influence decisions about the use of resources, commercial interests have become more informed and more intimately involved than ever. The public, too, is increasingly better informed and educated. They are more involved and alert to the issues, and they are more aware that somehow their fate depends on the fate of the natural environment.

It is this natural environment with which we are concerned. The information made available to planners and managers must be at least as good, and the choices and positions as solidly based, as those of commercial and public user interests. As Jim Cochrane (Forest Service Recreation Staff Director for Alaska) recently phrased it, "We live in a glass house, and the walls of our house seem thinner than most." Researchers have been helpful, but more and better focus, research, and communication are needed if we are to continue to do a better job of planning and managing.

In this paper, the candid observations of a professional who is both a researcher and a planner are described. These observations are about past, present, and future issues and the actual and potential responses that research can make to these issues. Mostly the focus in this treatise is on applied research. Other papers in this book examine some of the more basic science and theoretical perspectives of sociology, psychology and economics. This paper is an examination of how far we have come in research on the outdoor recreation aspects of behavior, administration and natural resources management. It is not a comprehensive literature—space and motivation are not adequate for that undertaking. The basic thrust is to identify the issues of greatest past concern, those that seem most pressing now, and those that likely will impact us most in the future. These issues are examined from the perspective of a researcher/planner who has wondered how well research has responded to the issues.

THE PAST

The Issues

Recreation research became a visible and viable pursuit, as well as a recognized need, in the late 1950s. This was stimulated in part by the Outdoor Recreation Resources Review Commission and persons such as Marion Clawson, Samuel Dana, and Grant Sharpe. Then, as now, there was an imposing array of management, policy and research questions (ORRRC, 1960). These questions generally fell into the five categories listed in Figure 1.

The more visible questions within these categories were:

• What are the social implications of providing various kinds of recreation opportunities either through the private sector or through government?

- How would alternative ways of financing recreation affect distribution of the public tax burden?
- What is the value of recreation as a natural resource use, relative to the value of using these same resources for commodity or developmental uses?
- Which land uses are more compatible with recreation from an aesthetic viewpoint?
- How do different types of recreational uses conflict with one another?
- How can recreation use fees most efficiently and equitably be administered?
- How can outdoor recreation be considered in benefit-cost analyses of water resource developments and what standards should apply?
- What methods can be used to forecast future outdoor recreation demands?
- What are the indicators of taste changes and what social variables will cause change in actual future demand?
- What are the effects of advertising and education on demand?
- How does recreation use affect resource conditions, and how much recreation use can a resource accommodate?

Figure 1
Categories of Management, Policy and Research
Questions of the '50s and '60s

1. Roles and Responsibilities
2. Conflicts and Compatibilities
3. Finance and Administration
4. Future Change and Planning
5. Resource Location and Condition

Source: Outdoor Recreation Resource Review Commission, 1960.

The Research Response

In the early 1960s, a wide array of agency and university research was begun. The emphasis was on gaining a better understanding of this new resource management interest in outdoor recreation. In May, 1963, V.L. Harper (1963) reported progress to date among federal agencies, including the Forest Service, Economic Research Service, Corps of Engineers, and the Public Health Service. The emphasis of agency research at this time was on describing "demand and the resources, income potentials, personal and social benefits, and methods for use measurement and for resource impact assessment." In the same proceedings, van der Smissen (1963) reported that university research on outdoor recreation was just beginning and was exploring "outing activities" and user groups, land use planning methods, tourism, inventory techniques, and carrying capacity.

By 1971, appreciable amounts of research had been undertaken and much more was on-going. The thrusts were in planning and development, site management, describing the user, some on behavior and communication, and a continued small emphasis on carrying capacity (USDA Forest Service, 1971). Visual perceptions, interpretation and education, vicarious benefits, and quality measures were beginning to emerge as research topics.

By 1976, just prior to the first Leisure Research Symposium, there was a substantial amount of outdoor recreation research being conducted by both agencies and universities. There had been noticeable productivity since the late 1950s. Among the more notable accomplishments were analytical models for landscape planning, methods for evaluating environmental interpretation, procedures for economic valuation of outdoor recreation, methods for estimating visitation, better understanding of the dual aspects of carrying capacity, behavioral and motivational aspects of hunting and other recreation, concepts of social benefits, principles of public involvement, methods for evaluating provider roles, tools for managing developed site impacts, and the beginnings of modeling recreation demand and supply for comprehensive planning (USDA Forest Service, 1976).

There seems to have been a genuine responsiveness by the developing research community. They were responding to the issues that were defined by ORRRC and others in the '50s, and '60s. Often the influence and uses of the information and tools provided through research have been subtle and not explicitly recognized. But the work and resulting influence of researchers such as Wager (and his father), Shafer, Tocher, LaPage, Burch,

Driver, Davis, Lucas, Clawson, Lime, James, Knetsch, Elsner, Litton, Bevins, Hendee, Clark, Moeller, and others cannot be overlooked. These researchers and their work have had a powerful influence on management, planning and research.

PRESENT

The Issues

The most crucial issues of the late '70s and of the late 1980s (Figure 2) were summarized during the 1979 National Conference on Renewable Natural Resources, by the Outdoor Recreation Policy Review Group (1983), and by the President's Commission on Americans Outdoors (1986). Those issues included:

Figure 2
The Most Crucial Issues of the Late 1970s and 1980s

1. Recreation interests are not organized.
2. The public is not sufficiently aware of the need to protect natural environments.
3. Quality of environments for outdoor recreation seems to be deteriorating.
4. Access limits recreation participation.
5. Essential and unique environments are being converted to developments.
6. Land leasing, liability and exclusive membership rights threaten availability of opportunities.
7. Tax based funding alone is not adequate.
8. The social importance of outdoor recreation is not fully understood.
9. Data bases, models, and the inherent analysis capabilities are inadequate.
10. Ability to forecast and to simulate is inadequate.

---

1. Recreation interests are not organized to be effective in presenting the case for outdoor recreation budgets, incentive legislation, and policy. Effectiveness in this context has many dimensions, including coalitions, credible and believable analyses, influential people willing to "take up the flag," and "stand-

ing" where money and political power confer entitlement to share in decision making.

2. Most of the public has little concern about protecting our natural environments. Values are oriented much more toward materialistic wants, upward career mobility, and the personal community. The President's Commission concluded that our natural environment is at the heart of quality and opportunity for outdoor recreation. This does not seem to be a general concern of the public.

3. The quality of the facilities, services and spaces provided for outdoor recreation seems to be deteriorating. While associated with protecting the "health" of natural environments, this concern is focused mostly on the managerially provided components of outdoor recreation opportunities.

4. Access, both physical and social, limits recreation participation and can disproportionately affect opportunities available to various publics. Many outdoor opportunities are rural and remote. Limited information about these opportunities and limited transportation to, money for, and social acceptance to use these rural opportunities can dramatically affect the social distribution of recreational access.

5. Greenspace, river, wetlands, shorelines, mountains, scenery and other essential or unique resources are being converted and not preserved for future generations. This issue may be the most crucial one of the 1990s and the next century. Without these unique resources and environments, outdoor recreation would be a much different experience.

6. Private land leasing and liability and the increasing incidence of exclusive membership rights to recreational spaces and facilities threatens the availability of recreational opportunities for the general public.

7. Tax-based funding alone is no longer a plausible option for financing the planning, acquisition, development and management of outdoor recreation resources. Decreased governmental funding has been accompanied by rationalizations that the private sector would fill the voids left by government retrenchment. But most forms of outdoor recreation cannot and will not be provided commercially. There are many who would be unable to pay even if these forms of outdoor recreation were commercially provided.

8. Lack of understanding of the importance of outdoor recreation in the sense of the social, personal and economic benefits it provides limit optimization in decision making. Particularly limited may be development of opportunities that are culturally, motivationally and behaviorally significant.

9. Data bases, models and analysis techniques are inadequate and incompatible. We spend millions of dollars unnecessarily on repetitious data collection. Often the resulting data are in error and usually they are not linked to other studies or results. The work of the President's Commission on Americans Outdoors exemplified the need for good information. The long-term effect of this Commission will in part be an outcome of the information that was available to it.

10. Ability to forecast and to simulate are inadequate. Prediction of future demand and supply and/or visitation shifts is much more of an art than a science. Simulation of the effects of demand changes, and resultant gains or losses of benefits are difficult to predict. Yet where policy, access, development, or information flows are to be decided, such simulation is needed. Population growth, demographic shifts, and cultural and taste changes are demand shifters whose effects are not well understood.

Of course, not all of the above needs for information, methods, actions, or better understandings are "research questions." For the most part, the "research questions" are embedded within these issues and deal with the need for theoretical or methodological underpinnings to enhance understandings of social and personal relevance, the need for credible information describing conditions and situations, needs for analytical methods for estimating benefits and effects, and methods and models for simulating and forecasting. In the following paragraphs, a brief commentary is provided on the research response to date to these issue-driven questions. This commentary is intended as an evaluative review, not as a comprehensive literature review. One of the principle sources of reference was the literature review developed by the President's Commission as compiled by Laura Szwak (The President's Commission on Americans Outdoors 1986).

The issues and questions described in Figure 2, and seemingly many others identified here, can be grouped as follows:

1. Appropriate and credible information for both planning and management.
2. The relative importance of recreation within society's hierarchy of needs and wants.
3. Sufficient and equitable access to all publics.
4. Quality and appropriateness of the recreational opportunities.
5. Protection of the environment and resources upon which outdoor recreation and our social and environmental health depend.

The Research Response

In the following paragraphs, an overview and observations are presented about the research community's contribution to the five issues above. Among these issues, information for planning and management, the relative place of recreation, and access are the three that seem to have been given the most attention in the literature. Research pertaining to each of the five issues is presented below in order of decreasing apparent state of knowledge and, therefore, increasing knowledge gap. Keywords or phrases are underscored within this text to help draw attention to the principal foci. The casual reader may wish to skip this section and continue reading the last section on future issues and research.

Credible Information for Planning and Management

Financing and communicating are two areas that have been of great interest. Much of this focus upon financing has had to do with fees. Thus far, only limited theoretical or practically applicable information has resulted. Communication, too, has been an area of attention. But aside from Wagar and a few others in previous years, we may yet be in the early stages of this work. This seems to be the case both regarding communications with users as well as communications with potentially supporting publics. Communication, of course, is the essential and key component of planning and managing.

Tourism, as a social and business concern, has also been of interest in outdoor recreation. There is a great deal of written material describing the tourism phenomena, how tourists spend their money, and how participation is motivated. But for the most part, tourism/recreation is an area that yet lacks explicit tools and methods for incorporating tourism demands and impacts into recreation planning and management.

Other advances include improvement in understanding urban settings and recreation. The urban setting is, of course, the origin of most tourists. But seemingly large gaps exist in describing the linkages between the day to day and the vacation components of outdoor recreation demand and consumption. This seems particularly true of urban recreation demand.

A large amount of information has been developed about participation patterns and the factors that affect participation choices. Among the many types of outdoor recreation participation, the greatest amount of research focus has been upon camping. These users and their attendant, complementary slates of activities are well identified. But many new activities, such as those classified as risk and adventure recreation are not so well understood. Only limited information has emerged to help understand and plan for the changing mix of future activities and seekers. There is also a less-than complete base of knowledge about the interregional and interspatial relationships among various outdoor recreation resources and uses how these relationships may be changing, and what has stimulated change.

Reasonably good descriptive data exist to describe equipment and license sales, travel, and other participation indicators. This includes equipment—intensive information regarding bicycling, off-road vehicular use, boating and other activities. Lacking are solid interpretations of the meaning of these behaviors as barometers indicating needed responses from the delivery system. Essential integrative work to better address interactions among activities involving various publics, resources, and providers—competitive, complementary, or otherwise—mostly is lacking. The literature discusses issues and the attendant needs of integrative models for planning. But mostly we have examined each part separately. Understanding the connections and mechanisms of exchange and of influence among these parts is yet to be done.

One area of accomplishment is that of measuring economic values and consequences in recreation. Since Hotelling first published in 1949, we have come a long way in developing the economics of recreation. We have methods for determining, credibly, the contributions of recreation to net economic development and the resultant distributions of economic activity. We are beginning to develop methods for modelling supply. While the "reconometric" methods that have been developed are still "data hungry" and expensive, one cannot overlook the significance of the advances that have been made.

The Importance of Recreation

Much of the research dealing with recreation within society's hierarchy of wants and needs has dealt with identifying benefits and the beneficiaries. Describing benefits in an understandable framework has helped in arguing for recreation programs and budgets. Showing magnitude of benefits from recreation relative to transportation or other public purposes helps determine recreation's budget share. Frequently, the managers and planners of recreation operations plea for defensible information on benefits or values. They seek "justification" for their budget requests and ammunition for asking for a larger share.

On the broadest of social scales, recreation, and especially preservation of outstanding or critical outdoor environments, confers aesthetic, appreciative, bequest, option, spiritual and other vicariously gained benefits. We know virtually nothing about the magnitude, distribution, or explicit nature of these vicarious benefits. Very little has been provided through research that justifies changing resource allocations based upon these benefits. Oddly enough, these vicarious benefits are suspected to be very "large." Their magnitude may in fact overshadow direct use benefits.

Documentation of social benefits from outdoor recreation is on a more concrete footing than is documentation of vicarious benefits. Evidence has been presented that family solidarity and productivity are among these benefits. Benefits from organized, institutional recreation have been best documented. But like many other research outputs, the integrative and interpretive aspects of these knowledge gains could be improved.

Much concern in the profession has been focused upon the benefitting publics. One such public is the emotionally disabled. Research on physical fitness and wilderness programs has documented that positive benefits are gained by the emotionally disabled. These benefits include improved self-concept and social functioning. One remaining question is how long these benefits persist. Another public is the physically impaired, estimated at 32 million in the U.S. in 1984. Available research findings indicate that for the physically impaired, outdoor recreation provides benefits such as improved self-esteem, social behaviors, and physical abilities.

Older populations are of increasing numbers, importance, and research concern. Research has shown that a definite positive relationship exists between recreation involvement and life satisfaction among older people. One particular benefit is a more positive morale. Research results suggest that not only does the quantity, but also the variety of recreational pursuits positively affect life satisfaction among older persons.

On the other end of the age spectrum are children. For children, recreation, through play, serves an especially beneficial role in individual development. Physical, cognitive, socialization, and personal identity, knowledges and skills are among the most prevalent developmental benefits resulting from children's play in outdoor environments. The experiences that most influence these developments include vacations, camps, home community, and school.

Research focusing on personal benefits has produced technology for measuring and ranking benefits. For example, there is good documentation of the personal benefits that result from activities that are specialized and/or are especially challenging. From this research we know that the physically or skill-demanding activities are often undertaken for the experience as well as the change that results. But this research is somewhat limited in that it does not usually provide measures of the "real" benefit or change that occurs. Typically, the selected response variable measures relative or perceived change. Understanding the meaning and long-term effects of those measured changes is a remaining challenge.

Sufficient and Equitable Access

As space for outdoor recreation becomes more scarce because more people are demanding it, the issue of access becomes more pressing. For example, exclusive rights to recreation opportunities obtained through leasing or organizational memberships seem to be increasing. These rights provide access to subscribing members, but they limit access to non-members. Barriers to participation and access can take many other forms. These forms may include lack of exposure and information, cultural contradiction, and inappropriate facilities relative to abilities. Other barriers may include perceptions about the environment, distance, personal attributes, social place, spending power, previous exposure, disability and non-responsiveness of the delivery system.

Barriers to recreation participation lie at the heart of concerns about equity. The issue seems to be that barriers are not uniformly limiting across various social strata. Research has begun to describe barriers, but understanding them and predicting their consequences largely are unknowns. We have begun to understand the complexity of the subject of barriers and that it involves both the perceived and the actual. Barriers are not mutually exclusive or separable. Access to recreation opportunities involves a combination of factors formed by who and where a person is at a time and place in life.

Another fundamental concern regarding access is that of how funding is acquired. The literature has documented many of the alternatives, including successes and failures. For example, third-party reimbursement procedures for therapeutic recreation, philanthropy, fees, and taxes are among the alternatives pursued to assure access. But research has done relatively little to evaluate efficiency and the distributional consequences of such means. Needed are models and methods suitable for evaluating financial alternatives.

Research has produced good descriptive information about who the recreation seekers are and the likely consequences of administering various forms of fees. Prediction of revenues and changes in participation rates are the contributions of economics. These accomplishments are the more notable among those which thus far have addressed the issue of fees.

Information can be either a barrier or a stimulant to recreation participation. It is obvious that lack of knowledge prohibits participation. Research has only begun to assess the different influences that alternative information dissemination strategies may have upon different social strata.

An appreciable amount of descriptive work has been directed toward access for certain population strata. For example, recreation access for native Americans has been described in the southwestern states. Some focus also has been devoted to access for older people; noting that access to a variety of activities is more important than frequency of participation in achieving life satisfaction. Most older people pursue sedentary, close-to-home activities because of physical, financial, mobility or other limitations. Aside from obvious physical constraints, research has not produced a depth of knowledge about why older people change participation habits and what actions can be taken to mitigate undesirable changes. Older people once were young, and as young people they learned a set of values and preferences. How these values and preferences carry through to influence participation in later years of life is a potentially enlightening research undertaking.

People with disabilities have also received some research attention from the perspective of access. Mostly this work has been applied and has not delved deeply into the situations and perceptions involved with recreation by the disabled. The physically disabled face imposing physical barriers. But like many other disabled persons, they also face attitudes toward them by other publics and by some managers that may act as barriers.

Among special populations, the economically disadvantaged are probably the most numerous. They occur across all other "labeled" special populations. Complicating access for economically disadvantaged persons is their lack of access to information, experience or exposure, transportation acceptance, equipment, and many other affiliate circumstances. More is known about the urban poor than is known about the rural poor.

The mentally retarded represent a different special population in that they usually do not make sovereign decisions. Access for this population strata is largely addressed through institutional programs and household facilitation. Interestingly, when unconstrained, participation patterns by retarded persons are very similar to the patterns of those who are not retarded. A typical difference is that participation is not as often. The barrier to more frequent participation has been shown to be in part due to a lack of friendship networking.

Conflict and on-site interaction among the many users of outdoor areas are increasing phenomena and can become barriers to recreational access. Interactions occur within recreation, as well as between recreation and other land uses. Progress has been made in describing interactions between recreation and other uses, particularly those that are visual and those affecting vegetation. Techniques have been developed to monitor on-site effects and to determine what is needed to meet recreation preferences. Tools such as the Recreation Opportunity Spectrum and Limits of Acceptable Change are among the applicable results of research. Through knowledge of how recreationists interact with sources and resource uses, access and satisfactions can be improved.

Quality and Appropriate Opportunities

Carrying capacity is a key concern in evaluating the quality of recreational opportunities. Resources and social and managerial factors interact to delimit capacity. Quality and appropriateness of recreational opportunities are both defined by and in turn define capacity. Too many people, incompatible uses, inappropriate management, and unrealistic user expectations are among the factors that enter into the quality/capacity interaction. Research and the thinking of researchers have greatly improved our understanding of capacity. But the linkage to quality is yet to be fully developed.

Information is one of the more important elements that affects the interaction between quality and capacity. Information for the user about opportunities influences choice of time, place, activity, perception, and behavior. Information about the user enables a better response by managers. Research has helped in understanding the use and importance of information from both perspectives. What seems to be lacking is a firm grounding in theory.

In addition to information, there are many facets of behavior and management that relate to the quality and appropriateness of the recreational opportunities as provided through our delivery system. Deviant behavior is one of these facets. Research in this area has dealt mostly with users' and managers' perceptions and with potential management strategies to cope with deviant behaviors. Most of the research has been descriptive, not experimental. Broadly generalizable and applicable results are not yet available.

The processes of planning and management as a research topic, beyond those aspects dealing with information and deviant behavior controls, have provided a number of concepts and tools. Among these, understanding that recreation is much more than mere numbers of people have led to better definitions of the outputs of recreation management. This output orientation leads to clearer statements and understandings of the appropriateness of various opportunity choices and of the components of quality.

One of the targets of planning is to better define the feasible and efficient set of management strategies. Research and the contributed thinking of researchers have greatly aided this process of defining strategies. Planning and management have been given a better set of tools by which to determine which outputs are most appropriate.

There has been an enormous amount of research focusing on wilderness management. This research has identified management and policy strategies. Similarly, intensive work has in past years focused on rivers as recreational resources. Most of this research has described the users, types of uses, equipment, site choices, and evaluations of quality. Among recreational settings, rivers (and lakes) are among the most highly attractive and popular. Absent is a holistic approach through research to developing clear definitions of what is being demanded and where.

Research focusing on quality and appropriateness of recreational opportunities related to trail recreation is less voluminous. Trail use is growing and research has developed some tools for monitoring this use and its effects. Studies have described the users, their attitudes, and physical trail wear. Translating this information into guidelines for maintaining a high quality of trail recreational opportunities is yet in the future.

Research on motivations has produced a better understanding of the role of psychological states (i.e., "frequency of the receiver") as an aspect of quality or satisfaction. From this perspective, structural variables including complexity and mystery, obtain greater meaning as stimuli in recreational participation. As a "transactional model," this approach acknowledges the interactive roles of users, the resource and managers in producing an appropriate mix and quality of opportunities.

One setting to which little research has been devoted is that of urban parks and recreation. In this arena, especially, there seems to be a strong need for applied research. The components of quality and the appropriate mix of opportunities for various urban publics is a particularly vivid issue. Much of the work completed has described users, external benefits, and the distribution of benefits. But knowledge of which factors affect quality for the many urban publics is inadequate. This is not to say that a considerable quantity of literature is not available. Much has been written regarding infrastructure, information, management, financing, program evaluation, liability and planning. But this writing has presented the professional's perspective, not the results of well-designed research. For example, recent financial pressures have made public/private partnerships an attractive option. No identifiable research has been conducted to evaluate the likely dimensions and consequences of this partnership.

Protection of Environments and Resources

Inadequate assessment methods are a principal limitation of more effective protection and management of environmental and natural resources. If the case is not first presented well, then fiscal and political resources may not be adequately mobilized. If solid evaluative results are not available, management and allocative decisions also may be off target. Research is beginning to provide guidelines for comprehensive examination, costing, and evaluation of resource employment alternatives including protection and preservation. The need for improved assessment and planning rationales and tools cuts across the spectrum of resource settings from the city to the most remote and wild environments. Recent works associated with the Renewable Resources Planning Act Assessment and of the Public Area Recreation Visitor Study Group, both national in scope, are beginning to contribute some significant advances. Planning tools such as rational, comprehensive synoptic, and transactive models have been the focus of some research. But a major deficiency in all of these is their focus on now and their apparent inadequacy in representing likely scenarios and values of future generations. This inadequacy reaches beyond public resources. There also is a paucity of good information about protection of the common interest in private lands.

A research need is consideration of non-recreational values and uses of wilderness and other wild, "undisturbed" environments. These values include scientific, ecosystem representation, subsistence, human developmental, habitat for critical threatened and endangered species, educational, and preservation of unique environments. These values are typically under-represented in allocative and management decisions.

Conflict between recreational and other resource uses is an increasing phenomenon. We have made some progress in providing methods for examining tradeoffs. But, one of the holes in guidelines and models based in planning theory is inadequate consideration of adjacent land values and uses. Air, water, acoustical and visual externalities are particularly problematic. Much of the visual resources assessment principles and methodology resulting from research relates to the near or local perspective, as opposed to the vista perspective.

In many instances, recreation itself is a threat to sensitive environments and the vegetation, soil, water, and fauna composing these environments. Vegetation and soil have been studied most, particularly with regard to developed sites and trail impacts. Bacterial content of water and off-road vehicular impacts on wildlife have also received some study. While we have learned a great deal, there remain many facets of the impact of recreation on environments for which we have little information. In particular there are needs to know more about impacts on microflora and fauna, about visual perceptions among different types of users, about loss of critical habitat, and about disruption of ecological balance.

At the very heart of environmental protection is the degree to which people are sensitive to or knowledgeable of nature ecosystems. Here our lack of research output is noticeable. What constitutes an adequate public environmental awareness? How can environmental education of the public be achieved? How much should we invest in environmental education and, if done, how would society now and societies of the future benefit— assuming that measures of the resulting human benefit provide an appropriate measure of environmental protection. Some of the work on public involvement has helped define the extent of the problem.

At a more basic level, there are simple questions such as how much, where, and how various environments should be preserved. Research has described to a limited extent what we have, what we have lost, and whether we could bring back some of the lost. Organizations such as the Nature Conservancy and the U.S.

Forest Service are working toward more comprehensive, systematic information about these questions, but the amount of work yet to be done is enormous.

THE FUTURE

Some Observations About the Future

In reviewing what research has contributed, several interesting and helpful insights became apparent. The most substantive one was the profound degree to which research and researchers have impacted the course of outdoor recreation. Stepping back and taking a selfless view of what research has contributed offers an impressive and almost overwhelming feeling of pride. This is far from saying that the work is finished, for it is not finished. The fact remains that the research communities of the past and present have been bountiful in the technology produced. This technology has seemed to make an enormous difference in the direction and ways the "delivery system" has responded to different publics of American society.

Also a Critique

In fairness, some of the insights gained through a review of past and present research have indicated opportunities for improvement. This is to be expected in a subject area that has grown from infancy to adolescence in only 30 short years. We are not a matured discipline and yet have a distance to go before achieving that maturity. It is often true that one is his or her own worst critic. Let a researcher offer some self-criticisms of research in outdoor recreation.

1. Often studies have been undertaken without making adequate ties to and thus benefiting from relevant previous work. Especially important are ties to other disciplines such as sociology, psychology, economics, geography, health, medicine, and engineering. A large portion of outdoor recreation research lacks this firm theoretical grounding.

2. There is a need for more follow-up research. It seems that many studies are "one shot" in nature and do not build upon preceding results and lines of investigation by the same investigator or group of investigators.

3.   A weakness of some studies is their need for better tools and methods by which studied phenomena can be more meaningfully and consistently described and quantified.

4.   Often interpretations of findings do not go far enough in providing management and planning tools and in identifying the implications of advancements of theory and methodology. This is another reason for better grounding our research in theory.

5.   There seems to be a disproportionately small emphasis on interactions and a much larger emphasis on singularly viewed phenomena and of change are not yet well understood.

Figure 3
Comparison of Research Accomplishments Cross Classified Among the Dimensions and Type of Information that Research has Produced

TYPE OF INFORMATION	BASIC ISSUE				
	Credible Information	Importance of Recreation	Access	Quality and Appropriateness	Protection of Environment
Managerial Process and Tool	273	204	168	120	36
Types of Demand and Benefits	276	204	168	120	36
Population Strata Needs and Equity	138	102	84	60	18
Settings and Resources	115	85	70	50	15
Interactions Among Users & Resources	115	85	70	50	15
Determinants of Change	46	34	28	20	6

Summary of Research Accomplishments and
Future Implications

Figure 3 depicts a subjective ranking of the accomplishments thus far gained through research in outdoor recreation/resource planning. This ranking is based on a count of published papers obtained from subjectively picked sources. The larger numbers in the northwest quadrant identify the greatest amount of written material and previous research effort. In this quadrant, which we could label as applied and descriptive, most of the product has addressed the issues of providing credible information for decisions and of accounting for the social and economic importance of recreation. The middle band in Figure 3 separates quadrants and depicts the crosswalk between types of settings and resources for recreation and access to these settings. The southeast quadrant appears to identify the issues and information needs to which research has thus far contributed least.

The smaller numbers in the southeast quadrant indicate that interactions between and among resources and resource user interests and the determinants of change in these resources and user interests are areas that are not well enough understood. Understanding interactions and determinants are major information barriers to more effectively and appropriately providing quality recreational opportunities and experiences and to better protecting critical natural environments. Understanding interactions and determinants of change may be our most pressing and challenging future problem. A particular, but not exclusive, future emphasis of research applying to outdoor recreation/ resource planning and management should be the quality and protection of natural resources.

Along with these research futures, greater emphases are needed on the issues of access to recreational opportunities and of improving the information that the "deciders" who influence the future have about the importance of recreation. Recreation is very likely to be more important and valuable in the future than it is now. This likely will mean that access will become more of an issue. In particular equitable access among population strata will be a concern. We know little about involvements among social strata in outdoor recreation and environmental issues. It does seem that these involvements are disproportionate. We can say little about why this is true or whether it is important. But without everyone's involvement in deciding the future of our natural environments, continued access inequities seem assured.

Further research across all of the issues and types of information listed in Figure 3 will certainly be needed. As the 21st century unfolds, there will be other concerns not yet foreseen. We must begin now to depend upon our best vision of the future, for there is a time lag between initiation of research and technology hand-off. As we think about this future for research specialists, we should be attentive to areas not yet fully addressed (i.e., the "southeast quadrant"). Research must be visionary if the influential role played by researchers of the past is to continue.

BIBLIOGRAPHY

Harper, V.L. (1963). Outdoor Recreation Research in Federal Agencies. In *Proceedings of the National Conference on Outdoor Recreation Research* (pp. 43-52). Ann Arbor, MI: School of Natural Resources, the University of Michigan.

Outdoor Recreation Policy Review Group. (1983). *Outdoor Recreation for America 1983*. Washington, D.C.: Resources for the Future.

Outdoor Recreation Resources Review Commission. (1960). In *Proceedings of the Second Joint Meeting*. Washington, D.C.: U.S. Government Printing Office.

The President's Commission on Americans Outdoors. (1986). *A Literature Review*. Washington, D.C.: U.S. Government Printing Office.

USDA Forest Service. (1976). In H. Ken Cordell (Ed.). *Proceedings of the Southern States Recreation Research Workshop*, Asheville, NC.

USDA Forest Service. (1971). In *Proceedings of Recreation Symposium*. Upper Darby, PA: Northeastern Forest Experiment Station.

van der Smissen, Betty. (1963). Outdoor Recreation Research in Federal Agencies. In *Proceedings of the National Conference on Outdoor Recreation Research* (pp. 43-52). Ann Arbor, MI: School of Natural Resources, the University of Michigan.

Management and Evaluation of Leisure Programs and Services

Past, Present, and Future Research

Lawrence R. Allen
Department of Parks, Recreation, and Tourism Management
——————— **Clemson University** ———————

INTRODUCTION

It is difficult to assess past, present, and future research in management and evaluation of leisure services because of a lack of clarity and/or consensus regarding several key terms associated with this task. Oddly, there appears to be a growing consensus as to what is meant by leisure programs or services, but confusion remains regarding the concepts of management, evaluation, and in particular, research.

For example, what is management? One's response certainly depends upon one's particular school of thought. Management entails the designing of jobs and tasks to insure efficiency of operation according to proponents of the scientific management approach. This is a somewhat dated view, but it still has application in some settings. Human relations advocates stress that management deals with human needs and social factors to develop a productive and satisfying work setting. Human resources enthusiasts would suggest that management is the action of providing a supportive and open environment, one in which the individual has the opportunity for self-direction and to optimize personal resources. Still others would suggest that management is "the process of planning, organizing, leading, and controlling the efforts of organizational members and the use of other organizational resources in order to achieve stated organizational goals" (Stoner and Wankel, 1986, p. 4). This classical school of thought was originally developed by Fayol (1949) and has continued to be a dominant framework for the study of management since the 1930s. Because of its broad acceptance and well-defined dimensions, this concept of management will provide the basis for discussion in this essay. Also, evaluation is viewed as the systematic assessment of the success or worth of some phenomenon based upon predetermined criteria and is a function performed in all areas of leisure services management (Carpenter and Howe, 1985).

Research is an equally difficult concept to clarify in one's mind. Is research only those activities in which formally developed hypotheses are tested in highly controlled settings to investigate the proposed relationship between natural or social phenomena? OR does it include methods of inquiry that do not subscribe to the very rigid positivistic paradigm of research? If one reviews standard definitions of scientific research, it is apparent that there are gradations or degrees inherent within the research process. For example, Kerlinger (1986) states scientific research is "the systematic, controlled, empirical, and critical investigation of natural phenomena guided by theory and hypotheses about the presumed relations among such phenomena" (p. 10). All who have been involved in "scientific investigations" realize that there are degrees of systemization and control in any scientific investigation; there are no absolutes. Also, some researchable issues do not lend themselves to hypothesis testing initially; are these not scientific investigations? Even though I conceptually understand and philosophically support scientific research as espoused by Kerlinger and others, I still have difficulty determining when it stops and other forms of investigation begin.

I also have difficulty with the implied difference in quality between applied and basic research efforts. Although many researchers in leisure studies suggest that applied research is less valuable or meritorious than basic research, the difference between the two approaches is not one of merit, but of purpose. The advancement of knowledge through theory development is the aim of basic research. There is little regard for immediate application in terms of problem solving, decision making, or policy development. Applied research, on the other hand, is problem oriented. It is every bit as rigorous as basic research, but is more oriented toward practical problems and concerns. Applied research does not adhere to the basic tenets of scientific research and its focus is on generalization and not site-specific solutions. Because of its problem-solving orientation, management research generally falls within the applied category, and thus is not considered a worthy area of investigation by some leisure researchers.

A third type of research also exists: action research. Much of the criticism of applied research is actually more descriptive of this research type. Action research marginally contributes to the advancement of knowledge, since it does not have the generalizability or the rigor of basic or applied research. Its orientation is the solution of a specific problem within a specific setting. It rarely uses the principles of the scientific method to which we traditionally subscribe. Thus, it fits into a nonscientific research category. Admittedly, much of the inquiry in management would fall into this category because of the proprietary and site-specific nature of the problems with which organizations deal.

An added problem in understanding research in management and evaluation, which does not exist in the study of leisure behavior is the need to initially formulate the delivery system for which theory can be developed. In other words, the professional service must be created before hypotheses can be tested regarding service management. With this in mind, what do we call all the early efforts that went into the development of our profession? These efforts should not be discarded or discredited completely because the scholars behind them did not adhere to the scientific method in its strictest sense. Rather, these individuals should be recognized for the tremendous thought and effort put into the conceptualization and operationalization of our profession.

Actually, one could consider management development in leisure services paralleling the stages of science. First, one describes the phenomenon in question. In our case, one initially describes and defines management and evaluation applications as they relate to the delivery of leisure services. Second, one attempts to explain the phenomenon. From a professional development perspective, the attempt is to explain why the initially developed management and evaluation procedures functioned as they did; what effect did they have on the delivery of leisure services? In this stage, theory building is initiated through the testing of preliminary hypotheses. However, more often than not, explanation actually evolves out of systematically gathering facts to describe management phenomena. This is the basis for grounded theory development. Today, management and evaluation research is just beginning to address the explanation stage.

The third stage of science is prediction. Formal hypotheses are tested and theory is developed to explain the interrelationships among phenomena for the purpose of explanation and prediction. From a management perspective, this would entail the testing of various managerial procedures and processes to determine their success and/or effectiveness as they relate to predetermined criteria. This stage of science has rarely been addressed in leisure services management research.

The advancement of science through a very strict positivistic view of research, is an area to which several philosophers of social science are now taking exception. Many contend in the areas of professional development and problem solving, where competing forces and interdependence of activities are common, the ends or proposed outcomes are ambiguous or not defined at all. Theory development under these realities does not lend itself to scientific inquiry as suggested by positivism. Simon (1972), Schein (1973), and Glazer (1974) have all cited the shortcomings of positivism to the advancement of professional knowledge. They advocate a more reflective and humanistic process that is better suited for the uncertainty, instability, and amorphous circumstances surrounding problems in professional spheres such as social work, planning, education, and management. They contend that this more reflective approach will overcome the pitfalls of the rigid scientific method, which lacks relevance to the practical problems and decisions professionals have to make in their work settings (Schon, 1983). Individuals investigating leisure services management should utilize alternative methodologies that are sensitive to complexities of management research but still maintain the rigor as suggested by the more traditional scientific method.

This discussion has presented some of the issues surrounding the analysis of management research. Although the discussion was by no means exhaustive, it did provide a basis for understanding the confusion relating to the quality of research in the management of leisure programs and services. Now let's turn to the topic at hand.

Past Research Efforts

The development of an efficient and effective leisure services delivery system has been an evolutionary process dating back to the late 1800s. Professional and scholarly writing in the field, however, was very limited prior to the creation of the Playground Association of America in 1906, which later became the National Recreation Association in 1926.

During these early years, the concern was with the definition of the profession. Early scholars were attempting to define the initial parameters of the service as well as establish procedures for carrying out its activities (Sapora, 1961). Most of the early writings did not deal with management or evaluation issues per se, but rather focused on the direct delivery of services and the recreation behavior of various subgroups. A bibliography of over 300 master's theses and doctoral studies complied by G. M. Goss (1940) of Louisiana State University records the type of investigations conducted prior to 1940. Almost all the studies were descriptive using a survey methodology or anecdotal approach. Examples of some of the studies investigating the recreation behavior of various groups include: "Leisure Time Needs of a Boys' Group as Revealed by a Study of Samples" (Bantz, 1928); "A Study of the Recreational Activities of 10th Grade Boys and the Relationship of Choice of Activities to Motor Ability, Intelligence Quotient, and Chronological Age" (Barnett, 1934); "The Leisure Time and Recreational Life of the Negro Boy in Columbus, Ohio" (Gibbs, 1934); and "Game Preference of 10,000 Fourth Grade Children" (Schwendener, 1932). Although some investigations would not appear to be appropriate in today's society, they generally were no different than investigations that are undertaken today.

A second focal point of early studies that was related more to management included efforts to describe, prescribe, and evaluate program services. Some of the titles include: "Effect of Discontinuance of Supervision on Certain Philadelphia Bureau of Recreation Play Areas Upon the Delinquency Rate of Boys Aged 16 to 20 years, Inclusive" (Balen, 1934); "Practice and Policies of the Administration of Outdoor Recreation in Los

Angeles Co." (Clark, 1939); "An Investigation into the Conduct and Financial Support of Playground and Recreation Activities in Selected States" (Davis, 1931) "A Study of the Organizational and Functional Relationship of Public and Private Recreation Agencies" (Fitzgerald, 1939); "A Survey of Play Spaces Municipally Owned and Supervised by Either Park Departments or Boards of Education in Incorporated Towns in the State of Washington" (Kinsman, 1934); and, "A Study to Determine the Effect of Campfire Membership on the Social Adjustment of Girls" (Truxton, 1932). Again, these studies were primarily descriptive, but there were initial efforts to investigate relationships among phenomena and the effectiveness of services. Although it was not possible to assess the quality of these investigations based upon the few studies that were available for review, I suspect these investigations were very systematic efforts of inquiry that subscribed to the basic tenets of scientific research.

As indicated by the sample of titles presented, there was some interest in addressing management issues during these early years. The profession, however, was not in a state of development that allowed formal testing of hypotheses for theory building. Nonetheless, these efforts were critical to advancing the body of knowledge to a point where hypotheses could be formulated. These early developments, however, were consistent with the first stage of science and did provide a basis for the development of grounded theory.

Goss's listing of master's theses and dissertations provides some indication of the scholarly activity during the earlier part of the century. It does not contain, however, research conducted outside the academic setting. One of the outstanding pieces of research, in the area of recreation management prior to the 1950s, was commissioned in 1925 by President Coolidge. As a sponsor of the First National Conference on Outdoor Recreation, he requested a nationwide study of municipal and county parks and their systems of administration. This national survey resulted in a document of over 1,000 pages titled "Parks: A Manual of Municipal and County Parks" (Weir, 1928). The manual is the most complete document of parks and recreation management principles in existence even today. It presents concepts and principles of management that have not changed since its publication in 1928. The study is a credit to the professionals of the

1920s, but certainly an indictment of later professionals, since we have not seen any comparable effort since that time. Another area of investigation that was very prevalent during this time was the extensive efforts in comprehensive planning of recreation services in municipal settings. Some of the most sophisticated planning efforts in our profession were conducted before 1940. For example, in 1925 the Buffalo, New York Planning Association completed a comprehensive recreation plan that included a detailed analysis of recreation opportunities provided by public, private, commercial, and industrial entities as well as a demographic profile of residents in each district of the city. Based upon this information and previously established recreation standards, recommendations for future facilities were developed along with procedures for administering and financing the city's effort.

A second example is the five-volume recreation plan developed for the Chicago Park District in 1940 (Todd, 1940). This document provides a total analysis of the recreation environment in the City of Chicago. Volume V provides a comprehensive set of recommendations for the Park District that is unparalleled today. Other cities, such as Madison, Wisconsin; Cincinnati, Ohio; Kansas City, Missouri; and Dade County, Florida conducted extensive recreation plans that were the forerunners of efforts today. Each had a significant impact on the development of public policy and management of recreation services.

It is clear that there was no lack of systematic inquiry into recreation management and administration on a generalized level during the early part of the century. This trend continued until the 1950s and 1960s when there appeared to be a growing interest in specific areas of management such as finance, personnel, and policy development as well as a more concerted effort to evaluate management principles and programs. Many of these studies remained descriptive, but they became more defined in purpose and began to explore relationships among various management principles and outcomes. Correlational and comparative studies began to appear that suggest, at least informally, an effort to move into the second stage of scientific inquiry, the explanation of phenomena. The interest moved beyond creation of the profession to analyzing and enhancing the profession. The field was evolving to the point that critical assessment could begin to take place. Examples of studies typical of this time, addressing management and evaluation issues, are: "The Development of Personnel Standards for Leadership Duties in Public Recreation" (Anderson, 1948); "Evaluation Criteria for the Appraisal of General Recreation Supervisor's Competencies" (Lokken, 1958); "Analysis of Administrative Problems in New York State Public Recreation" (Prezioso, 1954); and "A Study of an Experiment in the Use of School Subsidies to Promote Community Recreation Programs in the State of Washington" (Tappin, 1956). Unfortunately, the research of this time remained highly *ex post facto* with very little experimentation of procedures or assessment of impact. We lacked research that analyzed the efficiency or effectiveness of professional management.

Present Research Efforts

Present research in management and evaluation can be categorized as much the same as the efforts conducted in the 1950s and early 1960s. The quality and quantity of research in recreation and leisure in general, however, has been enhanced. This is due in part to the rapid growth of academic programs at this particular time, the consolidation of splintered professional groups under NRPA, and the creation of expanded scholarly outlets such as the *Journal of Leisure Research, Leisure Sciences,* and *Leisure Studies.* The basic methodology remains heavily oriented toward survey techniques. Certainly, this is a generalization, since there are isolated examples of research studies using other designs, such as quasi-experimental, experimental, or ethnographic.

Because of the rapid growth of recreation services in both the public and private sector during the 50s, 60s, and early 70s, there was a strong need to provide academic programs to train professionals as well as provide in-service training to many individuals lacking appropriate expertise by filling recreation positions. Research activity continued to grow, but it was not primarily in the area of management. The study of leisure behavior grew in sophistication and the study of program delivery continued, but the general areas of management seemed to stagnate except in relation to outdoor recreation management specifically. This area was well serviced by the interests of agencies such as the Bureau of Outdoor Recreation, Forest Service, National Park Service, and other federal and state agencies. We did see the growth of professional magazines such as *Parks and Recreation,* which were a primary vehicle for disseminating management information; but there was little impetus for the advancement of management knowledge and theory. The need to respond to practitioners' lack of knowledge diverted energies from the creation of knowledge to the dissemination of information. And, times were good, money was plentiful, so who needed to worry about effectiveness and efficiency of management systems.

The optimism of the 50s and 60s quickly faded in the 1970s. The energy crisis, litigation frenzy, tax revolt, and a general scrutiny of governmental services brought recreation professionals and researchers back to reality. Accountability, efficiency, and effectiveness became the buzz words of the late 70s and 80s. These circumstances as well as the growing sophistication of the academic community kindled a renewed interest in management and evaluation research.

We now have a cadre of researchers who have expertise and interests in specific areas of management such as marketing, personnel, finance, evaluation, and planning. Also, additional scholarly publications such as the *Journal of Park and Recreation Administration* have been initiated that are dedicated to the management of leisure services. These developments have helped increase the quality and quantity of management research.

Funding, unfortunately, remains a severe limitation to the advancement of the study of leisure services management. Federal, state, or local governments have never placed a high priority on management research, and most research conducted by the private sector is proprietary and action-research oriented. The American Academy of Park and Recreation Administration in cooperation with the National Recreation Foundation has begun to support management research, but the need is much greater than the resources that are presently available. The lack of a national advocacy research group also has severely retarded the quality of leisure management research. NRPA, The Forest Service, and the National Park Service have developed research agendas and policies; however, these efforts have not been strongly supported or promoted within these organizations, the profession, or the academic community. Hopefully, with the growing expertise and interest in management research and changing societal conditions, these constraints will change in the future.

Future Research Needs

Today is an opportunity for change. All indications are that we are moving to a service-oriented society. My question is: will leisure services be one of the services recognized and respected in this new society? We must grasp this opportunity and develop a firm foundation for our profession. Even in this new society, financing will remain a critical issue. Services will expand and competition for limited dollars will be stiff. The public will support those services that provide the greatest benefit in a cost-effective manner. Our research charge must be to develop a strong theoretical base that verifies the effectiveness and efficiency of our service as it relates to society in general.

In order to accomplish this charge, management research must be broader than the positivistic approach. Management issues are very complex and cannot necessarily be addressed through a reductionistic orientation heavily supported by the physical sciences. Further, our research approach cannot rely solely on survey research methods or *ex post facto* designs. I strongly encourage experimentation and analysis of management principles and concepts that address the complexity of the issues involved. Research approaches that recognize that competing forces and symbiotic relationships exist in management situations must be developed. Field experimentation, comparative analysis, case study, ethnographic inquiry, participant-observation, and document analysis are all alternative research approaches that may be more effective in addressing management and evaluation issues than simple survey techniques. These approaches need to be encouraged and supported by the profession.

In conjunction with being innovative in our research designs, we must be "on target" with our research questions. For example, we have maintained strict adherence to traditional industrial management principles. Recently, however, several authors have questioned the wisdom of blind acceptance of these principles. For example, Draper clearly states that "the tacit acceptance of industrial management studies appears not appropriate for social services including parks and recreation" (p. 54, 1983). It is assumed the social service worker has the same desires, satisfaction, and perceptions of the work environment as the industrial worker. Preliminary findings suggest that these assumptions may be false. If this is the case, we may be basing our management principles on totally erroneous assumptions. Gray (1983) also criticizes adherence to traditional American management concepts. Management by numbers, excessive concern for short-range gains at the expense of long-range potential and the lack of interest in research and development are all management practices of which the recreation profession is guilty. He suggests that parks and recreation professionals must explore alternative management philosophies such as those presented by the Japanese. Gold (1985) suggests that future research agendas must address the broader context of our profession as it relates to society as a whole. We must recognize societal changes that will affect the nature of our service and be accountable to the public. Frugality and austerity, consolidation and integration and the provision of "more with less" all have implications for the management of recreation services; each must be investigated. Godbey (1985) further emphasizes the point of accountability by stressing that success of leisure service management and evaluation must be assessed in qualitative rather than quantitative terms alone. It is not enough to be efficient; we must also be effective. For example our effectiveness can be enhanced if the extensive body of behavioral research is integrated into the delivery of leisure services. Presently there is little effort to integrate these two primary areas of leisure research.

There are other critical questions in management and evaluation which need further investigation and analysis. Certainly, models of alternative financing of recreation services must be explored. The role of revenue production in public recreation is a major philosophical and practical issue most practitioners are grappling with today. This issue, as important as it is, has never been comprehensively assessed and explored. Again, we have made little effort at solutions. Other major management issues include: public and private competition and cooperation, environmental deterioration associated with recreation use, civil rights and gender equality, unionization and the changing labor force, changing role of service providers, and ethical behavior of the professional (Bannon, 1985). Each of these issues has been well documented in the literature; now we need comprehensive efforts using innovative research approaches to explore solutions.

The concern no longer is one of identifying or detailing the problems but one of how to arrive at valid solutions; how do we conduct rigorous investigations that are relevant to the profession? In order to accomplish this, we need several changes of thought on the part of the researcher, the practitioner, and their profession. First, we need to bridge the abyss between the researcher and practitioner. They are both seeking the same goal, enhancement of the profession, but from different perspectives. A partnership must be established. The practitioners must become involved in the research process and the researcher must make his research relevant to the profession. For example, management research cannot be conducted in a sterile laboratory. The community is the researcher's laboratory. The practitioner must provide access to this laboratory.

Second, a willingness to explore alternative methods and solutions must be established within our profession. If we are to be one of the chosen services, the profession needs to accept research and development as an essential professional function and commit funds to carry it out. Within the business community, experimentation with different thoughts, ideas, and products is an accepted part of managerial activity. In many cases, this is the difference between a profitable and bankrupt enterprise. How many recreation departments have a research and development division within the agency? I can only think of a handful.

A third area that needs modification if relevant management research is to be conducted in our field is the reward system for the academic researcher. Academics are rewarded for the quality and quantity of their scholarly activity. Efficiency of time is a critical factor in determining the type of research methodology a faculty member will utilize. Unfortunately, some of the methodologies that are most appropriate for solving many of the management issues facing our profession are also the most time consuming. For example, field experimentation, ethnographic inquiries, case studies, and longitudinal studies are all more involved than conducting the traditional one-time survey. Because of the constraint on their time, academic researchers may be prone to address only those problems that are amenable to survey research methodology. I am not suggesting, however, that academics are so calculated and driven by promotion and tenure that they are not committed to addressing the difficult questions, but time certainly is a factor in determining research approaches.

A related issue concerning the reward system is the worth of engaging in management research that inherently may be very applied. This issue was addressed earlier, but it should be reinforced that applied research is an acceptable area of investigation for academic professionals. The issue is not whether a research question is considered applied or basic, but rather the quality of the research design. If an investigation is conducted in a systematic and rigorous fashion, it should be accepted and respected by academic peers, whether applied or basic.

Finally, we need to establish a strong advocacy group of academics and professionals that promotes leisure management research and pushes for the development of regional and national research agendas with an integrated network of investigators. In conducting the library research for this paper, I became intimately aware of the lack of coordination among recreation and leisure researchers. There is a tremendous body of knowledge that needs to be reviewed and integrated into new research questions. We cannot continue to repeat the same research questions while merely varying the setting and population. Coordination and cooperation among the research community is essential. We must establish research agendas that are relevant to the profession and then aggressively pursue these agendas.

In conclusion, research in the management and evaluation of leisure programs and services has been primarily of a descriptive nature and has been heavily influenced by reductionistic research orientation. Today, however, there is a question as to the validity of this approach given the ambiguities and uncertainties associated with management processes. More integrative research designs that recognize human motives, the realities of competing forces, and symbiotic relationships must be encouraged to advance the understanding of leisure services management. Future efforts must move beyond description. Analysis and explanation of management principles, leading to a firm foundation for service delivery, must be the focus of future researchers if leisure services, as a public service, is to survive in the future. The problems have been identified, the issues are clear; now we need a commitment from the academic and professional communities to address these challenges.

BIBLIOGRAPHY

Ackoff, Russell, L. (1962). *Scientific Method: Optimizing Applied Research Decisions.* New York: John Wiley and Sons, Inc.

Anderson, J. M. (1948). *The Development of Personnel Standards for Leadership Duties in Public Recreation.* Unpublished doctoral dissertation, New York University.

Balen, H. (1934). *Effect of the Discontinuance of Supervision of Certain Philadelphia Bureau of Recreation Play Areas Upon the Delinquency Rate of Boys Aged 16 to 20 Years, Inclusive.* Unpublished master's thesis, Temple University.

Bannon, J. J. (1985). Public Administration: Roots and Implications of Change. In T. Goodale and P. Witt (Eds.), *Recreation and Leisure: Issues in an Era of Change (Revised Edition).* State College, PA: Venture Publishing.

Bantz, R. D. (1928). *Leisure Time Needs of a Boys' Group as Revealed by a Study of Samples.* Unpublished master's thesis, Ohio State University.

Barnett, W. J. (1934). *A Study of Recreational Activities of 10th Grade Boys and the Relationship of Choice Activities to Motor Ability, Intelligence Quotient, and Chronological Age.* Unpublished master's thesis, University of Michigan.

Carpenter, G. M. and C. Z. Howe (1985). *Programming Leisure Experiences: A Critical Approach.* Englewood Cliffs, NJ: Prentice-Hall, Inc.

Clark, G. W. (1939). *Practices and Policies of the Administering of Public Recreation in Los Angeles, California.* Unpublished master's thesis, Los Angeles County Recreation Research Division.

Davis, L. W. (1931). *An Investigation into the Conduct and Financial Support of Playground and Recreation Activities in Selected States.* Unpublished master's thesis, New York University.

Draper, Debra J. (1983). The Adaptation and Implementation of Business and Industrial Management Strategies and Techniques. *Journal of Park and Recreation Administration* 1 (1): 51-61.

Fayol, Henri. (1949). *General and Industrial Management.* London: Sir Issac Pitman and Sons, Ltd.

Fitzgerald, G. B. (1939). *A Study of the Organizational and Functional Relationships of Public and Private Recreational Agencies.* Unpublished master's thesis, University of Minnesota.

Gibbs, G. F. (1934). *The Leisure Time and Recreational Life of the Negro Boy in Columbus, Ohio.* Unpublished master's thesis, University of Minnesota.

Glazer, Nathan. (1974). Schools of the Minor Professions. *Minerva.*

Godbey, Geoffrey, (1985). Urban Leisure Services: Reshaping a Good Thing. In T. Goodale and R. Witt (eds.), *Recreation and Leisure: Issues in an Era of Change (Revised edition)*. State College, PA: Venture Publishing.

Gold, Seymour M. (1985). Future Leisure Environments in Cities. In T. Goodale and R. Witt (eds.), *Recreation and Leisure: Issues in an Era of Change (Revised edition)*. State College, PA: Venture Publishing.

Goss, G. M. (1940). *Bibliography of Master's Theses and Doctoral Studies in the Field of Recreation.* Unpublished manuscript, Louisiana State University.

Gray, David E. (1983). American Management Lessons from the Japanese. *Journal of Park and Recreation Administration* 1(1): 1-6.

Kerlinger, Fred N. (1986). *Foundations of Behavioral Research, 3rd Edition.* New York: Holt, Rinehart and Winston.

Kinsman, T. (1934). *A Survey of Play Spaces Municipally Owned and Supervised by Either Parks Departments or Boards of Education in Incorporated Towns in the State of Washington.* Unpublished master's thesis, University of Washington.

Koontz, Harold and Cyril O'Donnell. (1972). *Principles of Management: An Analysis of Managerial Functions, 5th edition.* New York: McGraw-Hill Book Company.

Lokken, E. W. (1958). *Selective Criteria for the Appraisal of General Recreation Supervisors' Competencies.* Unpublished master's thesis, University of California-Los Angeles.

Prezioso, S. J. (1954). *Analysis of Administrative Problems in New York State Public Recreation.* Unpublished doctoral dissertation, Columbia University.

Sapora, Allen V. (1961). *A Basis for and a Procedure to Carry Out a Program of Research.* Unpublished manuscript, University of Illinois.

Schein, Edgar, (1973). *Professional Education.* New York: McGraw-Hill Book Company.

Schon, Donald A. (1983). *The Reflective Practitioner: How Professionals Think in Action.* New York: Basic Books, Inc., Publishers.

Schwendener, R. (1932). *Game Preference of 10,000 Fourth Grade Children.* Unpublished doctoral dissertation, Columbia University.

Simon, Hubert. (1972). *The Sciences of the Artificial.* Cambridge, MA: MIT Press.

Stoner, James and Charles Wankel. (1986). *Management, 3rd edition.* Englewood Cliffs, NJ: Prentice-Hall, Inc.

Tappin, Jr., W. R. (1956). *A Study of an Experiment in the Use of School Subsidies to Promote Community Recreation Programs in the State of Washington.* Unpublished doctoral dissertation, University of Washington.

Todd, A. J. (Ed). (1940). *Chicago Recreation Survey.* Chicago: Chicago Recreation Commission.

Truxton, S. (1932). *A Study to Determine the Effect of Campfire Membership on the Social Adjustment of Girls.* Unpublished master's thesis, University of Michigan.

van der Smissen, B. (1955). *An Analysis of the State Laws Pertaining to the Establishment of Public Park and Recreation Boards.* Unpublished doctoral dissertation, Indiana University.

Weir, L. H. (Ed.). (1928). *Parks: A Manual of Municipal and County Parks.* New York: A. S. Barnes and Co.

Statistical and Methodological Issues in Leisure Research

Past, Present, and Future Research

James E. Christensen
School of Natural Resources
—————— **Ohio State University** ——————

Nine years ago, a book appeared entitled Micromotives and Macrobehavior (Schelling, 1978). A purpose in writing that book was to explore "... the relationship between behavior characteristics of the individuals who comprise some social aggregate, and the characteristics of the aggregate" (Schelling, March 1978: 13). There are familiar examples of this kind of analysis. Smith (1937) characterized an economic system which, in the aggregate, seemed to work. It worked in spite of the fact that people were pursuing individual goals with no thought given to the total system. The economic system worked as if guided by an "invisible hand." Hardin (1968) illustrated the negative aspects of micromotives leading to macrobehavior which was, and still is, ecologically disastrous when he discussed the "Tragedy of the Commons." These examples show that what happens at the macrolevel may, or may not be, what is intended by the goal-seeking individuals at the microlevel.

An analysis is conducted here that focuses on the past, present, and future of statistical and methodological work in leisure research. A two-tiered approach is necessary to see if the investigations of individual scientists (microlevel) is producing progress in the field of leisure research (macrolevel). The paper is structured in the following fashion. In the next section a view is expressed on how "progressive research" (Lakatos, 1970) of statistical and methodological issues in leisure should occur. The third section examines, at the macrobehavior and microbehavior levels, the statistical and methodological work in leisure. This work is measured against the criteria of "progressive research." The objective is to gain some sense of the kind of progress that has been made in the study of these issues in leisure research. Finally, from the arguments presented in the second and third sections, it is explained why specific statistical and methodological issues for future research are not offered. What is offered, on the other hand, is a plan for the study of these kinds of issues in the future that would result in significant progress in leisure research.

It should be stated what not to expect in this paper. As just mentioned, the paper does not outline specific research topics. The paper is not a scientific analysis of statistical and method-ological issues such as others (e.g., Kapfer, 1964; Smith, 1964; Berstein and Freeman, 1975; McTavish, et al., 1976a; McTavish et al., 1976b) have conducted in other disciplines. Dibble (1973:51) states that "In the scientific style of thought there is a sharp distinction between cognitive statements and statements of value or of norms. . . . " It is not possible, in other words, to infer what ought to be by looking at what exists. A view is presented here of how statistical and methodological issues ought to be studied. Finally, despite suggesting what ought to be the approach to investigating these issues, it is recognized that other views exist. Conceding this point means that the arguments presented are not intended to change minds. Malone, at some point in the distant past, stated, "I have never in my life learned anything from a man who agreed with me." Some of the views expressed in the paper will not be agreeable to some, if not many, people in the field of leisure research. What is presented is a theory of how advances are made in studying statistical and methodological issues. It has been well documented that data, either supportive of a theory or not supportive of a theory will usually result in more belief in the original theory than seems warranted (Nisbett and Ross, 1980; Hoaglin, Mosteller, and Tukey, 1985). Mitroff (1974), as an example, studied the case of three scientists, each of whom had different theories of what the moon was like. None of those scientists changed their view despite data brought back during the Apollo mission that was not consistent with any of the three theories. Disagreement with the expressed views, in other words, will probably remain regardless of this paper. So it might be added to Malone's statement "I have never in my life learned anything from a man or woman who disagreed with me either." The ideas presented, therefore, are intended to provide a focus for thought with no hope that they will lead to a "scientific revolution" (Kuhn,1970).

A DISCOURSE ON HOW SCIENCE "PROGRESSES"

One View of "Progressive Micromotives and Macrobehavior"

Prior to measuring the past accomplishments, from the investigations of statistical and methodological issues in leisure, a definition of the standard used to measure "progress" is needed. This standard represents an "ideal" pattern of development of the issues. The ideal pattern chosen represented a "theory of scientific progress" (Ball, 1984) which suggests how matters develop in scientific analyses. The theory of scientific progress presented here has been shown to be more consistent with the history of science than, for example, the theory offered by Kuhn (1970) (Ball, 1984). It is against this "ideal type" that the developments in statistical and methodological issues are compared.

The theory was originally presented by Lakatos (1970) and later summarized by Ball (1984). It is not, therefore, an original theory. Reliance on the summarization of Ball (1984:35-38) in this presentation of the theory is acknowledged here.

Scientific progress only can be measured by looking at the successes and failures, not of single theories, but of successive series of theories. Such a series Lakatos calls a "research program." Each successive theory shares a common core of assumptions. An example of a core assumption in the study of statistics or methodology, accepted by some in the leisure field, is that leisure behavior can be measured quantitatively. A research program consists partially, therefore, of a "hard core" (Ball, 1984) of assumptions.

The hardness of these core assumptions is a methodological hardness; it is assured by the program's "negative heuristic." The negative heuristic is the methodological rule that criticism be directed away from the hard core of the program. Continuing with the illustration, we might take the assumption that quantitative models of leisure behavior are appropriate as a "given." These givens are necessary because developments do not occur when scientists dwell upon the "fundamental assumptions" of a theory or series of theories (Ball, 1984). The "hands-off" policy prescribed by the negative heuristic allows the scientist to get on with his or her work without having to constantly defend core assumptions. The program's "positive heuristic," by contrast prescribes the construction of a "protective belt" of auxiliary assumptions and hypotheses that serves to protect the program's hard core. It is assumed, for example, that whereas quantification is a legitimate enterprise (core assumption) in studying recreation behavior, then regression models (e.g., Elsner, 1971a; Elsner, 1971 b; Christensen and Yoesting, 1973; Field and O'Leary, 1973; Crandall, 1976; Christensen and Yoesting, 1976; Christensen, 1980), factor analysis (Romsa, 1973; McKechnie, 1974; Schmitz-Scherzer, et al., 1974; Hendee and Burdge, 1974; Smith, 1975; Ditton, Goodale and Johnsen, 1975; Ritchie, 1975; Beaman, 1975; London, Crandall and Fitzgibbons, 1977; Christensen and Yoesting, 1977; Duncan, 1978; Chase, 1979; Yu, 1980; Craefe, Ditton, Roggenbuck, and Schreyer, 1981), logit models (Stynes and Peterson, 1984) and other quantitative techniques are usable analytic tools or methodological paradigms (Carroll, 1972). It is these methodological paradigms that must bear the brunt of tests and get adjusted and readjusted, or even completely replaced, to defend the hard core. The spirit of this argument is captured, for example, in the work of Stynes and Peterson (1984). Those authors stated that "The recreation field has been dominated by linear and gravity models in some cases without very close scrutiny of the assumptions that underlie these mathematical structures or their suitability in a given application (Stynes and Peterson, 1984: 295). Stynes and Peterson proceeded to summarize the basic properties of logit models, contrasting them with more traditional linear and gravity models of recreation behavior. Additionally, they discussed the implications of the literature on logit models for recreation research. Under the conditions specified by Stynes and Peterson, linear models should be adjusted to logistic models, in some cases. Two points can be derived from this position. The first point is that theories are defended tenaciously. The task of keeping a theory (or series of theories) viable regardless of anomalies requires dogged persistence and ingenuity on the part of its defenders (Ball, 1984). The second point is that critics should be tolerant of attempts to "save" theories from "refutation." At times it appears that some individuals in leisure research think that this tenacity in defending a theory is very nearly a "crime against science" (Ball, 1984). Lakatos argues that the history of science is the story of bold conjectures and "decisive" counter evidence (remember the "moon scientists"!).

Theories, on the other hand, can be criticized and even, eventually, falsified. Criticism, however, must be directed against successive adjustments in the protective belt surrounding the hard core of that series of theories that constitutes a research program (Ball, 1984).

The critic must ask: are these adjustments "progressive" or "degenerating" ones *within the context of this particular research program?* (original emphasized) (Ball, 1984: 37). Lakatos defines progressive and degenerative adjustments in the abstract as follows:

> Let us take a series of theories T_1, T_2, T_3. . . where each subsequent theory results from adding auxiliary clauses to (or from semantical reinterpretations of) the previous theory in order to accommodate some anomaly, each theory having at least as much content as the unrefuted content of its predecessor . . . (A) series of theories is theoretically progressive (or "constitutes a theoretically progressive problem shift") if each new theory has some excess empirical content over its predecessor, that is, if it predicts some new, hitherto unexpected fact . . . (A) theoretically progressive series of theories is also empirically progressive (or "constitutes an empirically progressive problem shift") if some of this excess empirical content is also corroborated, that is, if each new theory leads us to the actual discovery of some new fact. Finally . . . a problem shift is progressive if it is both theoretically and empirically progressive, and degenerating if it is not. We "accept" problem shifts as "scientific" only if they are at least theoretically progressive; if they are not, we "reject" them as "pseudoscientific." Progress is measured by the degree to which a problem shift is progressive [i.e.] by the degree to which the series of theories leads us to the discovery of novel facts. We regard a theory in the series "falsified" when it is superseded by a theory with higher corroborated content.(Lakatos, 1970:118).

So long as this protective belt can be adjusted in "progressive" (i.e., content increasing) ways, the research program is in no danger. By the same token, a research program begins to falter when its protective belt can no longer be adjusted in progressive ways—when, that is, adjustments amount to no more than content-decreasing semantical ones and/or when they fail to anticipate new facts. Only then is the research program itself— hard core and all—in any danger of extinction. But no matter how water-logged it is, a research program will not sink and have to be abandoned until a better, more buoyant one comes along to replace it. In any case, the decision to abandon one research program in favor of another is not taken lightly, nor is it nonrational. It is at every step a critical, considered decision in the light of available alternative theories against which the progressiveness (or degeneration) of successive problem shifts is gauged. Science is, then, both rational and progressive.

PAST AND CURRENT RESEARCH PROGRAMS CONCERNED WITH STATISTICAL AND METHODOLOGICAL ISSUES IN LEISURE

Have they or do they Exist?

Against this backdrop the rhetorical question is asked "Have research programs existed and do they exist now in leisure?" The situation is first examined at the macrolevel of analysis. An examination at the microlevel will then follow.

Macrolevel Analysis

At this level the existence of research programs, as defined previously, can be detected. A judgment about the quality of this work is indicated in the discussion of microlevel research programs. Also existing at this level are some examples of directions that would not be defined as progressive in the examination of statistical and methodological issues.

From its recent start, the scientists in the field of leisure research have been refining our conceptual and methodological tools or building upon our "core" assumptions. We have had articles attempting to clarify key concepts in the field such as dimensions of leisure (Neulinger and Breit, 1969; Neulinger and

Breit, 1971; Kelly, 1972; Spreitzer and Snyder, 1974; Iso-Ahola, 1979a; Iso-Ahola, 1979b; Levy, 1979; Pierce, 1980; Roadburg, 1983; Mannell and Bradley, 1986), leisure attitudes (Ragheb, 1980; Ragheb and Beard, 1982), and the play concept (Barnett, 1978). The development of typologies has engaged a number of researchers (Romsa, 1973; Ritchie, 1975; Christensen and Yoesting, 1976; London et al., 1977; Gudykunst, Kantor and Parker, 1981). We have had development in the area of measuring leisure (e.g., Bull, 1971; Bull, 1972; Noe, 1972; Kelly, 1973; Ellis and Witt, 1984; Cosper and Shaw, 1985; Witt and Ellis, 1985). We have had developments on how to model recreation trip behavior (e.g., Wolfe, 1972; Cheung, 1972; Malamud, 1973, Fruend and Wilson, 1974; Beaman, 1974; Mednick, 1975; Cesario, 1975; McAllister and Klett, 1976; Beaman, 1976; Bell, 1977; Ewing, 1980; Darragh, Peterson and Dwyer 1983; Baxter and Ewing, 1986; Stynes, Peterson and Rosenthal, 1986). There have been developments in modeling visual preferences in outdoor recreation settings (Peterson and Neumann, 1969; Cook, 1972; Hamill, 1975; Thayer, Hodgson, et al., 1976; Buhyoff and Riesenman, 1979; Shelby and Harris, 1985; Buhyoff and Wellman, 1980; Schroeder and Brown, 1983). Methodological critiques of methods to measure aesthetic values for recreation settings (Kreimer, 1977) and critiques of these methods exist (e.g., Buhyoff and Wellman, 1979). There have been interchanges and articles building on understandings of statistical techniques such as correlations (McCuen, 1974; Christensen, 1979), canonical correlations (Christensen, 1983; Christensen, 1985), conjoint analysis (Cosper and Kinsley, 1984), structural equation modeling (Tate, 1984; Caldwell, 1985), discriminant analysis (Brown and Tinsley, 1983), regression analysis (Brown and Wilkins, 1976; Crandall, 1976; Christensen and Yoesting, 1976; Smith and Munley, 1978; Christensen, 1980; Beaman, 1982; Levine and Hunter, 1983), factor analysis (e.g., Romsa, 1973; Beaman, 1975; Ditton, Goodale and Johnsen, 1975; Duncan, 1978; Schmitz-Scherzer, et al. 1974; Kass and Tinsley, 1979; Romesburg, 1979; Graefe et al., 1981), and logit models (Stynes and Peterson 1984). We have built upon our understanding of principles involved in sampling (e.g., Brown and Wilkins, 1978; Becker, Gates, and Niemann, 1980; Oderwald, Wellman, and Buhyoff, 1980; Wellman, et al., 1980; Scotter, 1981; Mills, et al., 1981; Christensen, 1981; Brown, et al., 1981; Hammitt and McDonald, 1982; Perdue and Ditton, 1983). The list of accumulated knowledge could include more topics but the point would remain the same. In most cases cited, scientists have started with core theories and worked with the models that seem justified. The exchanges have not been whether the core theory is correct, but rather whether the resulting concepts or models like factor analysis, regression analysis, and so forth are *correct in their application* with appropriate adjustments being made. This work may be characterized as being less concerned with the question of whether methods are used poorly! Constant adjustments are made, however, without calling into question the core assumptions.

There are some issues, addressed in the field of leisure, which are not research programs in terms of the model of such programs presented. An illustration of the nature of these kinds of topics comes from writers suggesting "qualitative research methods" for the study of leisure. It is hoped that the illustration is not taken as an attack on the core assumptions of qualitative methodologists; it would be hypocritical to suggest that some things in research must be taken as "given" and then to try to discredit the "givens" of other scientists.

People advocating qualitative methodology spend a great deal of time examining the "hard core" of quantitative methodologists. First, this is not a legitimate enterprise because it deprives the field of development of quantitative techniques. More importantly, however, this kind of activity also deprives the advocates of qualitative methods. This deprivation results because they are not illustrating the use of the methods as much as they are restating their "hard core" of assumptions. Many of these core assumptions have been known for years (c.f., Kelly, 1980; Howe, 1985; Filstead 1970). It is true that ". . . we cannot know that any statistical technique we develop is useful unless we use it" (Box, 1976; 792). This fact is also true of qualitative methods. The development of these methods will come through the iterative process of use and adjustment (Box, 1976). It is important for qualitative methodologists to begin to deal with adjustments in their own "protective belt" necessitated by questions raised about qualitative methods. Questions concerning, for example, implicit bias entering into observations (Popper, 1962; Hanson, 1958; Spector, 1966a; Spector, 1966b; Feyerabend, 1970; Machamer, 1971; Machamer, 1973; Ball, 1984) or what Nietzche called ". . . the dogma of immaculate perception" and the bias of emergent theory (Huber, 1973). Needed adjustments in the leisure setting can only become evident, however, if the qualitative methods are put to use. I think more progress has been made in this respect in quantitative research than in qualitative research.

The point to be understood is that the study of leisure methodology is, like most other areas of academic focus, capable of supporting many paradigms (Eckberg and Hill, 1979). The development of those paradigms, however, comes from their use and adjustment. Developments are less likely to happen as a result of challenges to core assumptions of alternative paradigms and a redundant restatement of the core assumptions of one's adopted methodology.

Microlevel Analysis

In the discussion of progress at the macrolevel of analysis, "research programs" were said to exist. No mention was made of the quality of those programs. The quality of those programs is dependent on the quality of the "research programs" at the microlevel of analysis. Unless the streams of articles at the macrolevel are themselves a part of a research tradition at the microlevel, they do not represent a high quality research program (Eckberg and Hill, 1979).

Given this position, progress in addressing statistical and methodological issues in leisure cannot be defined as good. Few research programs exist at the microlevel. This conclusion must be qualified because 1) there are some research programs that exist and 2) there are some research programs that are developing. An example will illustrate a research program at the level of the individual. Buhyoff and Leuschner (1978) demonstrated that a linearized natural logarithmic function was the best empirical fit of the data in a study designed to estimate the aesthetic impacts of southern pine beetles. This result suggested a needed adjustment to the usual linear models employed in most previous research (Buhyoff and Wellman, 1980). Buhyoff and Riesenman (1979) followed Buhyoff's prior study and experimentally manipulated conditions and again a linearized logarithmic function was determined to fit the data well. This work, designed to specify an appropriate form of a function to estimate the aesthetic values of scenery, was finally generalized in a paper by Buhyoff and Wellman (1980). As an individual scientist, Buhyoff started with some core assumptions (e.g., people can express consistent preferences for landscape photographs and preferences can be determined, see Buhyoff and Riesenman, 1979) and proceeded to work on the form of the appropriate mathematical function for expressing those preferences. The quantitative paradigm was used to "... both generate and solve puzzles and thus generate a visible research tradition" (Eckberg and Hill, 1979: 935).

Contrast this model of research to what might be called the "threshold model" (Granovetter, 1978), or "critical mass model" (Schelling, 1978). The words critical mass are synonymous with the term critical number (Schelling, 1978). What all of the critical mass models have in common is that some activity is self-sustaining once the measure of that activity passes a certain minimum level.

According to this model, people make decisions to participate in an activity on the basis of the actual number of other people engaged in that activity. This characterization, however, ignores the variance in how much influence actual numbers may have on a particular person or, the various "thresholds" that exist for different people. Schelling (1978: 96) explains: " . . . it is typically the case that the 'critical number' for one person differs from another's. When people differ with respect to their cross-over points, there may be a large range of numbers over which, if that number of people were doing it, for a few but only a few among them, that number wouldn't be big enough, while the rest would be content." Much of the work done on statistical and methodological issues in leisure has resulted from such a "critical mass" phenomenon.

One illustration was used to indicate a good individual level research program (i.e., Buyhoff et al.). Space permits only one example of the critical mass approach to examining statistical and methodological issues in leisure. Recall the mid-1970s to early 1980s. During that time period factor analysis (or its variants) of leisure activities was in vogue both as a subject per se (e.g., Ritchie, 1975; Holbrook, 1980) and as a method for building "activity type" typologies (e.g., London, Crandall, and Fitzgibbons, 1977). From 1973 to 1980 at *least* thirteen articles (Romsa, 1973; McKechnie, 1974; Schmitz-Scherzer et al., 1974; Hendee and Burdge, 1974; Smith, 1975; Ditton et al., 1975; Ritchie,

1975; Beaman, 1975; London et al., 1977; Christensen and Yoesting, 1977; Duncan, 1978; Chase, 1979; Yu, 1980) discussing or using factor analysis, or one of its variants, appeared in the *Journal of Leisure Research*. Eckberg and Hill (1979: 930) state that a paradigm, methodological or otherwise, should be widely recognized as an achievement and it should " . . . conceptually define the course of future research." Constant adjustments to a "protective belt" of assumptions and models, in other words, characterizes a good microlevel research program.

An examination of the authors of all of the factor analytic studies cited reveals that none of them are mentioned more than once. A look at the content of these studies would reveal little elaboration and much redundancy. In short, these factor analytic studies were not used by individual scientists as a starting point for further research.

Conceptual adjustments rarely occur when a threshold model characterizes research. Schelling (1978: 97) observed that "When those few for whom the number is not enough drop out, they lower the number, and some more drop out and so on all the way." In the end nobody is doing the work on the statistical or methodological issue. There is very little, if any, work being conducted on factor analysis models in the refereed journals today. Other areas of statistical and methodological work in leisure research follow similar courses of "nondevelopment."

Discussion

There is reason for both optimism and pessimism in the examination of statistical and methodological issues in leisure. At the macrolevel the field seems to be advancing. It is not, however, advancing at a rapid rate. It was possible, for example, to state in 1984 that investigators still adhered to univariate methods in a field defined as multivariate in character (Tinsley, 1984). It is still possible to find research reports justified on the basis of an R^2 value in a field defined by a concept that is to have little "explained variance" (i.e., leisure) (e.g., McCluskie, Napier, and Christensen, 1986). A number of reasons can be advanced for this inappropriate application of different methods in the field of leisure; at least one of those reasons is that the appropriate statistics and methods have not been developed or introduced to the field (Riddick, DeSchriver, and Weissinger, 1984). Reliance on "older" methodologies, consequently, is a result. Although there is evidence of research programs at the macrolevel, they are less in both number and quality compared to other fields of research. This conclusion is a direct result of the lack of development of individual research programs.

There are, as a consequence, many areas that need study. It can be stated that concept development is needed in leisure research as it is needed in other disciplines like sociology (e.g., Blalock, 1979) or political science (e.g., Jones, 1984); it can be stated that the contribution that methodology can make to theory development is needed (e.g., Christensen and Christensen, 1974; Christensen, 1980; Saris and Stronkhorst, 1984); it can be stated that the role of quasi-experimental designs in leisure settings needs to be investigated (e.g., Roggenbuck, Hall, and Oliver, 1982; Christensen, 1985); it can be stated that the value of "exploratory statistical analysis" should be considered (e.g., Tukey, 1977; Leinhardt and Wasserman, 1979; Hoaglin, Mosteller, and Tukey 1985), suggested investigations of the form that mathematical functions of recreation phenomena take could be made (Peterson, 1974; Buhyoff, et al., 1978; Buhyoff and Reisenman, 1979; Buhyoff and Wellman, 1980; Stynes and Peterson, 1984; Stynes, et al., 1986); how the evaluation perspective might improve understandings of leisure over traditional research perspectives can be suggested (e.g., Guttentag and Struening, 1975); how the subtle aspects of our statistical procedures enter into our substantive conclusions could be examined (see e.g., Darby, 1979; Christensen, 1985); how quantitative literature reviews improve our summarization and understandings of previous research on leisure is a possible suggestion (see e.g., Rosenthal, 1984), the effect of how questions are asked upon the responses obtained in a survey might be suggested (see e.g., Schuman and Presser, 1979); and so on, ad infinitum.

All of these specific suggestions, however, would be arbitrary and superficial for any one person to state. A person building a research program builds depth instead of breadth. Innovation ". . . is the result of discovering new ways to conceptually organize previously known but puzzling and inexplicable phenomena" centering around a particular topic, well enough to suggest meaningful areas of research. Schelling (1978: 97) observed that ". . . some fraction of the population will engage in (an) activity independently of how many others do . . ." The leisure field needs more of these individuals with zero thresholds who know how to build a research program around statistical and methodological issues. A number of factors explain why there are not a larger number of people, than currently exist, who consistently work on statistical and methodological issues in leisure. It can be stated, however, that more tolerance for the work of this type of individual is required before the field can hope to advance in this important area of investigation. It is, perhaps, this issue of tolerance which is *the* issue surrounding statistics and methodology in leisure research (see e.g., Cottrell, 1976; Iso-Ahola, 1984).

Paper presented at the National Recreation and Park Association Research Symposium. Statistics and Methodology Session. September 1987. New Orleans, LA. Salaries and research support provided by State and Federal Funds appropriated to the Ohio Agricultural Research and Development Center, The Ohio State University. I wish to express my appreciation to Drs. E. Howard Linsley and John Heywood for comments on an earlier draft of this paper.

BIBLIOGRAPHY

Ball, T. (1984). From Paradigms to Research Programs: Toward a Post-Kuhnian Political Science. In H.B. Asher, H.F. Weisberg, J.H Kessel, and W.P. Shively (eds.) *Theory-Building and Data Analysis in the Social Sciences*, Knoxville, Tennessee: The University of Tennessee Press.

Barnett, L.A. (1978). Theorizing about Play: Critique and Direction. *Leisure Sciences: An Interdisciplinary Journal*, 1, 113, 130.

Baxter, M.J. and Ewing, G.O. (1986). A Framework for the Exploratory Development of Spatial Interaction Models: A Recreation Travel Example. *Journal of Leisure Research*, 18, 320-336.

Beaman, J. (1974). Distance and the 'Reaction' to Distance as a Function of Distance. *Journal of Leisure Research*, 6, 220-231.

Beaman, (1975). Comments on the Paper "The Substitutability Concept: Implications for Recreation Research and Management." *Journal of Leisure Research* 7, 146-151.

Beaman, J. (1976). Corrections Regarding the Impedance of Distance Functions for Several g(d) Functions. *Journal of Leisure Research*, 8, 49-52.

Beaman, J. (1982). Comments on an Article "The Relative Performance of Various Estimators of Recreation Participation Equations." *Journal of Leisure Research*, 14, 266-272.

Becker, B.W. (1976). Perceived Similarities among Recreational Activities. *Journal of Leisure Research*, 8, 112-122.

Becker, R.H., W. A. Gates, and B. J. Niemann (1980). Establishing Representative Sample Designs with Aerial Photographic Observations. *Leisure Sciences: An Interdisciplinary Journal*, 3, 277-300.

Bell, M. (1977). The Spatial Distribution of Second Homes: A Modified Gravity Model. *Journal of Leisure Research*, 9, 225-232.

Berstein, I. and H. Freeman (1975). *Academic and Entrepreneurial Research*. New York: The Free Press.

Biskin, B.H. (1983). Multivariate Analysis in Experimental Leisure Research. *Journal of Leisure Research*, 15, 344-358.

Blalock, H.M. (1979). Measurement and Conceptualization Problems. *American Sociological Review*, 44, 881-894.

Box, G.E.P. 1976. Science and Statistics. *Journal of the American Statistical Association*, 71, 791-799.

Brown, T.L. and B. T. Wilkins (1978). Clues to Reasons for Nonresponse, and its Effect upon Variable Estimates. *Journal of Leisure Research*, 10, 226-231.

Brown, T.L., C. P. Davison, D. L. Hustin, and D. J. Decker (1981). Comments on the Importance of Late Respondent and Non-Respondent Data from Mail Survey. *Journal of Leisure Research*, 13, 76-79.

Brown, M.T. and H. E. A. Tinsley (1983). Discriminant Analysis. *Journal of Leisure Research*, 15, 290-310.

Buhyoff, G.J. and M. Riesenman (1979). Manipulation of Dimensionality in Landscape Preference Judgments: A Quantitative Validation. *Leisure Sciences: An Interdisciplinary Journal*, 2, 221-238.

Buhyoff, G.J. and J. D. Wellman (1979). Environmental Preferences: A Critical Analysis of a Critical Analysis. *Journal of Leisure Research*, 11, 215-218.

Buhyoff, G.J. and J. D. Wellman (1980). The Specification of a Non-Linear Psychophysical Function for Visual Landscape Dimensions. *Journal of Leisure Research*, 12, 257-272.

Bull, C.N. (1971). One Measure for Defining a Leisure Activity. *Journal of Leisure Research*, 3, 120-126.

Bull, C.N. (1972). Prediction of Future Daily Behaviors: An Empirical Measure of Leisure. *Journal of Leisure Research*, 4, 119, 128.

Bull, C.N. (1972). Reply to Noe. *Journal of Leisure Research*, 4, 356.

Caldwell, L.L. (1985). The Application of LISREL to Leisure: A Rejoinder, *Journal of Leisure Research*, 17, 68-73.

Carroll. M.P. (1972). Considerations on the Analysis of Variance Paradigm in Sociology. *Pacific Sociological Review*, October, 443-459.

Cesario, F.J. (1975a). A Simulation Approach to Outdoor Recreation Planning. *Journal of Leisure Research*, 7 38-52.

Cesario, F.J. (1975b). A New Method for Analyzing Outdoor Recreation Trip Data. *Journal of Leisure Research*, 11, 92-101.

Chase, D.R. (1979). Activity Preferences and Participation: Conclusions from a Factor Analytic Study. *Journal of Leisure Research, 11*, 92-101.

Cheung, H.K. (1972). A Day-Use Park Visitations Model. (Journal of Leisure Research), 4, 139-156.

Christensen, J.E. and C. E. Christensen (1974). The Cognitive Dissonance Model as a Predictor of Customer Satisfaction Among Camper Owners: A Critique. *Journal of Leisure Research,* 59-65.

Christensen, J.E. and D. R. Yoesting, (1976). Statistical and Substantive Implications of the Use of Stepwise Regression to Order Predictors of Leisure Behavior. *Journal of Leisure Research,* 59-65.

Christensen, J.E. and D. R. Yoesting (1977). The Substitutability Concept: A Need for Further Development. *Journal of Leisure Research, 9*, 188-207.

Christensen, J.E. (1979). The Correlation Coefficient and Problems of Inference in Recreation Research. *Leisure Sciences: An Interdisciplinary Journal, 2*, 291-304.

Christensen, J.E. (1980). Rethinking 'Social Groups as a Basis for Assessing Participation in Selected Water Activities.' *Journal of Leisure Research, 12*, 346-356.

Christensen, J.E. (1982). On Generalizing About the Need for Follow-Up Efforts in Mail Recreation Surveys. *Journal of Leisure Research, 14*, 264-265.

Christensen, J.E. (1983). An Exposition of Canonical Correlation in Leisure Research. *Journal of Leisure Research, 15*, 311-322.

Christensen, J.E. (1985a). "Interpretational Confounding" and Canonical Correlation in Leisure Research. *Leisure Sciences: An Interdisciplinary Journal, 7*, 189-204.

Christensen, J.E. (1985b). Different Answers to Different Questions: Experimental Designs in Recreation Research. *Proceedings, Seventh Annual Southeastern Recreation Research Symposium.*

Cook, W.L. (1972). An Evaluation of the Aesthetic Quality of Forest Trees. *Journal of Leisure Research, 4*, 293-302.

Cosper, R. and B. L. Kinsley (1984). An Application of Conjoint Analysis to Leisure Research: Cultural Preferences in Canada. *Journal of Leisure Research, 16*, 224-233.

Cosper, R.L. and S. M. Shaw (1985). The Validity of Time-Budget Studies: A Comparison of Frequency and Diary Data in Halifax, Canada. *Leisure Sciences: An Interdisciplinary Journal, 7*, 205-226.

Cottrell, R.R. (1976). The Manager's Viewpoint: Research and Applicability of Results. Unpublished paper.

Crandall, R. (1976). On the Use of Stepwise Regression and Other Statistics to Estimate the Relative Importance of Variables. *Journal of Leisure Research, 8*, 53-58.

Darby, W.P. (1979). An Example of Decision Making on Environmental Carcinogens: The Delaney Clause. *Journal of Environmental Systems, 9*, 109-121.

Darragh, A.J., Peterson, G.L. and Dwyer, J.F. (1983). Travel Cost Models at the Urban Scale. *Journal of Leisure Research, 15*, 89-94.

Dibble, V.K. (1973). What Is and What Ought to Be: Comparing Styles of Thought. *American Journal of Sociology, 79*, 511-549.

Ditton, R.B., Goodale, T.L., and Johnsen, P.K. (1975). A Cluster Analysis of Activity, Frequency, and Environment Variables to Identify Water-Based Recreation Types. *Journal of Leisure Research, 7*, 282-295.

Duncan, D.J. (1978). Leisure Types: Factor Analyses of Leisure Profiles. *Journal of Leisure Research, 10*, 113-125.

Eckberg, D.L. and Hill, L. (1979). The Paradigm Concept and Sociology: A Critical Review. *American Sociological Review, 44*, 925-936.

Ellis, G. and Witt, P.A. (1984). The Measurement of Perceived Freedom in Leisure. *Journal of Leisure Research, 16*, 110-123.

Elsner, G.H. (1971a). A Regression Method for Estimating the Level of Use and Market Area of a Proposed Large Ski Resort. *Journal of Leisure Research, 3*, 160-167.

Elsner, G.H. (1971b). Using Error Measures to Compare Models on Recreation Use. *Journal of Leisure Research, 3*, 277-278.

Ewing, G.O. (1980). Progress and Problems in the Development of Recreational Trip Generation and Trip Distribution Models. *Leisure Sciences: An Interdisciplinary Journal, 3*, 1-24.

Feyerabend, P.K. (1970). Problems of Empiricism II. In Colodny, R.G. (ed.) *The Nature and Function of Scientific Theories*. University of Pittsburgh series in the Philosophy of Science, Vol. IV. Pittsburgh: University of Pittsburgh Press.

Field, D.R. and O'Leary, J.T. (1973). Social Groups as a Basis for Assessing Participation in Selected Water Activities. *Journal of Leisure Research, 5*, 16-25.

Filstead, W.J. (ed.) (1970). *Qualitative Methodology: Firsthand Involvement with the Social World*. Chicago: Markham Publishing Company.

Freund, R.J. and Wilson, R.R. (1974). An Example of a Gravity Model to Estimate Recreation Travel. *Journal of Leisure Research, 6*, 241-256.

Graefe, A.R., Ditton, R.B., Roggenbuck, J.W., & Schreyer R. (1981). Notes on the Stability of the Factor Structure of Leisure Meanings. *Leisure Sciences: An Interdisciplinary Journal, 4*, 51-66.

Granovetter, M. (1978). Threshold Models of Collective Behavior. *American Journal of Sociology, 83*, 1420-1443.

Gudykunst, J.A.M., Kantor, W.I., and Parker H.A. (1981). Dimensions of Leisure Activities: A Factor Analytic Study in New England. *Journal of Leisure Research, 13*, 28-42.

Guttentag, M. and Struening, E.L. (1975). *Handbook of Evaluation Research*. Beverly Hills: Sage Publications.

Hammitt, W.E. and McDonald, C.D. (1982). Response Bias and the Need for Extensive Mail Questionnaire Follow-Ups among Selected Recreation Samples. *Journal of Leisure Research, 14*, 207-216.

Hamill, L. (1975). Analysis of Leopold's Quantitative Comparisons of Landscape Esthetics. *Journal of Leisure Research, 7*, 16-28.

Hanson, N.R. (1958). *Patterns of Discovery*. Cambridge: Cambridge University Press.

Hardin, G. (1968). The Tragedy of the Commons. *Science, 162*, 1243-1248.

Hendee, J.C. and Burdge, R.J. (1974). The Substitutability Concept: Implications for Recreation Research and Management. *Journal of Leisure Research, 6*, 155-162.

Hoaglin, D.C., Mosteller, F., and Tukey, J.W. (eds.) (1985). *Exploring Data Tables, Trends, and Shapes*. New York: John Wiley & Sons.

Holbrook, M.B. (1980). Representing Patterns of Association Among Leisure Activities: A Comparison of Two Techniques. *Journal of Leisure Research, 17*, 242-256.

Howe, C.Z. (1985). Possibilities for Using a Qualitative Research Approach in the Sociological Study of Leisure. *Journal of Leisure Research, 17*, 212-224.

Huber, J. (1973). Symbolic Interaction as a Pragmatic Perspective: The Bias of Emergent Theory. *American Sociological Review, 38*, 274-283.

Huff, T.E. (1973). Theoretical Innovation in Science: The Case of William F. Ogburn. *American Journal of Sociology, 79*, 261-277.

Iso-Ahola, S.E. (1979a). Some Social Psychological Determinants of Perceptions of Leisure: Preliminary Evidence. *Leisure Sciences: An Interdisciplinary Journal, 2*, 305-314.

Iso-Ahola, S.E. (1979b). Basic Dimensions of Definitions of Leisure. *Journal of Leisure Research, 11*, 15-27.

Iso-Ahola, S.E. (1984). Editor's Notes: What is Appropriate for Publication? *Journal of Leisure Research, 16*, iv.

Jones, C.O. (1984). Doing Before Knowing: Concept Development in Political Science. In Asher, H.B., Weisberg, H.F., Kessel, J.H., and Shively, W.P. (eds.) *Theory-Building and Data Analysis in the Social Sciences*. Knoxville: University of Tennessee Press.

Kapfer, P.G. (1964). *Criteria for Evaluating Research and Their Application to Science Education*, Ph.D. Dissertation, Ohio State University.

Kass, R.A. and Tinsley, H.E.A. (1979). Factor Analysis. *Journal of Leisure Research, 11*, 120-138.

Kelly, J.R. (1972). Work and Leisure: A Simplified Paradigm. *Journal of Leisure Research, 4*, 50-62.

Kelly, J.R. (1973). Three Measures of Leisure Activity: A Note on the Continued Incommensurability of Oranges, Apples, and Artichokes. *Journal of Leisure Research, 2*, 56-65.

Kelly, J.R. (1980). Leisure and Quality: Beyond the Quantitative Barrier in Research. In Goodale, T.L. and Witt, P.A. (eds.) *Recreation and Leisure: Issues in an Era of Change*. State College: Venture Publishing.

Kreimer, A. (1977). Environmental Preferences: A Critical Analysis of Some Research Methodologies. *Journal of Leisure Research, 9*, 88-97.

Kuhn, T.S. (1970). *The Structure of Scientific Revolutions* (2nd Edition). Chicago: University of Chicago Press.

Lakatos, I. (1970). Falsification and the Methodology of Scientific Research Programmes. In Lakatos I. and Musgrave, A. (eds.) *Criticism and the Growth of Knowledge.* Cambridge: Cambridge University Press.

Leinhardt, S. and Wasserman, S.S. (1979). Exploratory Data Analysis: An Introduction to Selected Methods. In Schuessler, K.F. (ed.) *Sociological Methodology, 1979.* San Francisco: Jossey-Bass Publishers.

Levine, R.L. and Hunter, J.E. (1983). Regression Methodology: Correlation, Meta-Analysis, Confidence Intervals and Reliability. *Journal of Leisure Research, 15*, 323-343.

Levy, J. (1979). A Paradigm for Conceptualizing Leisure Behavior: Towards a Person-Environment Interaction Analysis. *Journal of Leisure Research, 11*, 40-60.

London, M., Crandall, R., and Fitzgibbons, D. (1977). The Psychological Structure of Leisure: Activities, Needs, People. *Journal of Leisure Research, 9*, 252-263.

Machamer, P.K. (1971). Observation. In Buck, R.C. and Chohen, R.S. (eds.) *Boston Studies in the Philosophy of Science*, Volume VIII. Dordrecht: D. Reidel.

Machamer, P.K. (1973). Feyerabend and Galileo: The Interaction of Theories, and the Reinterpretation of Experience. *Studies in History and Philosophy of Science*, May, 1-46.

Malamud, B. (1973). Gravity Model Calibration of Tourist Travel to Las Vegas. *Journal of Leisure Research, 5*, 23-33.

Mannell, R.C. and Bradley, W. (1986). Does Greater Freedom Always Lead to Greater Leisure? Testing a Person X Environment Model of Freedom and Leisure. *Journal of Leisure Research, 18*, 215-230.

McAllister, D.M. and Klett, F.R. (1976). A Modified Gravity Model of Regional Recreation Activity with Application to Ski Trips. *Journal of Leisure Research, 8*, 21-34.

McClaskie, S.L., Napier, T.L., and Christensen, J.E. (1986). Factors Influencing Outdoor Recreation Participation: A State Study. *Journal of Leisure Research, 18*, 190-205.

McCuen, R.H. (1974). Spurious Correlation in Estimating Recreation Demand Functions. *Journal of Leisure Research, 6*, 232-240.

McKechnie, G.E. (1974). The Psychological Structure of Leisure: Past Behavior. *Journal of Leisure Research, 6*, 27-45.

McTavish, D., Cleary, J., Brent, E., Knudsen, K., and Knudsen, K. (1976a). Predicting the Methodological Quality of Research. Paper presented at the Annual Meeting of the American Sociological Association, New York.

McTavish, D., Cleary, J., Brent, E., and Knudsen, K. (1976b). Assessing Research Methodology: Some Preliminary Findings on the Structure of Professional Assessments of Methodology. Paper presented at the Midwest Sociological Society Meetings, St. Louis, MO.

Mednick, H. (1975). A Markov Chain Model of Travel Patterns of U.S. Visitors to Ontario. *Journal of Leisure Research, 7*, 246-255.

Mills, A.S., Hodgson, R.W., McNeely, J.G., and Masse, R.F. (1981). An Improved Visitor Sampling Method for Ski Resorts and Similar Settings. *Journal of Leisure Research*, 219-231.

Mitroff, I.I. (1974). Norms and Counternorms in a Select Group of the Apollo Moon Scientists: A Case Study of the Ambivalence of Scientists. *American Sociological Review, 39*, 579-595.

Neulinger, J. and Breit, M. (1969). Attitude Dimensions of Leisure. *Journal of Leisure Research, 1*, 255-261.

Neulinger, J. and Breit, M. (1971). Attitude Dimensions of Leisure: A Replication Study. *Journal of Leisure Research, 3*, 108-115.

Nisbett, R. and Ross, L. (1980). *Human Inference: Strategies and Shortcomings of Social Judgment.* Englewood Cliffs: Prentice-Hall.

Noe, F.P. 1972. Comment on Predicting of Future Daily Behavior: An Empirical Measure of Leisure. *Journal of Leisure Research, 4*, 354-355.

Oderwald, R.G., Wellman, J.D., and Buhyoff, G.J. (1980). Multi-Stage Sampling of Recreationists: A Methodological Note on Unequal Probability Sampling. *Leisure Sciences: An Interdisciplinary Journal, 3*, 213-217.

Perdue, R.R. and Ditton, R.B. (1983). Sampling from Registration Files: The Problem of Duplicate Listings. *Journal of Leisure Research, 15*, 95-99.

Peterson, G.L. and Neumann, E.S. (1969). Modeling and Predicting Human Response to the Visual Recreation Environment. *Journal of Leisure Research, 1*, 219-237.

Peterson, G.L. (1974). Evaluating the Quality of the Wilderness Environment: Perceptions and Aspirations. *Environment and Behavior, 6*, 169-193.

Pierce, R.C. (1980). Dimensions of Leisure. III: Characteristics. *Journal of Leisure Research, 12*, 273-284.

Popper, K.R. (1962). Conjectures and Refutations. New York: Basic Books.

Ragheb, M.G. (1980). Interrelationships Among Leisure Participation, Leisure Satisfaction, and Leisure Attitudes. *Journal of Leisure Research, 12*, 138-149.

Ragheb, M.G. and Beard, J.B. (1982). Measuring Leisure Attitude. *Journal of Leisure Research, 14*, 155-167.

Ritchie, J.R.B. (1975). On the Derivation of Leisure Activity Types—A Perceptual Mapping Approach. *Journal of Leisure Research, 7*, 128-140.

Riddick, C.C., DeSchriver, M., and Weissinger, E. (1984). A Methodological Review of Research in Journal of Leisure Research from 1978 to 1982. *Journal of Leisure Research, 15*, 311-321.

Roadburg, A. (1983). Freedom and Enjoyment: Disentangling Perceived Leisure. *Journal of Leisure Research, 15*, 15-26.

Roggenbuck, J.W., Hall, O.F., and Oliver, S.S. (1982). *The Effectiveness of Interpretation in Reducing Depreciative Behavior in Campgrounds*. Unpublished Final Project Report.

Romsa, G.H. (1973). A Method of Deriving Recreational Activity Packages. *Journal of Leisure Research, 5*, 34-46.

Romesburg, H.C. (1979). Use of Cluster Analysis in Leisure Research. *Journal of Leisure Research, 11*, 144-153.

Rosenthal, R. (1984). *Meta-Analytic Procedures for Social Research*. Beverly Hills: Sage Publications.

Saris, W. and Stronkhorst H. (1984). *Causal Modelling in Nonexperimental Research*. Amsterdam: Sociometric Research Foundation.

Schelling, T. (1978). *Micromotives and Macrobehavior*. New York: W.W. Norton and Company.

Schimitz-Scherzer, R., Rudinger, G., Angleitner, A., and Bierhoff-Alfermann, D. (1974). Notes on a Factor-Analytical Comparative Study of the Structure of Leisure Activities in Four Different Samples. *Journal of Leisure Research, 6*, 77-83.

Schroeder, H.W. and Brown, T.C. (1983). Alternative Functional Forms of an Inventory-Based Landscape Perception Mode. *Journal of Leisure Research, 15*, 156-163.

Schuman, H. and Presser, S. (1979). "The Assessment of 'No Opinion' in Attitude Surveys." In Schuessler, K.F. (ed.) *Sociological Methodology, 1979*. San Francisco: Jossey-Bass Publishers.

Scotter, G.W. (1981). Response Rates of Unmanned Trail Registers. *Journal of Leisure Research, 13*, 105-111.

Shelby, B. and Harris, R. (1985). Comparing Methods for Determining Visitor Evaluations of Ecological Impacts: Site Visits, Photographs, and Written Descriptions. *Journal of Leisure Research, 17*, 57-67.

Smith, A. (1937). *The Wealth of Nations*. New York: Random House.

Smith, G.R. (1964). *Inadequacies in a Selected Sample of Educational Research Proposals*, Ph.D. Dissertation, Columbia University.

Smith, S. (1975). Similarities Between Urban Recreation Systems. *Journal of Leisure Research, 7*, 270-281.

Smith, V.K. and Munley V.G. (1978). The Relative Performance of Various Estimators of Recreation Participation Equations. *Journal of Leisure Research, 10*, 165-176.

Spector, M. (1966a). Theory and Observation. *British Journal for the Philosophy of Science*, May, 1-20.

Spector, M. (1966b). Theory and Observation. *British Journal for the Philosophy of Science*, August, 89-104.

Spreitzer, E.A. and Snyder, E.E. (1974). Work Orientation, Meaning of Leisure and Mental Health. *Journal of Leisure Research* , 207-219.

Stynes, D.J. and Peterson, G.L. (1984). A Review of Logit Models with Implications for Modeling Recreation Choices. *Journal of Leisure Research*, 6, 295, 310.

Stynes, D.J., Peterson, G.L., and Rosenthal, D.H. (1986). Log Transformation Bias in Estimating Travel Cost Models. *Land Economics*, 62, 94-103.

Tate, U.S. (1984). Convergent and Discriminant Validity of Measures of Job, Leisure, Dyadic, and General Life Satisfaction by Causal Modeling Methodology. *Journal of Leisure Research*, 16, 250-254.

Thayer, R.L., Hodgson, R.W., Gustke, L.D., Atwood, B.B., and Holmes, J. (1976). Validation of a Natural Landscape Preference Model as a Predictor of Perceived Landscape Beauty of Photographs. *Journal of Leisure Research*, 8, 292-299.

Tukey, J.W. (1977). *Exploratory Data Analysis*. Reading: Addison-Wesley.

Tinsley, H.E.A. (1984). Limitations, Explorations, Aspirations: A Confession of Fallibility and a Promise to Strive for Perfection. *Journal of Leisure Research*, 16, 93-98.

Wellman, J.D., Hawk, E.G., Roggenbuck, J.W., and Buhyoff, G.J. (1980). Mailed Questionnaire Surveys and the Reluctant Respondent: An Empirical Examination of Differences Between Early and Late Respondents. *Journal of Leisure Research*, 12, 164-173.

Witt, P.A. and Ellis, G.D. (1985). Development of a Short Form to Assess Perceived Freedom in Leisure. *Journal of Leisure Research*, 17, 225-233.

Wolfe, R.I. (1972). The Inertia Model. *Journal of Leisure Research*, 4, 73-76.

Yu, J.M. (1980). The Empirical Development of Typology for Describing Leisure Behavior on the Basis of Participation Patterns. *Journal of Leisure Research*, 12, 309-320.

Curriculum and Professional Preparation in Leisure Research

Past, Present, and Future Research

H. Douglas Sessoms
Curriculum in Leisure Studies and Recreation Administration
———University of North Carolina at Chapel Hill———

Fifty-seven years ago this December, a group of educators and practitioners met at the University of Minnesota to develop the ideal curriculum to prepare recreation leaders through our universities and colleges. The conference was sponsored by the University of Minnesota and the Recreation Division of the Works Progress Administration. The report is the first of a succession of national conferences and workshops devoted to curriculum development for park and recreation education. The conferees held that a functioning curriculum should address three concerns: training at the undergraduate level for those who wish to be professional workers, assisting recreation leaders in their work to become more effective in their dealing with participants, and providing general preparation in matters of leisure for all students (WPA, 1937).

Although some universities had been offering courses and course work on play and recreation since 1905 (Sessoms, 1993), no national conference had been convened to formulate a university curriculum designed exclusively to prepare students for employment in the field of recreation services until 1937. Granted that the National Recreation Association had operated a year-long certificate training program (1926-1936), and several universities had formulated their own course of study, there was no national movement to prepare recreation professionals through the university system until the Minnesota conference primarily because there was no advocate offering a rationale as to why recreation should be a part of the baccalaureate offerings of a major university. Edward Lindeman provided that rationale and leadership. He saw leisure as a national concern, an opportunity for the advancement of democratic practice and principles and thought it well that society prepare a wide range of social planners, including recreation leaders, who could give meaning to the advances resulting from science and technology (WPA, 1937).

> I surmise that the further development of democracies will be very closely associated with the new leisure of which I have so frequently spoken. . . . In this culture the people will have free access to all the arts; they will develop cooperative habits through recreation; their earned leisure will provide them with additional opportunities and continuing education and for civic participation. A democratic culture cannot be content with star performers and masses of spectators. Participation is the essence of the democratic process. But, a newly invigorated leadership will be needed for this leisure which is to become the seed-bed out of which the refreshed democracies are to build their cultures (pp. 14-15).

It is obvious from the report of the 1937 conference that there was very little ambiguity as to what recreation, play and leisure were about. Leisure was defined in the context of time, time away from work. Recreation and play were seen as activities, intrinsically motivated, which occurred during leisure. It was the responsibility of recreation leaders to design and conduct programs of recreational activity, activities that would be both pleasurable and move the participant toward a higher form of social existence. Teaching the skills of play and helping to develop an attitude that would allow for freedom of expression through recreation were the noble goals. Recreation professionals were to be teachers, social planners and social reformers.

What was the ideal curriculum? It was acknowledged by the delegate that the "Traditional college education has been concerned primarily with preparing students to make a living. . . . We affirm (also) that it is the function of education to equip persons to live effectively. We assert, furthermore, that to live effectively in our day, education for leisure is conceived" (p. 21). Therefore, they concluded that the curriculum should accomplish three things: to educate college students to manage their own leisure more effectively; develop leadership skills, even though their students might not become recreation professionals; and prepare them to become effective community planners. To accomplish this, approximately one half the curriculum should involve general education courses; the remaining course work should emphasize their professional development. As a part of that development, the conferees held that there should be experiences throughout the student's university life which would encourage participation in student government, co-recreational activities, and an understanding of "recreation and leisure in the modern world." Professional education was to occur primarily at the upper divisional level.

The mix of professional courses was an interesting one. It was assumed that there were common learning experiences required of all who might become recreational leaders. The basic training areas identified (p. 25-26) and which constituted the core were:

a. the study of the personality of the individual from the biological, psychological, and sociological view;

b. the study of community resources and community needs, with special attention being given to recreation;

c. the study of group organization and leadership in the field of recreation.

d. the study of physical and mental health, safety education and elementary first-aid.

e. advanced coursework in arts and crafts, including advanced courses that would add theory and techniques for community and group application, e.g., methods of teaching community music and directing drama; and

f. field work problems, including supervised and direct field experience.

Specializations would be allowed at the upper divisional level. However, the number and type of specializations identified were limited and stressed activity skills rather than knowledge of the particular setting in which one might work. The four most desirable specialties were: arts and crafts; dramatics; sports and games; and voluntary group enterprises. Furthermore, the conferees held that the "capstone of the training of recreation leaders is reserved for administrative curricula," which should occur at the graduate level and only for those who had experience as practitioners. They felt it was unwise to attempt to train for administrative and supervisory positions at the undergraduate level. "To offer such curricula at the undergraduate level is to do violence to the significance of the work involved. Such provision will also give unwarranted encouragement to immature and inexperienced students to anticipate administrative positions." (p. 27) The three basic curricula identified for graduate study were administration, supervision, and coordination of community work.

There was no equivocation among the group as to the role of the recreation leader. Recreation was viewed as a client-centered field of service that might be practiced in a variety of settings including therapeutic environments. Even the term "recreational therapy" was used. These early curriculum designers saw recreation as a community service not too dissimilar from that of social work, group work, and adult education. Yet they were conscious of the various settings in which recreation was practiced, acknowledging that:

a. all full-time recreation jobs do not have similar duties;

b. there are many jobs in recreation for which the conventional type of recreation training does not give preparation, for example, positions in forestry departments, national and state parks, agriculture extension services, etc.

c. there is little standardization in job titles—recreation jobs seem to be built around the individual, whereas in industry the individual conforms to the job; and

d. there are many jobs in commercially sponsored recreation similar to community jobs (p. 56-57).

The last observation was punctuated with the question: Shall we train for commercial recreation positions?

The issues of curriculum—intent, content, and importance—must be interpreted in light of the events of the mid 1930s. The world was in a serious economic depression; fascism and communism were "attractive" political philosophies, offering an alternative to democracy as a means of resolving the economic crisis. Unemployment was significant and so was the presence of new infant technologies: television, plastics, air conditioning, and agro-biology. It is not surprising that Lindeman would suggest recreation as a means to strengthen democratic ideals and practices or talk about leisure as earned, free time. His agency, the Works Progress Administration, was primarily interested in community development efforts that might improve the quality of life. Recreation services was a relatively new public responsibility and those promoting the training of its leadership as a university responsibility had their academic grounding in either education, physical education, or sociology.

Many of the pioneers in recreation education attended the Minnesota conference. Among them were Jay B. Nash, Elmer D. Mitchell, Neva Boyd, Dorothy I. Klein, and Gerald B. Fitzgerald. Few of them had doctorates; the issue of academic qualifications of the faculty appears to have been moot. The conferees seemed to have assumed that those involved in the training of recreation leadership should come from the applied fields and have a strong commitment to the end result of their effort. They were responding to a perceived need arising from the effort of governments to do something about life in a turbulent industrial world. Little did they realize that the model of professional preparation they were choosing would shape the public's acceptance of recreation as a field of work closely aligned to sports and physical education, a program to be completed at the baccalaureate level. Their model was that of education (teacher preparation), not that of public administration or social work.

Given the limited number of high school students who attended college in 1937 and the small number of those who would choose recreation leadership as a career, the baccalaureate model appears to have been appropriate. Also, the conferees seemed to be both philosophically and pragmatically opposed to the idea that undergraduates should be trained as managers and administrators. That responsibility was to be left to the few graduate programs which would emerge. Graduate education was for the more mature, those with practitioner experience, not for the 20-year-old. And, since practice teaching was a part of teacher preparation, it is not surprising that these early curriculum designers included field work as a basic ingredient in the training of recreation leaders. The baccalaureate degree was to be the entry level for the profession and the role of the professional was to provide leadership in the development of recreational skills and opportunities for play.

It should be noted that little attention was given to the preparation of those who might function as resource managers or protectors and interpreters of the environment. Parks was viewed as a separate and distinct area of service. The typical pattern of management of parks and recreation within a community was to separate the two services as independent governmental functions: there were park departments and commissions and there were recreation departments and commissions. Professional training in parks and resource management was the responsibility of schools of forestry, natural resources and the like. Park professionals were grounded in the biological sciences; recreation leaders were to be trained as teachers and social engineers, specialists in human and community development. There seems to have been some unanimity as to what to call these programs of professional training for recreational personnel. Regardless of the administrative unit which would supervise the recreation curriculum, the curriculum would be entitled "Recreation(al) Leadership."

One cannot help but to speculate what might have happened to the field of recreation services had the world not gone to war in 1941. But it did and it altered the course of history in every facet of life: work, technology, family patterns, educational systems, resource usage, living arrangements, sex roles, and our concept and use of time. The curriculum reports of 1946 and 1948 clearly demonstrate the metamorphoses which occurred as a result of the war, two of which were growing college enrollments and expanding governmental services. Consequently, additional responsibilities were cited as objectives of recreation leadership curricula. Among them was the development of an appreciation of recreation as a profession. G. B. Fitzgerald reminded those attending the January Recreation Institute, sponsored by New York University, that recreation educators should begin to think about the accreditation of college programs in professional recreation education as well as the need to certify recreation personnel (Gabrielsen, 1948).

These post World War II conferences urged recreation educators to include more course work and experience in the administration of recreation services. The legal aspects of recreation, budget and finance, personnel management, public relations, and planning and maintenance of recreation areas and facilities were seen as important learnings for undergraduates (AAHPER, 1948). Curriculum planners were also encouraged to offer a wide range of specializations to accommodate the various employing markets.

Camping, industrial recreation, penal institutions, hospitals, homes for the aged, student unions, and youth serving agencies were cited as fields, along with the more traditional local recreation services, seeking recreation graduates. Even so, activity preparation remained the major thrust of the baccalaureate degree program. Students were expected to be skillful in activity instruction and be competent in the use of group work methodologies. Graduate study was still reserved for those who wished to further their administrative skills or pursue one of the emerging specializations such as hospital recreation. Graduate study normally included the writing of a thesis although the level of research methodologies and statistics one was to master was at a beginning level, given today's understanding of these subjects. Graduate programs were encouraged to accept undergraduate majors who had a background in group work, physical education, and recreation as being academically prepared to do graduate work in recreation leadership (Gabrielsen, 1948).

The 1950s was a decade of transition. It saw the emergence of outdoor recreation as a major interest of the American public. Americans were on the move with their parks, lakes, and rivers as primary recreation destination sites. Local governments, in increasing numbers, were accepting recreation services as their responsibility and were turning to the universities and colleges for personnel, including administrators. Recreation leadership no longer seemed to be the appropriate description for what we were trying to do in our programs of professional preparation. Consequently, many curricula underwent a name change. Recreation Administration replaced Recreation Leadership. Several universities created graduate programs, using the professional degree mechanism—the Master of Science in Recreation Administration or the Doctor of Recreation—rather than as the more conventional Master of Science or Master of Arts degree approach. These new professional degree programs were more flexible, often allowing their students to elect a graduate internship or set of professional papers in lieu of a thesis.

The 1950s was also the time in which President Eisenhower created the Outdoor Recreation Resources Review Commission and charged it with the responsibility of assessing the demands for outdoor recreation activity and our ability and the national resources to respond to those demands. "Parks" and "Outdoor Recreation" were becoming synonymous in the minds of many politicians and some were recreation practitioners and educators. In community after community, independent park and recreation commissions were merged to form a combined park and recreation department or commission. Even our professional park and recreation organizations were discussing merger. Professionalization issues were coming to the front: certification and accreditation were on the move. The American Recreation Society, through its educators section, formed a committee in 1958 to develop plans for the accrediting of recreation curricula, building upon the work done by Dr. Cliff Hutchins at the University of Wisconsin. Yet, the ideal undergraduate curriculum remained much the same with approximately one-half the undergraduate work to be done in general education, the remaining 50 percent to be taken in the professional core and/or related course work. The supervised internship was increasingly being viewed as a means to acquaint students with the setting in which they might work with some educators recommending that their students do a preliminary practicum or fieldwork or have experience in several settings prior to their enrollment for credit for their supervised fieldwork; however, there was no general agreement on this point.

As mentioned previously, change must be interpreted in light of the events triggering and sustaining it. Such was the case in the 1960s. Among the several external events that had a significant impact upon park and recreation education were the publishing of Sebastian de Grazia's *Of Time, Work, and Leisure* and the reports of the Outdoor Recreation Resources Review Commission; the creation of a grant program within the Office of Vocation Rehabilitation to support the training of therapeutic recreation specialists; the merger of five national recreation and park organizations to form the National Recreation and Park Association; the publishing of the NRPA manpower study (1968); the civil rights movement; the increasing numbers of students attending college and electing Parks and Recreation as a major; and selected social reforms such as the "War on Poverty" and the environmental movement. Each of these had a pronounced effect on our programs of professional preparation. Much of what we do today and many of the problems that we are seeking to resolve are directly related to the effects of those events.

Until *Of Time, Work and Leisure*, most recreation educators had been content to view recreation as an activity that occurred during leisure, motivated by the satisfactions derived from the experience. Leisure was seen as time away from work; recreation was an expression of leisure. de Grazia's writings altered that perception. He defined leisure as a state of mind and recreation as a diversionary experience that was available for the masses while leisure could be achieved only by the elite, those willing to discipline themselves so that the state of mind could be achieved. His writings literally shook the recreation education community. His work was scholarly and stimulating. Were park and recreation educators dealing with the right subject? Should leisure be our concern, not recreation leadership? Would the study of leisure add to our academic credibility, strengthen our collegiate and interdisciplinary relationships? If so, what was the best type of preparation to move one toward the study of leisure? It is not surprising that our research journals have *leisure*, not *recreation*, in their titles.

Some would say that de Grazia's work ushered recreation education into the post-industrial world, that it gave birth to the discipline of leisure studies. Leisure became vogue; recreation, passé. Leisure was ethereal, intellectual, and exciting. Recreation was viewed as practical, pedantic, and activity oriented. The effects of this shift in perception were not fully felt until a decade later when those schooled in leisure and leisure research became a part of the available pool from which curricula could hire their faculty. For some park and recreation education administrators it came as a shock to learn that their faculty were not necessarily speaking the same language, that their newer faculty had a different academic agenda and perception of the role of the profession and professional preparation than that of their senior staff. In time, we would discover what had transpired and begin our debates about the separateness and distinctiveness of Leisure Studies as a discipline and Recreation and Park Administration as a program of professional preparation.

The ORRRC report called attention to the need to prepare resource managers to develop and administer our nation's outdoor recreation resources. In 1964, a national conference on the preparation of outdoor recreation specialists was held at Syracuse University (BOR, 1964). It was sponsored by the Bureau of Outdoor Recreation and Syracuse University; it, along with the 1937 conference and a conference of Therapeutic Recreation Curricula, are the only national conferences which have had federal sponsorship. All three have had a pronounced effect upon our curriculum patterns.

The similarities of recreation management and park administration were becoming obvious: both drew heavily upon the management sciences for their practice. This conclusion, coupled with the merger of such national organizations as the American Recreation Society, the American Institute of Park Executives, and the National Recreation Association, suggested that park professionals and recreation professionals were viewing themselves as a part of the same political and professional body, one that proclaimed as its mission the promotion of enhancing the quality of life through parks, recreation and conservation. Should not one educational approach, a common set of learning experiences, be undertaken to prepare people for this unified profession?

The answer was yes, in principle, but in practice, since there seemed to be unique patterns of activity depending upon the setting in which one worked and a continuing allegiance to special interests, we continued to remain a federation in thought and behavior. The National Park and Recreation Association attempted to accommodate both those who wanted to be a part of a unified profession and those who wished to retain their specialty identification by establishing professional branches. In doing so, it set the stage for the ensuing battles between those who view parks and recreation as their profession and those who identify more closely with the individual specialization as a separate profession, often represented through their affiliation with their branch rather than the parent body.

To some extent the move toward a common profession and curriculum pre-dates the NRPA merger since, in 1963, the Federation of Professional Recreation Organizations had created a committee to develop standards for the accrediting of park and recreation curricula. Those standards were completed and field tested at six institutions in 1969. Recognizing that there were strong loyalties to selected special interests, the framers of the accreditation standards cited three specializations that might require a unique configuration of learning experiences. They were recreation programming, which included the specialization of therapeutic recreation; administration of recreation and park systems; and recreation resources administration.

Recreation and park education was becoming complicated. In addition to the philosophical question of what should we teach—leisure or recreation; generalists or specialists; development of activity or administrative skills—there was the practical question of staffing our curricula to meet the growing numbers of students who wished to major in recreation. Recreation curricula were expanding in both numbers and majors, due in part to the influx of the baby boomers, a higher percentage of high school graduates attending college, an emerging humanistic perspective, and the report of the National Park and Recreation Association's manpower study (1968) which cited recreation as a growth area. Guidance counselors throughout the United States were encouraging students to look at recreation as a career. Our graduate programs were incapable of providing the needed faculty, teachers who had both the necessary academic and professional training. Consequently, university administrators had to look to related fields of study for personnel or appointed those with the Masters, only, as instructors in the hope that the latter group would later pursue the doctorate and the former group would grow in their interest and knowledge of recreation and parks as a profession. With both groups, promotions were easily obtained and tenure was rarely an issue.

The same phenomenon of expanding recreation demand was occurring in the many settings where Parks and Recreation was practiced. The need for personnel was so great that graduates of recreation curricula were often placed in administrative positions upon graduation; non-recreation graduates were being used as activity leaders and program specialists. Recreation and park professionals were being seen as administrators, no longer teachers and developers of recreation skills. That task could be left to others. Recreation and park education was becoming a management science field.

There was one specialization, however, within recreation service that did not follow the trend toward the management sciences. It was therapeutic recreation. In 1963, the Vocational Rehabilitation Administration, in response to some initiatives by President Kennedy and the Joseph P. Kennedy, Jr., Foundation, created a training grant program to support those institutions that had a strong interest in developing recreation specialists to work with the ill and disabled. Funds were made available to employ faculty and support students enrolled in graduate therapeutic recreation programs. The consequences of this action were significant. Not only were universities able to appoint faculty with a therapeutic recreation specialization, there was the tacit approval by university curriculum developers that therapeutic recreation was somewhat different from the other components of the profession. Six years later, at the termination of the VRA grant program, the Office of Education (Special Education Division) embarked on a similar program to support graduate study in recreation for special populations. Again, the number of students interested in this specialization, as well as the schools offering it, increased. With qualified faculty to teach therapeutic recreation, it was only a matter of time before the university curricula with graduate programming in therapeutic recreation would offer courses in therapeutic recreation at the undergraduate level. The students were there; so was the interest.

The humanistic spirit of the 1960s was ever present as well as its impact on curriculum reform. Baccalaureate programs, in general, were becoming more flexible; the traditional required liberal arts courses were being reduced in number. Students were able to take more electives, and electing to stay in school to pursue the graduate degree rather than entering the work force after four years of study. The availability of federal grants and loans made this an attractive alternative to work. For literally thousands of recreation and park majors, the Masters became the entry-level professional degree.

One other trend of the '60s needs mentioning. It involved the changing composition of recreation graduates. Whereas previous generations of recreation majors were males, the '60s saw an increase in the number of females choosing our field as their major (Stein, 1984). Many were interested in the humanistic element of recreation services, especially services to special populations, but this was not the sole cause nor area of their interest. Their presence had several effects on park and recreation education, one of which was to shatter the stereotype that recreation was for jocks only. Another was the appointment of female faculty members, especially in those programs that had a therapeutic recreation option. The demographics of recreation education were changing: a different student body, faculty and curriculum emphases.

The 1970s saw an acceleration of the trends of the '60s. The separateness of therapeutic recreation was given additional support through two national conferences on therapeutic recreation curriculum development (AAHPER, 1973; Jordan, 1977). Both were supported by the Bureau for the Education of the Handicapped. The curriculum patterns continued to change: more students, more females, more graduates seeking the Masters prior to entering the work force, and more appointments of faculty to recreation and park curricula often without the faculty having had lengthy experience as practitioners or a strong identification with parks and recreation as their profession (Stein, 1984; Sessoms, 1993).

The rapid expansion and growth of recreation enrollments had several effects. For the first time, there were enough majors to justify the offering of highly specialized electives within the major, an action that encouraged the proliferation of special emphases within the baccalaureate degree major. But, unlike the specializations identified in the 1937 curriculum conference, these special emphases did not relate to development of particular program skills; rather, they furthered one's understanding of the setting in which the student might seek employment and the problems and practices associated with that setting. This trend was supported, in part, by the demise of the prescribed general educational requirements. It was a permissive time in higher education and we responded, as did our colleagues in other academic units, by offering and requiring more courses in our major.

Accompanying this expansion in major course work was the need for course texts and reading materials. Several major publishing companies established park and recreation series. Our body of knowledge expanded considerably as did the number of texts with leisure and/or recreation in their title. The profession created its first refereed journal, The *Journal of Leisure Research* (1969) and a second one, *Leisure Sciences*, in 1977. But all was not well; major divisions were rising. The debate as to whether we were dealing with leisure or recreation which has blossomed in the late 1960s prospered in the newcomers, those trained in other academic fields, or those interested primarily in leisure, not recreation and park practice. The politics of our national organizations and the actions of various federal agencies, along with the expanding number of undergraduate specializations within parks and recreation seemed to be fracturing rather than unifying the field. The one force that seemingly was seeking to strengthen the common bond was the accreditation process.

With the field testing of its standards and procedures completed, the Federation of Professional Recreation Organizations "willed" the accreditation project to the National Park and Recreation Association. It, in conjunction with the American Association for Health, Physical Education, and Recreation, made application to the National Commission on Accreditation in February of 1973 to have Parks and Recreation be approved as an accredited area of study. However, rather than giving its approval to the accrediting of park and recreation curricula, the National Council suggested that NRPA institute its own program of accrediting recreation curricula until such time as it had evidence of a need for accreditation and its ability to administer an accreditation plan. This we did, and in 1977 the Council on Accreditation for Recreation, Leisure Services and Resources Education was created. Nine years later, the process was approved when the Council on Postsecondary Accreditation, the successor to the National Commission on Accreditation, accepted the NRPA/AALR Council on Accreditation as a constituent member.

As cited previously, the framers of the initial accreditation document had developed criteria and standards for three undergraduate and three graduate specializations. They referred to these as professional emphases. At the undergraduate level the emphases were: (1) Recreation Program Administration, with seven sub-emphases (including therapeutic recreation); (2) Recreation and Park Administration; and (3) Recreation Resources Administration. The graduate areas of specialization were: (1) Recreation Programming; (2) Administration of Recreation and Park Systems; and (3) Recreation Resources Administration (AAHPER, 1974). By 1977, the system of emphases had been refined with a break-out of therapeutic recreation as a specialization in its own right. It seemed that the major goal had been accomplished: we were moving toward accreditation and appeared to be accommodating the diverse backgrounds of those involved in the professional preparation of park and recreation students. Correctly or not, we assumed those trained in the biological sciences had the same perception of the role of the profession and professional as did those trained in the social sciences or education. A few questioned this assumption (Reid,

1976) but no research was undertaken to test it. In fact, nearly all of the actions taken regarding curriculum content—the core and the special emphases—have been done with minimal data other than "truths" gleaned through group discussions, conventional wisdom and logic, and an occasional job analysis.

Even though most park and recreation professionals were pleased with the movement toward accreditation, new problems were confronting our colleges and universities that would affect our training efforts. By the end of the decade, it had become apparent that the permissiveness of the '60s and the decline of the required general education curriculum had exacted a price. Students seemed to be less able to write, have a sense of place and history, or be able to handle basic academic requirements. The American Council on Higher Education, the Carnegie Commission, and similar bodies created committees to study the problem (Sessoms, 1986). Then, too, the demographics of the early 1960s were catching up with higher education. The last of the baby boomers were entering college; college enrollments were declining. With fewer students, Parks and Recreation could expect fewer majors; that attrition began in the late '70s. However, it was probably another element of social change that had more effect on our curricula than did the declining birth rate or the problems confronting higher education. It has not only affected our numbers but also our course content.

America was becoming more conservative. The conservatism was seen in both political and social behaviors. Whether it was a reaction to Watergate, our views toward the Vietnam War, oil embargoes or inflation, America was turning toward the political right. Humanism was being replaced with pragmatism and skepticism. Students were becoming more interested in careers that would provide them with economic security than with opportunities to be of service or care for the environment. Both educators and politicians were calling for the return of excellence and there was a general revolution against governmental control. Decentralization was the mode and personal autonomy the watch word. Terms like "free enterprise," "entrepreneurship" and "privatization" began to appear in our literature and we began offering courses in recreation and the private sector, tourism, and marketing leisure service.

Once again, recreation education was in a state of flux and the questions and issues posed were not unfamiliar. They were and are the same that confronted our earlier curriculum planners and reformers. They pertain to the nature of our enterprise, the structure and content of our curricula, the relations between professional education courses and general education requirements, and our role in higher education. They also suggest inquiry into the relationship which exists between what and how we teach and the social and professional issues which society at large, and the profession in particular, have undertaken. To some extent this has been the agenda for the '90s.

Without enumerating all of the concerns confronting park and recreation educators today or discussing the many facets of each issue, may it suffice to acknowledge only a few and cite the writings of a select number of scholars who have devoted some time and energy to this problem in this decade. The list is not exclusive, but representative. There is the work of SPRE with *Schole* and its annual curriculum studies (Thomas A. Stein, Richard J. Gitelson, M. Deborah Bialeschki), which are the best accounting of changes in curriculum demographics and organizational patterns: the number of students majoring in parks, recreation and leisure studies; the size and academic background of our curriculum faculties, the gender size and academic background of our curriculum faculties, the gender of our students and faculties, the ratios of faculty to students, undergraduates to graduates; and the administrative locations of park and recreation curricula.

There is a debate as to the significance and viability of Leisure Studies as a discipline separate from Parks and Recreation education. In one of the issues of the *Journal of Leisure Research* (Vol. 17, No. 2, 1985), Geoffrey Godbey, Rabel Burdge, and Stephen Smith critically analyzed the issue and its relevance. For many, Leisure Studies has become an equal to professional preparation as the basis for what we are doing; for others, the professional preparation mission remains central. The choice we make regarding the relative importance of each of these functions has significance for staffing, accreditation and university role relationships. Several educators including Louis Twardzik (1984), Miriam P. Lahey (1986) and Karla A. Henderson and Leandra A. Bedini (1989) have written on the ethical and moral responsibilities of park and recreation educators and park and recreation curricula. They are concerned about values, particularly those affecting the delivery of services and how we impart these values in our curricula. The need for research in each of the areas of concern is obvious. Decisions will be made whether we have sound data or not.

Although there were no curriculum conferences in the '80s, curriculum changes have occurred, often without input from the profession. For example, university administrators and reformers are requiring more general educational courses of all majors. Course work in history, rhetoric, philosophy, and the biological and physical sciences, especially courses in math and computer science, are becoming standard fare for all freshmen and sophomores. Many institutions are requiring their upper divisional students to take special educational perspective and capstone courses. Consequently, the number of courses in the major or as electives has been diminished by these increased general education requirements. Where there was professional input it largely resulted from the work of SPRE through its teaching institutes and *Schole*, the first professional journal (an annual publication) devoted entirely to issues of leisure studies and recreation education.

Compounding the problem of curriculum content is the continuing debate among park and recreation educators as to the focus of undergraduate preparation. Should we be encouraging our students to seek a specialization at the baccalaureate level or give attention only to the professional core? The Council on Accreditation has attempted to give leadership in this area by reducing the number of recognized specialization options to four: Recreation and Park Administration; Recreation Resource Management; Recreation Program Supervision; and Therapeutic Recreation. But with increased demands for more general education, where will the cuts in the recreation and park major occur: the general core or the specializations? Or will we, too, move toward a five-year program? Then, too, how much duplication is there within the content of the various specializations and the core? Is not program planning, program planning, regardless of the setting? Must we rely only on our courses to prepare our students for their "professional risks," be they management or counseling or should we be drawing upon the resources of other departments and disciplines for some of the professional preparation of our students—an issue discussed in 1992 by Ronald D. Riggins and Frank B. Butts (*Schole*).

Perhaps the larger issue is what are we preparing students to be: job ready for their first position or education professionals? Even more critical is the question that Bill McKinney at the

University of Illinois has been addressing: Does recreation and park education make a difference? (McKinney, 1987) Are graduates of park and recreation curricula better able to perform as professionals than those who come into our field from other courses of study, and what are the effects of certification and our National Certification Examinations with their prerequisite educational requirements? This is a fertile research field.

A limited number of studies of the attitudes and behaviors of recreation and park educators have been conducted. Tony Mobley (1984) and his colleagues at the University of Indiana have looked at faculty attitudes toward publications, the role of faculty in decision making, and their views of the profession while John Kneiss's dissertation (1986) looked at the views of recreation education administrators with those of college administrators regarding the merits and effects of our accreditation efforts. The results of these studies say something about our current patterns and issues, our perceptions of tenure, need for publications, status within the university and future within the university community. On the other hand, the work of Arnold Grossman (1991) and Thomas Goodale (1992) have explored our views toward social responsibility and our attitudes toward sensitive issues. There is much for us to learn about ourselves as we also look at the effects of our effort.

As mentioned earlier, there are also a good number of behavioral changes in park and recreation curricula that merit scrutiny. One of these is the title by which curricula are known. I suspect that many of our colleagues throughout the university system do not know who we are; we so often change our name. Some might say that it is because we are more accurately defining and describing our work, but could it be that our chameleon character is more motivated by marketing objectives than by academic grounding? What is the communality of a profession in which the accredited programs are known by such titles as Parks, Recreation and Environmental Education; Recreation Management and Youth Leadership; Leisure Management and Tourism; and Leisure Studies and Services? Other professional bodies and disciplines tend to concentrate on one or two titles to describe their effort. Should not we? The same might be said about our seemingly uncontrolled urge for "cell division." We create specialization (emphases) at a rate which equals that of a budding amoeba.

Another current interest is teaching behavior and the effectiveness or consequence of how we teach and what resources and technologies we use. Several studies including those of William D. Murphy and Ellen Weissinger (1990), Karen M. Fox and Karen J. Warren (1990), Ruth V. Russell and Anne M. Rothschadl (1991) and Michael A. Kanters (1992) have looked at learning strategies, critical thinking and approaches to learning but few studies on the effects of new technologies have been done.

Duplication technologies, combined with the rising cost of texts and our tendency to want only to use that which is most recent, have contributed to this phenomenon. The consequences are several. Who will write the texts in the future? In our rush to read only the most recent will we continue to ignore our history and the views of those who may have seen the issue from a different perspective? Texts tend to give students a sense of continuity and understanding that is lacking with the readings approach. Students get to know the views of the writer; observations about the subject area may be interpreted in context; schools of thought are developed. The readings approach tends to lack this—depth and continuity are secondary to currentness and expediency. Others may judge our literature performance and failure to use texts as an indicator of our lack of academic discipline. Experiential learning is fine but scholarship comes from delving into the writings of others and attempting to develop our own theses with supporting data. Both types of readings are important, as is the need to have our students become better writers and disciplined thinkers.

Speaking of the views of others, to what extent do they see our effort as a part of the general educational thrust of the university? Do they believe we can contribute to the education of their majors? Has our baccalaureate level professional approach with its heavy concentration on professional courses and emphases labeled us as non-scholars, as trainers rather than educators? We are in an international environment: what we do is affected by what others think of us and allow us to do as well as what we want to do and have the ability to do.

Finally, there is the issue of accreditation and its role in shaping the future of park and recreation education. The Council on Accreditation is mindful of its responsibility to improve the quality of learning through the adherence to standards and patterns of performance. It does not seek to make all programs alike; yet, there is that tendency by the very nature of the accrediting process. The task of maintaining curriculum relevance and program flexibility is too large for the Council alone. That must come from many sources including output data and an occasional curriculum conference in which practitioners and educators join together to discuss the issues confronting the profession and their relationship to park and recreation education, tempered by the unique mission of each institution. The educational component cannot be divorced from the practice component nor from the goals of the universities and colleges which house us. The curriculum planners in 1937 understood that. Do we?

What happens to park and recreation education is beyond our control. Demographics, values, technologies, and catastrophes have a way of shaping our destinies. Parks and recreation education is influenced by changes in the thinking and practice of university administrators and those political processes which influence educational systems. We are also influenced by what happens in our field of work, the delivery of park and recreation and leisure services, for we are an element of that system. If society or the profession defines its role differently in the future than it does at the present, then we will be affected. If the public seeks a different mandate for parks and recreation than it has in the past, we will be affected. If the profession changes its view as to the role of the professional in the delivery of services, we will be affected.

But a part of our future is also in our hands. We are the influencers of the system through our writings and teachings, through the instruction we give those who will, in time, assume leadership roles. What we will become will depend upon how we deal with the issues and questions at hand, the kinds of data we develop to assist us in decision making, and our willingness to come to grips with who we are and what we want to be. Each day we create our tomorrow just as our predecessors have created our today.

BIBLIOGRAPHY

Burdge, Rabel J. (1985). The Coming Separation of Leisure Studies from Parks and Recreation Education. *Journal of Leisure Research, 17*(2), 133-144.

Bureau of Outdoor Recreation (1964). *Proceeding of the National Conference on Professional Education for Outdoor Recreation*. Washington, DC: US Government Printing Office.

Butts, Frank B. The Leisure Studies and Recreation Undergraduate Curriculum. *Schole*, Vol. 7, 74-80.

Fox, Karen M. and Karen J. Warren (1990) The Conception and Practice of Leisure: The Role of Critical Thinking. *Schole*, Vol. 5, 15-40.

Gabrielsen, Milton A. (1948). *Report of Eighth Annual January Recreation Institute*. New York: New York University.

Godbey, Geoffrey (1985). The Coming Cross-Pollination of Leisure Studies and Recreation and Park Education: A Response. *Journal of Leisure Research, 17*(2), 142-148.

Goodale, Thomas L. (1992). Education in Social Responsibility. *Schole*, Vol. 7, 8-91.

Grossman, Arnold H. (1991). HIV/AIDS Education: The Professional and Social Responsibility of Recreation Educators. *Schole*, Vol. 6, 1-13.

Guidelines for Professional Preparation for Personnel Involved in Physical Education and Recreation for the Handicapped (1973). Washington, DC: American Association for Health, Physical Education and Recreation.

Henderson, Karla A., and Leandra A. Bedini (1989). Teaching Ethics and Social Responsibility in Leisure Studies Curricula. *Schole*, 4, 1-14.

Jordan, Jerry J. and others (1977). *Theory and Design of Competency-Based Education in Therapeutic Recreation*. Philadelphia: Temple University.

Kanters, Michael A. (1992). Teaching the Professor to Teach. *Schole*, Vol. 7, 55-64.

Kelly, Jerry D. and others (1976). *Therapeutic Recreation Education*. Urbana, IL; University of Illinois at Urbana-Champaign.

Kneiss, John M. (1986). *A Comparison of the Perceptions of Department Heads of Recreation, Leisure Services, and Resource Curricula with Chief Academic Officers of Selected Institutions Regarding the National Recreation and Parks Association's Accreditation Process*. Unpublished doctoral dissertation, University of Georgia.

Lahey, Miriam P. (1986). Teaching Values and Ethics to Recreation Students. *SPRE Annual on Education*. Arlington, VA: National Recreation and Park Association, 172-187.

McKinney, William R. (1987). Accredited Versus Non-Accredited Curricula: Is There a Difference in Professional Preparation? *SPRE Annual on Education*, Vol. 2. Arlington, VA: National Recreation and Park Association, 82-99.

Mobley, Tony A. (1984). Faculty Development for a Maturing Profession. *Leisure Sciences, 6*(3): 351-358.

Murphy, William D. and Ellen Weissinger (1990). Application of Cognitive Instructional Techniques in Leisuré Studies Curricula. *Schole,* Vol. 5, 1-14.

Professional Preparation in Recreation. *The National Conference on Undergraduate Professional Preparation in Health Education, Physical Education and Recreation* (1948). Washington, DC: American Association of Health Education, Physical Education and Recreation, 26-34.

Recreation Education. *Professional Preparation in Dance, Physical Education, Recreation, Safety Education and School Health Education* (1974). Washington, DC: American Association of Health, Physical Education and Recreation, 67-91.

Reid, Leslie M. (1976). Parks and Recreation: Should They Separate? *Park Maintenance, 29*(4), 15-20.

Report of College Conference on Training Recreation Leaders (1937). Washington, DC: Works Progress Administration.

Riggins, Ronald D. Liberal Education and Professional Studies at the Undergraduate Level: Still Circling Moose Jaw. (1992). *Schole,* Vol. 7, 5-16.

Russell, Ruth and Anne M. Rothschadl (1991). Learning Styles: Another View of the College Classroom. *Schole,* Vol. 6, 34-45.

Sessoms, H. Douglas (1984). Research Issues in Park and Recreation Education: An Overview. *Leisure Sciences, 6*(3), 327-336.

Sessoms, H. Douglas (1986). Trends in Park and Recreation Education. *SPRE Annual on Education.* Arlington, VA: National Recreation and Park Association, 1-18.

Sessoms, H. Douglas (1993). *Eight Decades of Leadership Development,* Arlington, VA: National Recreation and Parks Association, 144.

Smith, Stephen L. J. (1985). An Alternative Perspective on the Nature of Recreation and Leisure Studies: A Personal Response to Rabel Burdge. *Journal of Leisure Research, 17*(2), 155-160.

Stein, Thomas A. (1984). Recreation Education in the United States and Canada: A Look at the Past, Present and Future. *Leisure Sciences, 6*(3), 337-350.

Training Programs, Resources and Challenges. (1974). *Educating Tomorrow's Leaders in Parks, Recreation and Conservation .* Washington, DC: National Recreation and Park Association, 24-32.

Twardzik, Louis F. (1984). A Case Study of Ethics in Professional Recreation. *Leisure Sciences, 6*(3), 375-385.

— Epilogue —
To Our Health

Past, Present, and Future Research

Thomas L. Goodale
Health Sciences Program
——————— **George Mason University** ———————

As with the initial (1988) version of *Research About Leisure,* authors have included with their reviews critiques of research to date on their respective subject areas, and some suggestions about how to improve our research and increase our understanding. There is much insight in those critiques and suggestions and many interesting questions are raised; questions about the subject and also about research into the subject. Those portions of the chapters perform part of the function of an epilogue in providing reflective commentary on what has ended and what may occur next.

Unlike the initial version, there are chapters here on marketing, consumption, feminist perspectives, leisure and culture and other, comparatively recent avenues of research about leisure. Insights are plentiful and interesting questions are raised in these chapters too. But the new chapters, per se, contribute to the epilogue in another way, as they represent the evolution of leisure research in recent years, and the maturation of some of the sub-fields explored by leisure researchers.

On a more material level, this version is the result of the initial version being out of print. That a book on research about leisure would be sold out would still surprise many observers, however small the print run, however scarce or weak the competition. An out-of-print research book is epilogue enough.

Since the initial version was compiled, much else has happened that attests to the vitality of research about leisure. Research symposia, in the U.S., Canada and in other countries continue to flourish and to welcome criticism and debate about paradigms, methods, relevance and the like. Publications in recent years reflect increasing pluralism in methods and perspectives, increasing interest in summing up and setting agendas, increasing interest in interpreting leisure research not only to practitioners but also to the public and to those who make policy.

Should there be a third edition, and should it appear six or seven years after this, what might be said about the next interval? Should we expect more and better of the same?

Perhaps not. That we are soon to enter not simply the twenty-first century but also the third millennium anno domini should give us all pause, if events of the recent past have not already done so. That is because, as everyone grants, research about leisure is shaped by social, political and economic forces, and it appears those forces have become increasingly intrusive in recent years. One need only note the epidemics of violence in urban America and AIDS everywhere, and how they affect leisure directly and leisure research indirectly, to appreciate the point.

The most pervasive force is surely the economy, particularly the recession we have been experiencing for a number of years, and changes in the distribution of wealth that began in the 1970s. Inflation-adjusted wages declined for most people. Work and work-related time increased for those employed full time. Unemployment rates increased as did welfare payments. With sixteen million or more people seeking full-time employment, people and policy are even more than typically focused on job creation, not leisure creation. There may be a subtle dampening on leisure as well. Reduced spending on leisure may be accompanied by a more defensive posture about life in general among those no longer assured of getting ahead and anxious about falling behind. Maybe that is just aging. Maybe not.

The direct and indirect impacts on leisure are obvious, the impacts on leisure research only slightly less so. The cost of a college education has increased dramatically, especially tuition, as the proportion of support from public funds decreased equally dramatically. The economy also intrudes directly to the extent that funds overall or for certain lines of inquiry become increasingly scarce. It also impacts directly on the career paths students (and their parents) perceive as viable. The financial squeeze has resulted in the reconfiguration or elimination of programs of study, including some leisure studies programs, through even the doctorate level. Leaving aside any discussion of program or student quality, there has emerged a legitimate concern about the number of students interested in and prepared to conduct research about leisure. Who will do leisure research in the future? What will be their orientation and preparation?

People who appreciate leisure in their own lives and in those of their children and friends, usually do so from the privileged positions of those with secure jobs and incomes. Anxiety about jobs and incomes dampens the enthusiasm for leisure and for leisure research, especially among politicians and policy makers. We cannot, some Senators recently argued, build swimming pools for inner-city youth, what with the budget deficit, unemployment, health care costs, and all . . .

The years to come promise no reduction of the impacts of these external realities. We may be seeing only the leading edge of larger forces still. There is, for example, much discussion and debate about free trade, currently focused on NAFTA, the North American Free Trade Agreement. Everyone understands that entails the loss of manufacturing jobs which, many believe, will be made up by jobs created by increasing exports to our trading partners, particularly Mexico. Such "dislocations," even if temporary, determine how work, jobs, income and free time, and thus opportunities and constraints are distributed. They also illustrate the decades-old reality of an international labor force and, increasingly, division of labor, and instantaneous movements of massive amounts of capital worldwide. That severs employers' ties to any locality and ties between employers and employees. That, clearly, affects leisure.

The shift from manufacturing to services, especially white collar service, severs even more ties, since much white collar service can be rendered independent of place. The information age may sever even more ties, not only separating producers from consumers but eliminating many of both. The information age, so far, has produced no jobs.

The shift of manufacturing and now also much service work from cities to suburbs has left scars on our cities and the city people lacking mobility and the skills for what jobs remain. One obvious effect has been to diminish opportunities for the urban poor. Absent secure jobs and steady income, social problems, present even in the best of circumstances, are magnified. With those problems go costs of many kinds. At the same time, revenues from the loss of corporate, property, sales and other taxes erode. Transfer payments from senior governments erode as well. Funds available for public leisure services erode, as do funds for services of other kinds. Those who can afford alternatives pursue them by moving to the suburbs, joining private clubs and resorts, sending children to private schools, and resisting taxes for public services they no longer use. Even the public services, under these conditions, serve the comparatively well-to-do better than those with limited means and no alternatives. That affects leisure too, along with the distribution of so many other goods and services, housing and health services among them.

Besides the impact on college and university programs, enrollments, funds, and time for research, do these economic forces and resulting conditions affect leisure research? If this book is an indicator, the answer has to be, not much, or perhaps not much, yet. Should the researchers and research thrusts represented here change? Probably. But not necessarily in dramatic, wholesale fashion, and not necessarily in response to the evolving conditions just described.

Surely there come times when lines of inquiry return less and less of theoretical interest or practical use and mining the same veins or pits is no longer feasible. No doubt researchers continue in certain directions because of momentum rather than any remaining contribution to theory or practice.

Research is an evolving process in which interests are constantly reshaped by information or the absence of it. All the preceding chapters speak of veins being exhausted and abandoned as potentially more rewarding veins are uncovered. That will and should continue, but that is not enough.

What is also needed, as has been said so many times before in the preceding chapters here and elsewhere, is more research of different kinds, involving different concepts of leisure, different paradigms, questions, methods and the rest. In particular, more veins must be opened where the unit of analysis is greater than one, and things other than individuals have to be conceived as something other than shapers of individual choices. Social psychologists should continue studying intrinsically motivated behavior. It is an important part of leisure research and will remain so. And often it is done well, as is the case with the editor and authors here. But leisure is more than what social psychologists study, however, and now that the social psychology of leisure is well established, as is evident in many ways, we can further encourage and even begin ourselves to risk further exploration of units greater than one, and leisure defined in other ways.

There is some work in which couples or families are the units of analyses. There is some work on groups organized around work, common characteristics, or enthusiasms of different kinds. Work in which neighborhood, community and society are units of analyses is less common. There are a number of conjectures as to why there is a lag in studies of these kinds. It may be because these units are much more complex, even ethereal. For positivists attempting to control variance, they may be the stuff of nightmares. It may be that these units cannot be studied by the methods most familiar to us; methods designed to gather and analyze many observations, quickly, and by dividing labor in assembly-line fashion. Research on communities and societies may require more of the ploddings of the scholar and her tolerance for ambiguity and uncertainty.

The comparative lack of studies of units larger than one may, finally, reflect avoidance of the social, economic and political colorations inevitable with such studies. Somewhere a balance must be struck between freedom and equality, between rights and responsibilities, and between the individual and the collective. That is because leisure defined as an individual's perception of freedom is as much a political and cultural statement as an empirical one. Other research focused on units other than individuals and on other concepts of leisure is needed to enrich and enliven the conversation and balance the perspective.

In so many ways, the national preoccupation with illness, increasingly and necessarily focusing on prevention rather than treatment, provides a bedrock value, health, on which all can agree. This preoccupation with health promotion and health maintenance may have salutary affects on leisure and leisure research. It clarifies the importance of recreation and leisure, and thus also the importance of leisure research. It encompasses all units of analysis: we can speak of healthy relationships, communities, institutions, and environments as readily as healthy individuals, and we can operationalize the concept of health for all these units.

The preoccupation with health also leads to more research in which leisure, however that may be operationally defined, is the independent variable. Research on benefits, which may have a salutary affect on the survival of leisure research, is essentially research on health.

There is yet a third salutary affect of the focus on health. It enables us to refocus on a concept abandoned many years ago in the midst of unprecedented economic growth, affluence and abundance. That is the concept of need. We succumbed to the consumer society imperative of manufacturing and satisfying wants. It has become increasingly clear that such a society cannot be sustained and that people are not sustained by such a society anyway. Do people need leisure? Do families? Communities? If the answer is no, then the society does not need leisure research. If the answer is to be yes, then we have to be able to specify the consequences if the need is met and the consequences if it is not. Is that consequence health, broadly writ, if the need is met, illness, broadly writ, if it is not? Is not the health of leisure research, then, a function of its ability to demonstrate its contribution to health? If so, the study of individuals' motives, perceptions and behaviors is necessary and important, but probably not enough. We need, as our health depends on it, to be enriched and enlivened by multiple perspectives of and approaches to leisure.

The final salutary affect of focusing on health and refocusing on need is that it restores to leisure its high status in an ethical order of things. Lack of place in an ethical order was discomforting for too many colleagues and allies who, if leisure research is to matter, must help inform and direct it.